Why Appeasement Failed

Also by Andrew Sangster and in print with Pen & Sword Books

'Pug' – Churchill's Chief of Staff (2023)
How Hitler Evolved the Traditional Army Establishment
(with Pier Paolo Battistelli) (2024)
Hitler's New Command Structure and the Road to Defeat
(with Pier Paolo Battistelli) (2024)
Major Blunders of the Second World War (2024)
'Make Germany Great Again' (2024)
From Stalingrad to Italy – Von Senger's War (2025)
Exploring Nationalism (2025)

Why Appeasement Failed

The Ignored Evidence

Andrew Sangster

Pen & Sword
MILITARY

First published in Great Britain in 2025 by
Pen & Sword Military
An imprint of Pen & Sword Books Limited
Yorkshire – Philadelphia

Copyright © Pen & Sword Books Ltd 2025

ISBN 978 1 03613 583 6

The right of Andrew Sangster to be identified as
Author of this Work has been asserted by him in accordance
with the Copyright, Designs and Patents Act 1988.

A CIP catalogue record for this book is
available from the British Library.

All rights reserved. No part of this book may be reproduced,
transmitted, downloaded, decompiled or reverse engineered in
any form or by any means, electronic or mechanical, including
photocopying, recording or by any information storage and
retrieval system, without permission from the Publisher in writing.
NO AI TRAINING: Without in any way limiting the Author's
and Publisher's exclusive rights under copyright, any use of this
publication to 'train' generative artificial intelligence (AI) technologies
to generate text is expressly prohibited. The Author and Publisher
reserve all rights to license uses of this work for generative AI training
and development of machine learning language models.

Typeset by Mac Style
Printed in the UK by CPI Group (UK) Ltd, Croydon, CR0 4YY.

The Publisher's authorised representative in the EU for product safety
is Authorised Rep Compliance Ltd., Ground Floor, 71 Lower Baggot
Street, Dublin D02 P593, Ireland.
www.arccompliance.com

For a complete list of Pen & Sword titles please contact

PEN & SWORD BOOKS LIMITED
47 Church Street, Barnsley, South Yorkshire, S70 2AS, England
E-mail: enquiries@pen-and-sword.co.uk
Website: www.pen-and-sword.co.uk
or
PEN AND SWORD BOOKS
1950 Lawrence Road, Havertown, PA 19083, USA
E-mail: uspen-and-sword@casematepublishers.com
Website: www.penandswordbooks.com

Contents

Acknowledgements	viii
Preface	ix
Foreword	xi
Introduction	xiv

Part I: Appeasement and Divided Opinions 1
The Minefield of Historical Viewpoints 1
The Political Scene 3
Diplomats and Civil Servants 26
Munich, Round One, Berchtesgaden 32
Munich, Round Two, Bad Godesberg 36
Munich, Final Round 38
Post Munich 43
1939 and War 45
The Immediate Aftermath 54
The Different Opinions 58

Part II: Literary Efforts to Reveal the Truth 61
Role of Journalism in the 1930s 61
Dorothy Woodman 68
Nature of the book *Hitler Rearms* 69
Conclusion 74

Part III: *Mein Kampf* 75
Introduction 75

Chapter 1   Hitler, the Man and His Views 79
Hitler's Ability to Convince the Germans 79
Personality 80
Some of Hitler's Views 81

Chapter 2 His Special Hatreds — 89
Anti-Semitism — 90
Marxism — 92
France and Russia — 94

Chapter 3 Pan-Germanism — 95
Nation and Race — 96
Hitler and His Homeland Austria — 98
Democracy — 98
England — 99
Lebensraum — 100

Chapter 4 Idealism and Foreign Affairs — 101
Hitler's Idealism — 101
Foreign Affairs — 103
Eastern Policy — 105
Final Observations on *Mein Kampf* — 106

Part IV The Man Who Was Ignored — 111
Introduction — 112

Chapter 1 The Early Days — 117
The Man Hitler — 117
Hitler's Major Henchmen — 121
The Nature of the Early Nazi Movement — 123
So-called Philosophy of National Socialism — 125

Chapter 2 Four Years of Power — 127
Technique of Revolution — 127
The Growth of Party Organisation — 128
The Eclipse of the Brownshirts — 133
The Army and Hitlerism — 135
A Nuremberg Rally — 138

Chapter 3 The Economics of Hitlerism	140
The Doctrine of Self-sufficiency	140
Financial Jugglery	141
The Internal Boom	142
The Fight for Raw Materials and Substitutes	143
Schacht Versus the Extremists	144
The Agricultural Fiasco	145
Chapter 4 The Balance Sheet of Hitlerism	147
The Youth Movement: the fight for the first 18 years	147
The Labour Service: the fight for young men	148
The Labour Front: the fight for workers	149
Women and Population: the fight for the race	151
Public Works and Great Roads: the fight for employment	152
The Drive for a Common Mentality: how a nation is hypnotised	153
The Present Place of Jews	156
Swastika Versus Cross	157
Law as a Political Instrument	159
Chapter 5 Hitlerism and the World	161
General Foreign Policy	161
The Soviet Bogey in Theory and Fact	164
The Lost Germans	164
The Southern Danger Zones	166
The Baltic Pressure Points	168
Germany and Western Europe	169
The Colonial Question	170
Conclusion by Roberts	172
Part V: Final Observations	175
Notes	182
Bibliography of Cited Texts	187
Index	189

Acknowledgements

Over the years I have been very grateful to those who work and administer the various archives, and for the work of fellow historians with their various insights and perceptions.

However, I am exceptionally grateful to my wife, Carol Ann, for her incredible patience as I disappear into archives and rarely emerge from my study. I am also grateful for the support and encouragement of my friend and colleague the Revd Dr Canon Peter Doll, Vice-Dean of Norwich Cathedral.

Preface

Many books have been written on the Chamberlain years of appeasement, and historical judgments have changed and counter changed as the years pass by. They range from condemning the appeasement lobby to seeing it as *Realpolitik*, and these lines of thought have been major features of some studies. In looking back in history with the benefit of hindsight it is easy to dwell on the mistaken judgments of the past, and in the study of the appeasement years this has multiplied. For many the conundrum is that Chamberlain's policy was based on the moral basis of wanting peace in Europe, even if it meant re-addressing some of the problems resulting from the Treaty of Versailles after the First World War. If his policy had worked there would have been no war, but this hope was 'pie in the sky'.

The question arose in this writer's mind as to what Chamberlain missed, why did he think Hitler could be reasoned with and appeased. The missing component he and many others missed was the nature of the man Hitler himself and the Nazi regime which reflected Hitler's way of thinking. Knowledge of a potential opponent or enemy is critical, even in sport let alone war. A chess player finds it useful to know whether the opponent is prone to accepting draws, uses gambits, the style of attack, but that is nothing compared to the police who need to know something about the psychology or personality of a potential criminal and his *modus vivendi*, in other words, using a colloquial expression, 'having his number'. Not seeking this information in the case of Hitler could be seen as a sin of omission, not least because the necessary evidence was there waiting to be properly read and understood, the information was available in print at the time and was ignored or overlooked. This book explores the appeasement era to provide the setting, explores the literary efforts which could have supplied the necessary indicators of Hitler and his regime, and concludes with a critique of two books available at the time, which provided the necessary information which would have been critical for being aware of Hitler's warped personality, his driving forces, his potential criminality, his lack of any sense of moral standards, and his intentions.

Foreword

By Dr Pier Paolo Battistelli

On a personal basis I have always attributed an immense value to history, which I consider as the true *magistra vitae* [Life's teacher]. We learn from our own misjudgements, and as a society we should learn from the mistakes made in the past by the people in charge, which, admittedly, rarely happens. Recent events clearly show that people seem unable to learn from the past being thus condemned, as written by George Santayana, 'to relive it over and over again'. As I read Andrew Sangster's book, I realised this is not a sin of the present age, but a recurring mistake repeating itself during human history. As Sangster remarks it is easy today to criticise Chamberlain's politics of appeasement, but at the same time it is not so easy avoiding making the same mistakes, for a variety of reasons.

The crucial issue is whether it is possible to understand that the choices one has made are wrong, and by correcting one's own course of action before the mistake materialises towards disaster. Hitler, for instance, made the same mistake Chamberlain had made, albeit in a different context. His decision to attack the Soviet Union in 1941 was based, amongst others, on a series of reasons related to the potential danger the country represented for Germany in case the United States entered the war. This sort of pre-emptive war was based on Hitler's view of Stalin and of the Soviet Union, regardless of the fact that the country was tied to Germany by a non-aggression pact. This prompted Hitler to a war he thought would be victorious. This fatal error of judgement, which eventually led to Germany's defeat and to the end of the Third Reich, bears similar hallmarks of Chamberlain's idea that appeasement was the best solution to preserve the peace in Europe. Both relied on a distorted view of the other side, Stalin in Hitler's case, Hitler himself in Chamberlain's case, and on errors of judgement based on mistaken evaluations and ignoring the available evidence of the day.

Chamberlain's approach to the appeasement politics seems to have more than one issue in common with Hitler's decisions. The idea of peace was not entirely a pipe dream, since Hitler himself wanted to avoid war with the Western Powers in order to have time to prepare to wage war against them. Both France and Great Britain relied on the period of peace following the Munich agreement to rearm, their eventual failure in 1940 being dictated by their lack of preparation and other reasons. Chamberlain's politics does not always appear as a mistake but rather, as Sangster remarks, more like *Realpolitik*, with all its pros and cons. The question, raised by many, is whether a pre-emptive war waged by France and Britain against Germany at a time when they were not ready for war might not have prevented the subsequent events, namely the Second World War. From the historical perspective the question belongs more to the 'what if' history approach and, as such, it could be debated practically forever.

The interesting point made by Sangster in his book is not what might have happened if Chamberlain had avoided his appeasement politics when facing the September 1938 crisis, but rather why at the time the people in France and Britain – in particular those in a position of power – failed to understand the true nature of the National Socialist regime and in particular Hitler's intentions. As Sangster clearly shows, thanks to a unique research based on the sources of the time, neither Hitler nor his acolytes never made a mystery of their intentions. Starting from Hitler's *Mein Kampf*, which was widely diffused in Germany and known abroad as well, the intent and purpose of Hitler's Germany should have been clear, if not in their true extent at least in their aims. This issue begs the question as to whether Chamberlain's appeasement politics was a mistake based on an error of judgement, or was it based on some sort of acceptance of Hitler's political vision. The question, uncomfortable as it is, might at the same time explain why after all this time history seems to repeat itself with all its doubts and uncertainties. Because while assuming that Hitler's intentions were not fully understood by some, one must also face the fact whether others actually understood and accepted what certainly was a vision of the world shared by many others, in Europe as well as in other parts of the world.

It is therefore essential to understand the true nature of Chamberlain's politics and, as Sangster highlights in his book, the many signals which might have revealed to those who needed to see fully what the future held as likely to come. Understanding the potential enemy and being aware of who they are, and their intentions remains critical to the current day, and not overlooking the available evidence.

Introduction

When the American journalist William Shirer first observed Nazi Germany, he noted all that was happening in Germany during the 1930s. After having attended a Nuremberg Rally, he wrote that 'I heard no mention of the loss of personal freedom and of other democratic rights. Apparently, this is not much of a sacrifice. They couldn't have cared less. They had committed themselves to Adolf Hitler and his barbarian dictatorship. The liberal democratic West did not yet realise this, nor did the Soviet Union to the east'.[1] He felt there was a pervading ignorance about what was developing within this huge central country of Europe. Later he added the observation that 'the German people, on the whole, had accepted the Nazi tyranny, and were helping to make it work. A newly arrived American correspondent had to recognise that startling reality. The outside world still did not believe it – or – when we began to report it'.[2] As it will be explored in Part Two of this book being a foreign correspondent in Germany was a difficult if not dangerous task, but there were some 'telling reports' which often led to foreign journalists being expelled from Nazi Germany. Despite all the available evidence Shirer was shocked on a visit home that his American friends appeared to know little about what was fermenting in the growth of the new Germany, the Third Reich, and the fact it did not appear to bother them. More to the point he was uncomfortably aware that in Europe itself, on the very doorsteps of Germany, the Western democratic countries and the Soviet Union seemed to be in ignorant bliss of the realities of Nazi Germany.

This study begins by exploring the background of the 1930s in an effort to understand why when the Second World War started in September 1939, it came as such a shock. Some people were aware of the imminent dangers, some ignorant, and some who always felt the threat could be dealt with diplomatically. This complex area is worth investigating because 'what is around the corner' is an issue which every generation has to face, and ask the question, 'what are we missing, or what should we be looking at?' In personal terms a person may use the colloquial expression 'I have your number', meaning they may know all about the person in question, their personality, their views and attitudes, their plans and intentions, their hopes, and their fears. In international terms this is the role of the diplomatic service, for apart from consulting with their host country, they also inform their home governments of what is driving their hosts, and although most embassies deny it everyone knows they have an Intelligence staff stationed with them. 'Awareness' is the key word, aware of what is happening in neighbouring countries, whether it a place for safe commerce, for binding treaties, or a place which may offer future threats. As with today the information is not always secure, often causing a lack of awareness of the key issues.

During the 1930s there were major divisions of public and political opinions in Britain and France, and an atmosphere of indecision, emanating from this lack of awareness. During the First World War an estimated 16 million people had died in the blood bath of an industrial type of war which shook the world. There was understandably and justifiably an ardent desire to avoid such another conflict, and the arguments for pacifism were more strongly expressed than ever before, permeating every level of society. However, as is typical of human life, the decision of war or no war rested in the hands of a few people, namely those who govern. This was true of democratic countries who had to listen to the voters, but who were equally divided on the issues regarding the sudden growth of Nazi power in Germany. This raises several questions which still have ramifications in today's world, not simply who has the final power of decision making, but being able to know the truth of what is happening on an international level or even across a boundary in a neighbouring country.

Today the television broadcasting system alerts the publics of the world to what is happening in the Russian attack on the Ukraine, Israel's attack in Gaza and a myriad of other areas of concern within the community of nations. Nevertheless, it all leads to a division of opinion at every level of society as no one can predict the future with certainty. 'Awareness' is the key word, trying to establish the truth of what is happening, discerning the intentions of another nation's leaders, and how far the general publics are aware of the issues or dangers. If the bulk of a population are for or against a particular emerging problem this has major ramifications in a democratic society and even in a totalitarian state, albeit to a lesser extent.

This key point raises the issue of what was happening in the 1930s with the dangers perceived by the rise to power of Adolf Hitler. At the political level it led to division and indecisiveness with the general public equally uncertain. This area of vagueness which dominated the 1930s has had the attention of many historical studies, and the point of this study is first to give a brief outline of the critical issues and clashes, but also to raise the question as to why two books, one published in the 1920s and the other in 1936 were not read, because both revealed the truth of what would happen, both providing an awareness of Hitler's thinking and his intentions. The later book (1936) was professionally written by a gifted academic, and easily read but generally ignored, the former was boring and difficult to read, but it laid bare the character of the man Adolf Hitler and outlined his intentions, because it was Hitler's own political autobiography. 'Awareness' of these two books could have led to more decisive action on the part of the Western powers, not least in an earlier reaction to the Nazi threat if only by appropriate military preparation and necessary diplomatic arrangements. These two books would have removed the ignorance and speculation about Nazism, and so the main thrust of this study is to review these books and see what was missed by those who should not have ignored them, and also try to explain why they were ignored.

Part I

Appeasement and Divided Opinions

Author's Notes: *In this Part One there is a brief outline of the historiography of the appeasement era, a brief reflection on the change of views of postwar historians and public reaction. This is followed by looking at the political scene, diplomats, Civil Servants, the tensions with Germany, the problems of the French and British working together. This is followed by the Munich Conference, its failure, and the consequences and the aftermath following the declaration of war, until the time that appeasement was seen as a hopeless cause. Many major books have been devoted to this delicate era of British history, one of the best being Tim Bouverie's 'Appeasing Hitler', but this section of the book is a mere summary of the well-known facts. Part One outlines the background, but it raises the main thesis of this study as to what was missed by politicians and public alike, namely an awareness of who Adolf Hitler was, and his intentions. The facts, figures, and other data are one thing, the psychology of Hitler's warped thinking process another, and they were overlooked despite available evidence.*

The Minefield of Historical Viewpoints

After the war in 1945 there were various views of the appeasement lobby expressed in the various historical studies and also reflected in the public reaction. The first reaction was the book published in 1940, *Guilty Men*, which condemned the government and remained the popular view for a long time.[1] Historians often change their perspectives (revisionist history) based on new documents revealed in the archives or the arrival of new revealing autobiographies and diaries. There may follow further shifts of opinion or a return to the older views, sometimes they are seismic shifts other times splitting hairs. One historian pertinently wrote that 'The appeasement debate has revolved around two contrasting viewpoints, grounded in two of the most archetypal forms of narrative emplotment: a negative one emphasising contingency, agency and morality, and a positive one emphasising determinism, structural constraints and *Realpolitik*'.[2]

Much of this period reflects the conundrum around the figure of Chamberlain. There are the negative aspects that his insistence on appeasement led to a war which could have been avoided by earlier military action, or working more efficiently with the French, or preparing the military for war. Sometimes the various angers over Chamberlain are softened by emphasising that his intentions for peace were honourable and he was quintessentially a good man. Others suggest he was too domineering, too self-assured, believed he was always right, disliked criticism because he saw himself as the man of power, yet too ill-informed to see the errors of his policies. On the other hand, it was later argued that he was a man of *Realpolitik*, basing his policies on practical objectives rather than ideals. Britain was weakening, economically in trouble which had brought about the ten-year rule about when it was right to put money into the military. He had to be cautious about the reaction of the major Dominion countries (generally the large white populated colonies), and there was a notable shortage of dependable allies. He was facing a strategic dilemma in an impossible situation, not only regarding Germany, but in the almost universal fear of Communism. It has been argued that his passivist attitudes held the moral high-ground and his efforts were at least in God's direction. He believed in reconciliation, understanding the other's point of view and maintaining the peace of nations.

In the historiography of this period there are various forms of Historical Revisionism followed by counter changes and various shades have followed one after another. It is up to the reader to try and unpick the complex tapestry of historical viewpoints and arrive at his or her own conclusions. In the brief summary of this era, both sides of this historical puzzle are delved into, but for this writer the tendency is not to see the appeasers as fools, but like most others, they were people who failed to see the truth of Nazism and be aware of the potential dangers. The expression 'keep your friends close and your enemies closer' has uncertain origins, but in many occupations makes sense, and despite available evidence during the 1923–1939 era, the main issue boiled down to failing to be aware of Hitler's personality and his obsessive intentions which had been well documented but overlooked.

The Political Scene

For six years politicians were indecisive, even on 2 September 1939 when the Poles were suffering from the onslaught of German forces the British were prevaricating, mainly because of the difficulty in gauging the nature of French cooperation for an agreed time of declaring war. This level of uncertainty and debate was the hallmark of the 1930s in political circles in both Britain and France.

One politician stood out, Winston Churchill, who had campaigned since as early as 1932–3 that Nazism was a serious danger. He was virtually treated as a political outcast (*The Wilderness Years*), known as the man who had crossed the floor of parliament (changed political allegiance), and was often seen as an unwanted bellicose figure. When Hitler became Chancellor in 1933 most politicians saw little consequence as German Chancellors came and went as rapidly as the musical chairs of the French governments. *The Times* and other newspapers barely recorded this event regarding it as of minimal interest and little consequence. It was the same reaction in France, but because it was known that Hitler was known for his obsessively intense anti-Bolshevism this gave for many people a degree of hope, as Communism was regarded as the greatest threat to world stability. Britain and France had found working with the fascist Mussolini possible, and their greatest fear remained international communism. Even Churchill, who detested the concept of communism had admired the dictator Mussolini not least because the Italian supremo held the same views of Bolshevists. For many national leaders, the occasional rise of a dictator was of less consequence than communism, mainly because a dictator was an event in a singular country, whereas communism was looking at global expansion and most European countries had political communist groups in their midst, a cause of growing concern.

Even when it was heard that there was violence on German streets as the SA hunted down communist opposition, that Dachau concentration camp had been opened to give 'protective imprisonment' to any form of opponent, and anti-Semitism was reaching barbaric levels, it was seen by many as merely 'German business'. Beaverbrook (the newspaper magnate) visited Berlin in March 1933 returned to Britain 'convinced that the stories of Jewish persecution are exaggerated'.[3] There were many in Britain who had a degree of sympathy with Germany on many grounds. There were those who wanted a friendship between old enemies, some saw the French as the more traditional enemy than the Germans. Others sympathised with the way Germany had been treated, and amongst these were a few who had predicted the Versailles Treaty had been too harsh, including David Lloyd George. Others admired the German sense of order and obedience, there were a few who were anti-Semitic, and some who admired what they called strong leadership. The British Union of Fascists had appeared in 1932 led by Oswald Mosley, and in 1936 changed its name by adding National Socialists to its title. Sir Oswald Mosley was an aristocrat who had a small degree of support but was mainly opposed, not least after he travelled to Germany to meet Hitler. He carried many of the hallmarks of the Nazi Regime, with Gladys Langford writing in her diary on 28 September 1939, that 'several walls are decorated with his Fascist sign and bear slogans, "Mosley for peace. Why fight in a Jews' War, Britons in Khaki, Jews in Air Raids Precautions"'.[4] At least his public rallies met with violent protest, especially in the east-end of London, where Mosley had thought he would find support.

For many of the public, Germany was not seen as a potential enemy, and what was happening in defeated Germany was either ignored, not known about, or believed to be 'their business, not ours'. This broad sweep of the brush is a generally accepted view of the early and mid-1930s. It was the same with politicians who were desperate to avoid another catastrophic war which was their driving motivation until it was too late. This made Churchill and his few supporters an insignificant opposition, but always a thorn in the side of the government because his eloquence and use of English was much feared in the Commons.

It was a forlorn hope that the Germans would follow the broad outline of the Versailles Treaty, and having signed the 1925 Locarno Treaty, they had been allowed to join the League of Nations, and hopefully the 1928 Kellogg-Briand Pact which made war illegal would mean a future of peace. The latter agreement to outlaw war would be welcome in any generation, but as in any friendly school playground there are always a few who will assert themselves and become the bullies, assuming their own version of authority. It is tempting if not cynical to note that in human history this was dreaming in cloud-cuckoo land, and only Churchill and a few others had identified the emerging international bully in Hitler.

The brittle nature of French-German relationships was critical, the French had in recent years twice been invaded by Germany, and Hitler had no bones about his hatred for this neighbour. The British were often seen as the middleman between these two countries, having been at war with both, and not land neighbours with either. Many British, including the Prime Minister Ramsay MacDonald often saw France as the main problem, though this would change as the decade developed. For their part, led by Hitler, the Germans made it clear, it seemed, that all they wanted was peace and a degree of equality, a message which was greeted with pleasure in Britain, even though a few suspected that Hitler was being criminally deceptive. It would take the Prime Minister Chamberlain until after the 1938 Munich Conference to realise that Hitler was not a gentleman who kept his word, while the French tended to be more cynical. However, there were some French leaders, who like Pierre Laval, looked to the easing of tensions with Germany, but later during the war, Laval took this a step too far.

When Hitler had withdrawn from the Disarmament Conference, Churchill was equally opposed to British participation, and as early as 1932 publicly warned the government in the Commons not to believe the peaceful overtures of the Nazi regime and Hitler. Churchill's boldness in his views made himself something of a 'has-been recluse' sitting on the edges of the political benches, somewhat isolated. He would not be silenced, raising the issue of Nazi hatred towards the Jews, and the barbaric nature of the new German regime, demanding the government put more into the army and air force. However, pacifism and the need for international peace remained the dominant theme, which after the First World War was understandable albeit later denounced. There was a general belief that disarmament was the only way forward and had the full support of the Labour Party and many others, even though for some it was mere Utopia. Even Stanley Baldwin (Prime Minister three times and a dominant politician during this era) who was no pacifist, was horrified at the possibility of air warfare when cities could be obliterated within hours of a war starting, warning Parliament of this possible prospect.

Churchill was right in noting the anti-Semitism in Germany as this grew in barbarity, presenting for some observers a serious picture of the racialistic nature of Nazi thinking. Anti-Semitism was sadly and irrationally a feature in many European countries. In Britain, the government minister Leslie Hore-Belisha, when appointed Secretary of State for War in 1937, was rightly interested in army reform and mechanisation, which was necessary, but he was unpopular mainly because he was Jewish. Later commentators noted that Leslie Hore-Belisha was attempting the necessary reforms in the army, but some, probably quite rightly, detected this degree of anti-Semitism amongst Leslie Hore-Belisha's critics. Others thought that because he was Jewish, he might become 'a target for the Germans'.[5] This turned out to be true, when Goebbels' diaries were translated, he referred on 18 January 1940, having fastened onto the Commons debates, writing in a reference to Hore-Belisha, 'to cap it all the Jew issues a weak statement', drawing attention to Hore-Belisha's race.[6] Either way anti-Semitism was ridiculous even when social, but in Germany it was becoming widely known there were more sinister ramifications happening with its Jewish minority. Anti-Semitism was a feature in most European countries, pogroms in Tsarist Russia and Poland had been aggressive and even in Western countries it may have been only some form of social snobbery, but it was dangerous. In the issue which has been termed the 'Eastern Jews', who were constantly fleeing for their lives, in a conversation between Chamberlain and Édouard Daladier they both expressed concern that these refuges if allowed entry to their countries might cause concern with their current assimilated Jewish populations.[7] The ruthless idea of sending Jews to Madagascar is well known, but probably not the fact it had been in the air since the 1880s. In 1937 the Polish government had approached the British and French about sending to them a million Jews or to British South Africa. The British declined, but Léon Blum the French Prime Minister of the day, enabled a Jewish expert to visit Madagascar to see if it made sense, only to be told it could accommodate some 500 families not the anticipated thousands. In 1938 the French Foreign Minister Bonnet suggested to Ribbentrop that Madagascar might resolve the problem, and in 1939 Chamberlain and Roosevelt wondered whether Italy could accommodate Jews in Abyssinia. The so-called 'moderate anti-Semitism meant the Nazis interpreted this as evidence of an anti-Semitic consensus'.[8] The later Nazi annihilation of Jews was to shock the world, but the barbaric signs were appearing in Germany, and many parts of so-called civilised Europe carried some of the blame because of similar attitudes about Jewish people.

Another issue engaging the minds of leading politicians was the downturn in economics as experienced across the globe. During the First World

War 'the British National Debt increased by a factor of twelve. By 1927 it was equivalent to a crushing 172 per cent of gross domestic product'.[9] Chamberlain as one time Chancellor of the Exchequer was acutely aware of the state of the country's finances, which had meant deep cuts especially in military spending as no war was anticipated. To keep these cuts the well-known 'Ten Year Rule' policy (1919) was introduced, meaning military expenditure would increase only if a war were likely within the given time span, and Chamberlain had been part of this policy rule. However, it should be recalled that the financial downturn in the early interbellum years had been far worse in Germany and the USA than in Britain, though even in 1937 there was a serious fear of a major recession. Although the military expressed early concerns, little was done until halfway through the decade of the 1930s, then slowly if not half-heartedly. Churchill kept on demanding from Baldwin that more was needed to be spent on the air force, and this time he was greeted with more cheers from his Tory colleagues. Many critics saw Baldwin's time as one of lethargy, and he has been criticised for a seeming lack of interest in matters arising overseas. Baldwin's lack of concern in international matters had already been noted by the German regime, and it struck the Germans that 'Chamberlain seemed much livelier'.[10]

The Chiefs of Staff continued to apply their pressures to spend more on the military, but Neville Chamberlain who was Chancellor at the time managed to block such extravagance. There was possibly the feeling of putting too much reliance on the French at this stage, as they had the largest army in Europe and the second largest air force. They had built their Maginot Line which envisaged another static war, and not the mobile war, an innovative approach which had been prepared a decade before by the German General von Seeckt during Weimar Republic days. In addition to this French politics was somewhat volatile with governments collapsing one after another.

More to the point it was becoming widely known that the much-feared German air force was growing at a rapid rate, and Baldwin was obliged to defend the government policy of not spending more on the RAF. Throughout 1934 Churchill hammered home the warnings that unless the RAF received more money to expand then Britain would not be able to withstand a German air attack. The Labour Party accused him of warmongering, others accusing him of creating unnecessary panic, while others in political style accused him of trying to resurrect his lost political importance. This heated debate over air power was further darkened when it became known that the German army now stood at 300,000 and was still rapidly expanding. It is historically curious that with all these warnings the government continued on its course of trusting Hitler's promises, a problem this study underlines given the precise knowledge supplied, not only by its own Intelligence Services, but by books being published about the dangers in the mid-1930s. One of the accusations levelled at Churchill by Sir Samuel Hoare, was that he had less knowledge of the German facts and figures than the government, and so there was no need for his sense of panic. It may be true that Churchill often exaggerated the numbers, but with the benefit of hindsight, he was undoubtedly correct to sound the alarm bells, and he had his own often clandestine informants within the Civil Service, Military, and elsewhere. There were signs that Churchill's support was increasing, and the former Foreign Secretary Sir Austen Chamberlain had accused the Nazi regime of being a reincarnation of Prussian Imperialism but with more savagery. At first the anti-appeasement lobby was small, but it increased as the 1930s unfolded.

In 1935 Sir John Simon, Foreign Secretary (1931–35), anticipated a visit to Germany to see if high-level talks might resolve some of the gathering issues over defence expenditure. However, Hitler chose the moment to announce German conscription was back which simply overturned the Treaty of Versailles, which seriously alarmed the French who had just voted for a two-year military service along the same lines. Sir John Simon continued to press for the visit which delighted the German regime as it appeared as if France and Britain were parting company. It was not the case, but John Simon was only wanting the talking to persist, to use Churchill's later phrase, somewhat ironically, about 'jaw-jaw, not war-war'. Eventually Hitler welcomed Simon alongside Anthony Eden (Foreign Affairs Minister) and Eric Phipps (British Ambassador to Germany at that time) as if they were potential allies. Various issues regarding foreign policy were raised, with Eden reporting back that it was impossible to influence Hitler. Hitler's interpreter, Paul Schmidt, who was nearly always present at such meetings in his autobiographical account recalled that while France was busy creating a system of security pacts to face future problems, 'the British had decided to seek clarification of the German intention through talks'.[11] He had the distinct feeling that England was friendlier, contrasting him to the French Ambassador, who had suggested that all ambassadors should be recalled setting up a common defence policy against Germany. Schmidt had attended the talks of Simon and Anthony Eden with Hitler, noting 'there were friendly smiles and handshakes all round' and that for Hitler 'the British guests were a triumph for him'.[12] Hitler, knowing the one thing they all had in common was their distrust of Communism, and consequently, in his usual monological style hammered away at this issue, claiming that National Socialism had saved Germany and was willing to do so to protect Europe. Schmidt noted that Simon 'looked at Hitler with by no means unsympathetic interest', with an expression of 'fatherly understanding'.[13] Following the discussion of an 'Eastern Pact', Eden wondered whether it could be combined with a system 'of bilateral non-aggression pacts or agreements of mutual assistance'.[14] Eden was virtually accepting a war in the East of Europe was acceptable, but not in the West. When Simon raised the question of Germany leaving the League of Nations, Schmidt was surprised that Hitler was by means as intransigent as he had anticipated. Schmidt recalled that the British were avoiding any antagonism and Hitler was extremely moderate in tone, demanding parity with Britain and France, which meant increasing the Luftwaffe only to match that of the Soviet Union. It was so friendly Hitler was invited to dine at the British Embassy, which was his first visit to any foreign embassy. In a revealing note Schmidt did not see the same friendly look in Eden's eyes as he did in Simon's. He was right as Eden was growing suspicious of Nazi Germany, whereas Simon, following government policy was always hopefully looking for areas of potential agreement to create a sense of unity and therefore peace. For Eden, his political attitudes would later move away from Chamberlain which would later cause problems between them, but never of a personal nature. Eden described Chamberlain's appearance and speech as 'stiff and forbidding...this had nothing to do with the real man, who was warm-hearted, considerate, and generous. He was incapable of a mean action and conscientious to a fault'.[15]

However, there were signs appearing that Britain's insistent efforts to negotiate with Germany were causing minor strains in the relationship with France. When in mid-April 1935 the French and British prime ministers met Mussolini in Stresa to form a collective agreement against the sudden upsurge of Germany, some mild form of agreement was reached. Then a couple of months later Britain signed the Anglo-German Naval Treaty which virtually appeared as if Britain were joining Germany in overturning the Versailles

Treaty. The British either overlooked or ignored the question of German submarines, which would in a few years cause serious problems. Hitler's interpreter was at the Naval Meeting, acting for Joachim von Ribbentrop (although Ribbentrop's English was good), who expressed astonishment the way Ribbentrop opened the proceedings with the threat that unless the British government did not agree at once, then the meeting would be useless. Schmidt did not think it was an intelligent start, and he was surprised by the friendly attitude of the British and the way they cooperated.[16] At this stage this military agreement pleased Hitler as for him it was noticeable that he was making headway with the British. Had Hitler been concerned about the Stresa agreement this Naval agreement by Britain may have calmed his nerves. The Italians felt let down, and the French led by Laval at this time were angry, and Eden was sent to France to calm the situation. He was the right man as he had some sympathy for the French, noting in his memoirs that 'France's distrust of the Nazi Government seemed to me justified'.[17]

Schmidt noted in his memoirs that 'at the time it was not possible to see that he [Hitler] owed his success less to his own statecraft than to the lack of decision and disunity amongst his opponents', which was an incisive view at the time.[18] At home in Britain by 1935 there were still sharp divisions of opinion on how to deal with the now recognised growing power of Germany, and more disagreements as to how serious Hitler was in his placatory peace ramblings. There was, it appeared, no sure knowledge, as far as the government could see, nor any signals of his intentions in terms of German foreign policy. The so-called Stresa front failed while the ink was still drying, and while the Western powers were unaware of the man Hitler, they had not realised that Mussolini had his own empire building plans. The frailty of the Stresa front was weakened when Mussolini suddenly invaded Abyssinia (1935–6), one of the few independent African nations at that time. The more astute outsider must have known that this was on the cards, as Mussolini was trying to emulate the expansionism of the ancient Roman Empire, always calling the Mediterranean 'our sea'. It was a ruthless onslaught against a country of tribesmen crushed by air power and the Italians even used gas-warfare. In this growing era of political instability, the British and French politicians had created what can only be described as yet more fiascos. The invasion of Abyssinia was against the stated principles of the League of Nations and its concept of international law on which so much hope had been based.

It had been Mussolini who had encouraged Abyssinia to join the League which, like NATO today, had ruled that an attack on one of its members was an attack on all.

In Britain Ramsay MacDonald had retired and was succeeded by Stanley Baldwin, and Samuel Hoare had replaced John Simon as foreign secretary. It was a time of political tension as the two Western powers of Britain and France had been wooing Italy in support as at the Stresa Front, and now their hoped-for friend had broken the very rules they feared about Nazi Germany. To try and iron out the crisis as fast as possible it was Eden who had first suggested the idea that Abyssinia cede part of her territory in exchange for slithers of land elsewhere in northeast Africa. In Britain there was public concern that it might lead to another war, and this time over generally unknown remote desert areas. Even the British King George V threatened to abdicate if Britain involved itself in a military conflict. Churchill was unhappy because he thought, correctly as it transpired, that this whole episode would thrust Mussolini, a hoped-for ally against Hitler, into Hitler's arms. The government of the day felt the same way, and were desperate to avoid an outright conflict, as peace was the priority of the day. The League of Nations had responded by imposing sanctions on Italy, with France under Laval and Britain supporting this, but with some provisos to try and keep Italy onside. It may have been a crisis for Abyssinia but in Britain and France their crisis was hanging on to Italy's support against Germany. This resulted in the infamous Hoare-Laval agreement of accepting what had happened by encouraging Abyssinia to accept other areas as mentioned above, which when it became known created public outrage, and was simply regarded as a shady deal. This created a major public storm of almost unprecedented anger. Samuel Hoare had no option but to resign, the United Nations which soon lifted the sanctions was seen as ineffective, and Hitler was undoubtedly pleased with the prompt uselessness of the Stresa Front. The way both British and French politicians had reacted was not only indecisive and muddled, but clearly indicated an ineptitude at a time when sound and clear decision making was essential.

Confusion and indecision continued when in early March 1936 German troops re-occupied the Rhineland. It was all part of Hitler's irredentist nationalism to reclaim Germany territory removed by the Versailles Treaty, and it was believed that French Intelligence knew this was likely, but they were still surprised when it happened. Eden had replaced Hoare as Foreign Secretary and had suggested the Rhineland would be the next area of concern. There were foreign observers who thought that Hitler was justified, including many British MPs, others were concerned that the absence of a response would strengthen Hitler in his plans, and many if not most in the West wanting to sweep it aside in the hope of peace. For their part, the French military also did not want to risk an all-out war. The French press was against retaliation on the grounds that France needed peace, as in Britain with the majority of the Commons wanting peace at all costs. Eden suggested every effort should be made to discourage any French military reaction which indicated he was out of touch with French popular opinion who would have agreed with him. However, he was undoubtedly in touch with his French equivalent Pierre-Étienne Flandin (French Prime Minister 1934–5) who wanted to challenge the Germans, if necessary, with the military. Hitler had been advised by both military and men like Schacht this move could spell disaster, but Hitler had correctly read the West's overwhelming desire for peace. The British hope for peace and the news that the French wanted to challenge the Nazis did not help the relationship between the two allies. Flandin made every effort to convince the British the French were correct, but was ignored. Postwar analysis has often suggested that had the French Army retaliated it would have succeeded (having at that moment the largest army in Europe) and it may well have led to the downfall of Hitler. This incident 'has often been identified as the crucial point at which Hitler's revisionism could and should have been nipped in the bud'.[19] This was a possibility but falls into the category of 'what if' speculation. Schmidt, Hitler's interpreter recalled a friend in the Foreign Office, from where he worked, who had told him 'If France attaches the slightest value to her security, then she must march into the Rhineland right now', and Schmidt added that he heard Hitler say many times that 'the forty-eight hours after marching into the Rhineland were the most nerve-racking in my life'.[20] It remains a complex puzzle which must always remain speculative.

The British were adamant that what is called 'appeasement' was the only way forward, and blocked Flandin's efforts, causing him and many others to wonder whether Britain was pro-German. Flandin wrote in his diary 'the peace current is still very strong. The idea of war is running up against strong opposition'.[21] Many in France and Britain were strongly pacifist and did not see this German reclamation of old territory as a cause for war. Following Abyssinia and the occupation of the Rhineland, the League of Nations appeared to have lost any realistic grip, there were tensions between France and Britain, and Hitler felt stronger, not just because of having successfully challenged the West and increased his popularity at home, but because Mussolini was emerging as a potential ally. There were amongst the two major western democracies serious political problems and divisions resulting in a high degree of indecision and lack of cohesion. The French did not help the situation with their political instability, frequently changing their governments, once cynically dubbed as the game of musical chairs, and in Britain prime ministers and senior posts such as foreign secretaries were too often changing, which was unusual for the traditional British sense of constancy, suggesting this was an era of uncertainty.

In Britain, these surprise shocks had reawakened the need to improve British arms which Churchill had been consistently demanding. In 1936, the year before he died, Austen Chamberlain (a former Chancellor of the Exchequer and also foreign secretary) had strongly criticised the government for not giving sufficient attention to this vital area of national interest. Churchill was pleased with the growing criticism, but still personally angry that he had not been given any form of governmental seat. It had been anticipated that Churchill would be the new government's defence minister, but this went to a Thomas Inskip, much derided but who managed his post well, especially with the RAF now becoming recognised as a critical branch for the defence of the realm. The problem for Churchill was that in the past he had created too many political enemies, but this never stopped him from attacking the government on failing to spend more on the military, and by demanding preparation for a war and not appeasement. The government was taking steps, increasing the size of the Royal Navy and Air Force, but seeming to give less attention to the army. For the government it was the constant concern of economics and the belief that Hitler could be won around, asking why it was necessary to impoverish the nation when peace could be maintained. There was always the constant rumour that in a new war, victory or defeat would come from the air not armies, which was entirely misleading, at it would be finally recognised that 'feet on the ground' was the decisive factor, although air power changed the nature of war. The Conservatives were edging towards rearmament, but at this stage were opposed by the Labour

Party. Churchill remained persistent, continuing to receive information from well-placed Civil Servants and often talking with officers from the military. He made the most of his position as a member of the Government's Air Defence Committee raising questions and issues at every opportunity, but as far as the government was concerned, he was just an ongoing nuisance.

However, the RAF was beginning to expand, probably because of the fear that aerial warfare was seen as an increasing menace. Austen Chamberlain and Churchill came together to demand a secret session in the Commons which was intended to demonstrate the main problems so reporters would be kept in the dark to make sure other nations had no inside knowledge. There remained the great divide between Churchill with his supporters and the government who could not accept Churchill's argument that Nazi Germany was a serious threat. There were some on the left-wing of the House who were now beginning to stand alongside Churchill, probably helped by the start of the Civil War developing in Spain, making Europe appear even more unstable, with concern that perhaps that it meant in another major country the rise of yet another dictator in the person of Francisco Franco. Even though the bombing by German planes caused considerable destruction and civilian deaths, as well as problems at sea with Italian submarines sinking boats suspected of carrying Russian supplies to Spain, it was still felt that European security was not threatened by Germany's military growth. Franco's anti-republican side was opposed by communists and had Russian support, plus the International Brigade made up from many nationalities, while Franco was in turn supported by both Mussolini and Hitler. At about the same time war broke out between China and Japan, all of which clearly sent messages that the world was entering a serious state of unrest and Europe in particular was appearing unstable.

In the midst of this gathering maelstrom of events in May 1937 Prime Minister Baldwin resigned, proposing Neville Chamberlain as his successor, who was already 68 years old. He was generally seen as a thorough gentleman with exacting standards and a man of determination. Unlike many of his political contemporaries, he had not fought in the First World War, but he was all too conscious of the deaths of many friends. His previous role had been Chancellor of the Exchequer, and the economy had dominated his thinking and would always be part of his political thinking processes. There was no love lost between Chamberlain and the Labour Party, it was clear that they detested him as much as he did them, and few were prepared to support him, and because of his style of dress and general demeanour he was often nicknamed 'the coroner'.[22]

The policy of appeasement is nearly always associated with Neville Chamberlain, but he was continuing the work of his predecessors which as a strategy was often used in British diplomatic history. It has often been claimed the policy of appeasement caused war, which is fundamentally untrue, it was war which produced appeasement as it was an effort to stop it starting or spreading. When Chamberlain had taken over there had not been the slightest progress with Germany, except for the much-maligned German-British Naval agreement. Even when Hitler introduced major conscription into the forces Chamberlain still remained in hope. He continued to believe that by diplomatic negotiations he could prevent war. The British government was becoming aware that Hitler was probably planning the *Anschluss* with Austria, and the return of German territory lost after the First World War. Many in the appeasement camp thought that these demands were reasonable, but Austria was not Britain's business, as it was an old and traditional country with its own history. Whereas the lost territories of the Versailles Treaty could be returned, but only with the agreement of other powers over which there had been international agreements. Chamberlain, as noted, was a man known for his determination, and he was entirely convinced that appeasement was the right policy, and he intended to pursue it despite the growing number of critics. He was accumulating information about German rearmament, he knew of the frustrations generated by the Versailles Treaty, what he did not appear to know was the true nature of Hitler the man, nor his henchmen, and the Nazi regime. The Nazis were as determined as he was but facing the other way, because their plans could not be fulfilled without war.

Another British politician of this era was Viscount Halifax (Edward Wood) who was highly respected and a powerful landowner, close to the Royal Family, having their support and appreciation. He was seen as a committed Christian with, as is well-known, Churchill dubbing him with the nickname of the 'Holy Fox'. Later, when he had met Hitler, the German dictator described him as the 'English Parson'. He was an avid follower of hunting and shooting and opted to visit Göring who was the master of ceremonies in the German pursuit of this sport, and who was holding an exhibition on this social 'upper crust' pursuit. This meeting was grasped by Chamberlain who was desperate to try and form some relationship with the Nazi Germans. Halifax had recently been fairly successful with Ghandi in India, and it was anticipated he could repeat his success in Germany. Halifax went to Germany where he was greeted by Göring on whom he much later passed some interesting and incisive judgements. Henry 'Chips' Channon in his diary of 5 December 1937, noted that he had met Halifax after his return from Germany, and was told that 'he liked all the Nazi leaders, even Goebbels… he thinks the regime absolutely fantastic, perhaps even too fantastic to be taken seriously…and he thinks good will come of it'.[23] Like many others Halifax came under the spell of 'Nazi charm', and for a time it worked until he changed his mind because of developing events, and later he joined the anti-appeasement lobby. With the benefit of hindsight, Halifax was far too amenable, generally accepting Nazi views on Russia, and the eastern area of Europe and Austria. His tendency was to see Britain as an island with an overseas empire, and the continent as of little importance for British interests. He once wrote that 'he could not bring himself to condemn nationalism or even racialism as either unnatural or immoral' and commended the Nazis for their hatred of communism.[24] Some of these views exposed him as more of a fox than a 'Holy Fox'. Chamberlain wrote in his diary that 'the German visit was from my point of view a great success…creating an atmosphere in which it is possible to discuss with Germany the practical questions involved in a European settlement'.[25] However, during his meeting with Hitler, it dawned on him that offering Hitler free action in Europe and bargaining over the lost colonies was evidently a wasted effort. Halifax 'the holy fox' was meeting a werewolf, prepared to lie, blackmail, and to gain his way. For Hitler it appeared that Britain was weak, and France was in turmoil with its political divisions, and he was beginning to see Britain more as a possible enemy than a potential ally. Hitler regarded his own views on the Western Powers could be a major pressure point with which he could persuade some of his more reluctant generals, who kept warning him that war against France and Britain might be catastrophic. Halifax, who was determined for a peaceful solution, nevertheless pursued the policy of appeasing Hitler by agreeing with his views, hinting that anything was possible unless it required force of arms. He later described Hitler as a sincere man who believed in everything he said, which could also be attributed to any mafia boss. Halifax arrived at the conclusions as he saw them, of needing agreement with Germany, knowing it would cost, including the return of some colonial territories. In Halifax, it appeared that Chamberlain had recruited another resolute politician to the cause of placating and befriending Hitler. While Hitler was undoubtedly viewing England as an enemy, Chamberlain and his cohorts were digging their heels in to ensure peace in the West. Halifax for all his abilities had recognised Hitler's stubbornness, but he had failed to see what sort of man Hitler was, and he had swept too casually over Hitler's plans and intentions.

In 1938 there were serious divisions at the political level, with Chamberlain rejecting the American President Roosevelt's offer to appeal for peace to the rising dictators to avoid friction within Europe. Although in a period of isolationist nationalism across the Atlantic, the Americans were aware not only of issues between Japan and China, but the rising tensions in Europe. Roosevelt was proposing an appeal for peace, suggesting a disarmament agreement with a new system of equal distribution of essential raw resources and material. Since the First World War America had kept itself to itself, but suddenly had re-appeared on the world stage out of concern emanating from Japan and Germany. Chamberlain had asked him to refrain on the grounds that he was personally doing the negotiating which did not please Eden, who was on holiday at the time, with the prime minister stepping into his role as Foreign Secretary during his absence. This was the start of the breakdown between these two leading men in the government. Eden was convinced that keeping America onside was critical and having just been on holiday with Churchill this was no surprise. Eden wrote 'I wanted to strengthen our hand by every means, amongst which, closer Anglo-American relations had a first place'.[26] Chamberlain appeared to be uncertain about American influence, and later said 'Heavens knows I don't want the Americans to fight for us; we would have to pay too dearly for that if they had any right to be in on our peace.' Fortunately the part-American Churchill made the right decision.[27]

Chamberlain had by hook and by crook been trying to meet with Mussolini to form a good relationship between the two countries. The machinations for this meeting involved the widow of his brother Austen who was in Rome and friendly with Mussolini, and a letter was received which was supposed to be from Mussolini, but which had probably been written by the Italian politician and diplomat Count Dino Grandi. Eden always found it a source of deep irritation that 'Lady Chamberlain had been visiting Mussolini and Ciano and reading to them another letter from the Prime Minister'.[28]

Eden objected to this type of outside interference, but not with the American President who had expressed concern of the dangers to European democracy. Eden wrote that 'it seemed to the President that as the bandit nations drew together, their respective policies became more and more clearly synchronised'.[29] It was known that Mussolini intended to visit Hitler and the diplomatic dancing continued unabated. Grandi wanted to meet Mussolini to discuss the situation between Italy with Britain and France, but Mussolini was more concerned about France than Britain, and expressed the opinion he could not care if Britain continued to rearm. From Ciano's (Mussolini's son-in-law and later Italy's Foreign Secretary) diplomatic papers it is now clear that although Ciano and Grandi supported Mussolini, they both feared Nazi Germany and later turned against Mussolini. It was Grandi who later in the war years made the proposal for the downfall of Mussolini for which Ciano was executed, but Grandi saved himself by going abroad. At this stage of events there seems little doubt that Grandi wanted a rapprochement with Britain.[30] However, when Grandi expressed concerns that any agreement with London was unlikely, Ciano told Grandi he agreed, adding the curious note to his diary that he concurred with 'the *Duce* that on a historical level the Italian British conflict is inevitable'. Ciano had demanded that Dino Grandi expedite the matter, but he was up against Eden, now well known for his reluctance to deal with dictators. Later, a worthless agreement was signed in April 1938, of no value because the agreements were contingent upon Italy withdrawing troops from the Spanish conflict, and throughout this year relationships with the British were never easy, especially when an Italian submarine sank a British ship just off the Spanish coast during the civil war in that country.

When the meeting eventually took place, it was clear that Chamberlain was probing the Italian emissary, not only to discover Mussolini's attitude, but what Hitler was planning. It was Grandi's opinion that Chamberlain was pleasantly accepting his replies, but he noted there was obvious tension between the prime minister and Eden. He was astute in this observation, with Eden recalling that 'Chamberlain did not want me to be present, but I insisted, Grandi having ducked me for several days'.[31] It was now widely known that Eden was hostile to any form of dictatorship. Eden questioned Grandi over the Italian contribution in Spain, the so-called issue of volunteers, the matter of piracy in the Mediterranean, and informed Grandi there was no question of Abyssinia being recognised with all these other causes of aggravation. Grandi turned to Chamberlain, and following Ciano's advice, explained that the *Duce* 'is more anxious to clasp England's hand than he was yesterday'.[32] There was a clash over the venue for further proposed talks, Grandi insisting on Rome and the British on London. Grandi claimed that Rome had been agreed and produced the necessary papers to prove his point. In his telegram to Rome, Grandi outlined the difficulties and tensions between Eden and Chamberlain, the two arguing in front of him as if he were not there. Grandi wrote that 'Eden, for his part, did not scruple to reveal himself fully in my presence…as an inveterate enemy of fascism and Italy.'[33] The line that Grandi was proposing was that Italy wanted the gains in Abyssinia recognised and not to be treated as a pariah State.

However, Grandi had witnessed firsthand the growing clash between Chamberlain and Eden, reflecting serious tensions within the British government. Although Eden at this stage had some hopes of an appeasement with Germany, he was rapidly changing his mind, and he was outraged by Mussolini's behaviour, as well as Chamberlain for toadying to the dictator, and by contacting Roosevelt without him as Foreign Secretary being aware. The arguments between Eden and Chamberlain were diverse and heated. He warned Chamberlain that his rebuttal of Roosevelt's offer of help would send America back into the safety of isolationism and pointed out that regarding Mussolini it was only politically safe to negotiate with a person he trusted, with Chamberlain responding that he trusted the Italian dictator. There was no doubt that these tensions were not only noted by Grandi, but others which would have caused joy in Berlin. Given these circumstances Eden resigned, and Chamberlain in the Commons defended his policy of keeping the peace. Eden, however, was fairly popular in the public eye, and it was clear that not only was the government divided over the issue of appeasement but so were the public. It was clear from this rift in government that Britain's political leadership was divided and was leading to a degree of internal instability. Postwar, and with the benefit of hindsight it was more than apparent that Hitler did not understand the nature of negotiations, and Mussolini would follow the winner in the international scene, and these insights remained a mystery to most of the politicians of those days, with the exception of Churchill and a few of his intimates.

Chamberlain remained convinced that Mussolini could be won over, but the main thrust of governmental planning was the effort to keep Hitler onside and under some form of control by political agreements. There was even a degree of anticipation about which high-ranking Germans could be invited to King George VI's coronation which caused heated debates and discussions. Chamberlain was hoping with others like Halifax that Hitler could be appeased by handing back some selected colonies which caused further debate. Had he read *Mein Kampf* properly it would have been clear that Hitler had next to no interest in the colonies as he wanted to dominate eastern and southern Europe, becoming the lead nation in Europe, not Africa. It appeared Hoare knew Hitler would not be happy with such an offer, and the debate in Britain rumbled on both in public and behind closed doors.

From Intelligence and other sources, it was known that the Nazi news was focusing on two high-ranking German generals (Blomberg and Fritsch) who had been involved in trumped up charges and dismissed, mainly because they had objected to some of Hitler's plans, and consequently the OKW (Oberkommando der Wehrmacht) was established. More worrying was that Hitler had made himself the overall commander, which with the Prussian discipline of obedience carried many ramifications. A fanatical politician who once reached the rank of corporal was now to be obeyed in all military matters. In Britain, during the war years, Churchill often came up with military proposals, but they had to be vetted by the Imperial General Staff, and Alan Brooke's (Chief of this Committee) diary exposed the fact that Churchill could only suggest or advise and not dictate, which led to many heated discussions.* In Germany it was widely known how Hitler could quickly convince people he was right in all his judgements, it had worked with many British visitors, diplomats, and later his control over traditional sound-thinking German generals, and it was often dubbed 'the command bug'. Although not widely recognised at the time it was like having a psychopath as the pilot of a large passenger plane. When these changes happened in Germany the outside world was puzzled, if not bemused, but the possible ramifications were not explored. Also still brewing in the background was the potential *Anschluss* which was known about and concerned Britain,

---

* See Alanbrooke Field Marshal Lord, *War Diaries 1939–45* (London: Weidenfeld & Nicolson, 2001) and Sangster, Andrew, *The Unknown Field Marshal* (Oxford & Philadelphia: Casemate, 2020)

France, and Italy. When it was discussed as to whether Hitler should be warned off, Ambassador Henderson warned that it would put Hitler off listening to British overtures. Eden had now resigned as foreign secretary, and Halifax had observed that the Germans would be more amenable with Eden gone. Halifax met Ribbentrop and underlined that Britain wanted friendship with Germany, but regarding Austria and Czechoslovakia and German plans for these countries, it would be risky. It was evident that some members of the public who had greeted Ribbentrop with jeers were absorbing the issues at stake. There were rumours that German troops were gathering near the Austrian borders which was hotly denied. Ribbentrop and his wife, while being entertained as German Ambassador, was asked about Austria. Ribbentrop simply denied the possibility of a German occupation. When news then came through that it was actually happening Ribbentrop simply replied that it had to be for the best. It astonished the outside world, but there seems little doubt that the Austrian public greeted the Germans and Hitler with open arms, and furthermore visitors and foreign journalists were shocked in the way that the Austrians suddenly turned their venom on the Jews, with some describing it as worse than in Germany. The British appeared uncertain about the whole business, some thinking it was a natural union of the same speaking people, some reading about the rapture of the Austrian public, a few claiming it was their business not ours. Other saw it as an attack on a distinctly different country, some regarding it as part of the Nazi dream of expansionism, and Churchill saw it as further proof of what he had claimed about Nazi plans. Chamberlain, determined as ever, wanted peace at any cost. The rift in Britain and amongst its politicians was all too clear, with some, especially in the upper echelons of society being pro-German, while lower down the social strata there was often the sense that 'it was overseas' and nothing to do with us. Halifax started the tune that if the *Anschluss* were done peacefully then all would be well, and the Austrian welcome to the intruding Germans appeared to confirm his thinking. Chamberlain, still anticipating cooperation from Mussolini, when informed of the Austrian greeting retained his hope for a peaceful settlement with Hitler. The Archbishop of Canterbury even 'welcomed the union of Germany and Austria on the grounds that a continuing sore at the heart of European politics had been removed without any bloodshed', neglecting the fact that Austria had always been an independent State, and its government forcibly toppled.³⁴ In Britain it stirred little public interest, with one journalist writing that when the news came through last night, 'this morning's placards are equally excited about the fight [boxing match] between Farr and Baer. We fiddle while Vienna burns'.³⁵

After the Anschluss everyone knew Czechoslovakia was probably Hitler's next target. It was a new country formed after the collapse of the Habsburg Empire covering the old territories of Bohemia, Moravia, and Silesia and consisted of a vast number of languages and different nationalities, including Germans. One of the strengths of the Habsburgs was their willingness to accept all nationalities within their empire. The area of greatest concern was the Sudetenland with a large German population and a dedicated National Socialist Party led by Konrad Henlein. It was widely accepted that Hitler was in nationalistic terms irredentist and with his pan-Germanism concept wanted post-First World War German territory back. There was a degree of sympathy for this possibility, but irredentist nationalism is only a small step away from aggressive nationalism, which seeks expansionism in countries with any political excuse of justification. It appears that a few people at this time thought Hitler's demands were fair and were possible, despite Hitler's *Mein Kampf* boldly stating the need for *Lebensraum*. Hitler had already expressed his anger at the way Czechoslovakia was like having a dagger in the back of Germany. Through a 1925 treaty, the French had promised to come to the defence of Czechoslovakia and recommitted it in March 1938. In Britain, as the rumours circulated there were the usual divisions of opinion, with some thinking that more aggression by Germany meant war, with some hoping that it would not affect Britain at all, and some with a degree of sympathy for Germany reclaiming lost territory. Churchill wanted a Grand Alliance, but the cabinet met and decided it was best for the Czech government to talk with Hitler and find a solution.

This all rose to the surface because thousands of troops were rumoured to be gathering along the Czech borders. The Home Secretary Samuel Hoare raised the issue as to whether Britain should walk alongside France, but in both countries, despite French promises, it was considered that from a practical point of view there was little that could be done if the invasion started, not least in Britain where the army was not only ill-prepared but low on numbers. Maurice Hankey pointed out that the Czechs' best resources for industry, its best defences were in Sudetenland. However, the general feeling was one of resigned helplessness. There was still the hope that Hitler's wishes would soon be satisfied (or appeased), and peace would reign. Even when the French minster of defence asked that Britain should stand by France, it was rejected, but the general feeling in France was similar to that of Britain where it was believed that nothing could be done, and which, with the benefit of hindsight, may have been correct. This raises the problems of making promises which cannot be kept as with Poland in September 1939.

Meanwhile Chamberlain had thought himself successful with the Anglo-Italian treaty in Rome on 16 April 1938, but with Italy's involvement in Spain it proved to be a waste of paper and time. He was also convinced that Hitler could be kept onside, despite the alarms being sounded with many reports of German troop movements constantly arriving close to the Czech borders. The Germans from General Keitel to Ribbentrop kept denying this was happening, but the Czechs were preparing their military. As it was the crisis did not materialise except in helping Britain and France into further political differences, though the French were now more alongside the British in thinking the Czechs should 'talk' to Hitler, probably because they realised that they would be seen as breaking their promises.

After the fright that Hitler was going to invade Czechoslovakia political opinion in Britain and France and also at the public level remained divided. Churchill long seen as the leader of anti-appeasement lobby had some supporters in the Commons, but many remained cautious of associating with him given his political record. His main supporters tended to be Harold Macmillan and Brendan Bracken, and while others may have understood where he was coming from, he was a person whom the politically sensitive felt best to avoid. There was still the overall belief that Communism was much more to be feared than any dictator, and Chamberlain's constant assertions that he was in control gave many a sense of assurance. Anthony Eden, when he had resigned, had taken a lengthy holiday, and although a growing anti-appeaser, wanted to keep out of the limelight. Eden had criticised Chamberlain about upsetting Roosevelt's offer of help and was undoubtedly right, and there was growing consternation in America about what was happening in Europe. The American Ambassador to London, Joseph Kennedy, was cynical about the British, believing they had misjudged many things, but fortunately for later war years Churchill recognised the power of America's size and resources. There were critics in America who believed that Britain's upper echelons in society were terrified that they would lose their sense of grand prestige if the communists or left-wing flourished, so to retain their positions they were prepared to come to terms with the dictators. There were some who may have fitted this proposed pattern, but in British society from the House of Lords, through the Commons and down to the pubs and streets there were a myriad of opinions which given the state of confusion was not surprising.

Chamberlain held the power and at times almost behaved in a dictatorial fashion, using the Whips to ensure his views were upheld, which amounted to a tight rein on demanding total support from Party members. He was self-assured that his diagnosis of Hitler and Mussolini was correct, and he had no time to listen to what he saw as the warmongers. It transpired to be a serious flaw that he always 'assumed the existence of moderate elements within the Nazi regime that could be strengthened through conciliation'.[36] Somehow, he and many others totally failed to understand Hitler's true nature, even though there was available evidence which would have made Chamberlain and others aware of the man they were dealing with.

Following the First World War there was a genuine and understandable hope to avoid another world war, an increasing fear of bombing by the rapid development of air power. In 1935 the film *Things to Come* based 'on H. G. Wells' novel, warned of the effects of air power and of weapons of mass destruction' and the resurgence of pacifism was no surprise.[37] The next war it was believed would not involve battles in faraway places but civilians and cities. The Italian air theorist Giulio Dohuet's theories, which had been published in the United States (*Il dominio dell'aria* – Mastering the Airspace) was widely read abroad with its theory of demonstrating large scale bombing of civilian areas to stop industry from supplying their military.

There were now growing numbers who were suspicious of Hitler and wondering whether his peace overtures were honest. It is easy with the benefit of hindsight in the post Second World War era to be critical of these divisions, perhaps the only valid one, which is part of the theme behind this study was the failure to understand the man Hitler and explore the Nazi Regime, when there was known published evidence, and which is explored later in this book.

The political divisions within Britain and France continued, but now the focus was over Hitler's intentions regarding Czechoslovakia, for many people a country of which little was known. It was understood that the Germans in the Sudetenland were restless and that the Nazi Party was active there, and Hitler wanted it back within German boundaries. There were constant reports in the German press as to how badly the Sudeten Germans were treated, and although it is now believed the Czechs could have been more amenable, the Nazi propaganda typically exaggerated the situation.

Despite the earlier crisis many were convinced that the issue would not be resolved until Hitler had his own way, and Ambassador Henderson reminded the government of this within his diplomatic messages, and as will be explored in the next section, it was becoming clear that the British Ambassador was too friendly with the Nazi regime. There was a high degree of sympathy for the German claims which even found some support in the British press. The so-called discussions between the Czech and Nazi governments were slow, mainly because the Czechs knew they were up against a now powerful military country, and the Nazi regime knew that it was only a matter of timing. Chamberlain was sticking to his pacifist diplomatic hopes and demanding support from the Commons. It was, as far as Chamberlain was concerned a matter of being able to talk to the Germans face to face. He was therefore overjoyed when Hitler's personal adjutant, a Captain Fritz Wiedemann met Halifax with suggestions of exploring the possibility of Göring coming to London. Perhaps because of their lack of knowledge of Hitler's power, it was not recognised that all his henchmen, Göring, Goebbels, and Himmler would only repeat that ordered by Hitler, the only difference was that Göring smiled more and was conventionally more acceptable. Any hope produced by this visit soon evaporated, and Lord Runciman (known as the Runciman Mission) would travel to Czechoslovakia to function as a mediator. It was met with hope, but it was pointed out in the Commons that the Sudetenland was where the Czech borders were well fortified, and if they came to Germany the way to Prague would be wide open. It was a prescient warning of things to come, but it was ignored with the fervour for peace. There were also doubts about whether Runciman was the best choice, but for many the mission offered some hope. It was dampened somewhat by consistent Intelligence reports that there was a great deal of military activity happening in Germany. It was clear that Germany was preparing for war and supported by the news that some German generals, especially the respected Ludwig Beck had resigned, an ominous note.

Diplomats and Civil Servants

When Hitler took over the reins of power the British Ambassador in Berlin was Sir Horace Rumbold, (1928–1933) who although a mild-mannered gentleman had quickly warned his government about Hitler's propensity for the use of violence to gain his way. He was one of the few who had read *Mein Kampf* (not translated into English until 1933) and realised Hitler's overall intentions, not just for organising popular German support, but his policies towards *Lebensraum* and his embittered hatred of France and Jews. He also placed considerable emphasis on Hitler's passion for building up a strong military for more than just defence purposes. It was sent to the Foreign Office and then his report was given to the cabinet. However, it was clear that despite Rumbold's efforts it was not given top priority which remained maintaining the peace and keeping Hitler under control. Sir Robert Vansittart (Under-Secretary at Foreign Office from 1930 to 1938) did his best in circulating Rumbold's memorandum and became well-known for his anti-appeasement stance.

The French Ambassador in Berlin, François-Poncet was more nonplussed as he knew that Hitler at the time was portraying himself as a man of peace, but he also had read *Mein Kampf* and knew of Hitler's long-term plans. He, like many others, was disturbed when Hitler withdrew Germany from the League of Nations and the ongoing Disarmament Conference, which gave the French more powder for their anti-German keg.

When Rumbold retired as British Ambassador he was replaced by Sir Eric Phipps, who held little trust in the Nazi regime, but as the British Ambassador reflected his government's wishes, which meant trying to keep relations calm and peaceful, even though he evidently despised Hitler. Pacifism and the need for peace were the political orders for the day, though not all the Civil Servants agreed. Vansittart, Robert Fisher (Head of Treasury) and the well-known Maurice Hankey (Cabinet Secretary) asked the Cabinet if a warning should be sent to Germany about her massive buildup of arms. Churchill had already drawn attention to the need for preparation for war, and necessary raw materials (1933) which seemed to reflect a book by Dorothy Woodman published in 1934 and explored under the chapter on 'Literary Efforts'. The government were aware of the buildup of the German military, but they decided that because Hitler wanted peace he could be trusted, and all was well. The first British Ambassador in Hitler's time, Horace Rumbold would not have agreed having read *Mein Kampf* more studiously than most.

A Major Desmond Morton, a Civil Servant who had much to do with the Intelligence services, broke the Official Secrets Act, and often supplied Churchill with detailed information about what was happening in Germany. Another source of information for Churchill within the Civil Service was Ralph Wigram who worked in the Foreign Office, clearly indicating that some senior Civil Servants were opposed to their masters' policies, and they had identified Churchill as the one man who could help. The Civil Servants known for their education and high intelligence were technically expected to stand apart from the political parties, serving those governments currently in power, but many became important tools, not only on questions of conducting a given policy, but their advice was often sought. Churchill had a formidable team of such support behind him, but so did Chamberlain with his particular guiding light of Sir Horace Wilson, whose rooms adjoined those of Chamberlain and whose influence over the prime minister was widely known, but not always appreciated by his many critics at the time, and since.

Central to understanding the Nazi regime's intentions was knowing the man Hitler, and in his interesting and revealing account of *Appeasing Hitler*, Tim Bouverie devotes a chapter to those British citizens who travelled to Germany to meet this leader, who was often surrounded by his Nazi cohorts and always guarded by the black-uniformed SS guard, which was seen as a form of Praetorian Guard. One of the major figures from the past was Anthony Eden who was in Geneva as a British representative at the Disarmament Conference. When he found himself dining with Hitler, they both discovered they had fought in the same sector in the First World War, and at one time had probably been in opposite trenches. This soon evolved into a friendly conversation about the circumstance of their mutual experiences, sometimes even tinged with a sense of humour.[38] The British Ambassador had warned Eden of Hitler's ability to charm people. There is no doubt from wide historical research that Hitler was able to captivate anyone if he chose to do so. People often commented on his eyes and the way Hitler could almost transfix the person to whom he was talking. Later he would use what has been described as his mesmeric gaze to convince German generals that he was right and should be instantly obeyed, dubbed, as noted above, as the 'command bug'. Eden was won over for a time, and his first impression was that Hitler was a man of peace, and all he wanted was a better air force. His message home to Britain was one of hope. This was promptly contested by Vansittart, who had initially considered that it was necessary to ease some of Germany's Treaty of Versailles issues, but by the 1930s had become an implacable enemy of the Nazi regime, which led to some temporary friction between himself and Eden. There had been many key-figures in Britain who had felt the Versailles Treaty had too many reprisals and predicted that it would be damaging in the near future. John Maynard Keynes the famous economist was one, and Churchill also wrote that 'the economic clauses of the treaty were malignant and silly to an extent that made them obviously futile'.[39] In 1919, a *Daily Herald* cartoonist, Will Dyson, had sketched a picture of the Versailles meeting with a baby crying in the corner with the label '1940 Class', which was truly prescient.[40] It has long been stated that the allies imposed a clumsy peace settlement at Versailles, but it has been recently argued that had the 'Germans instead been dictating the terms as victors, European freedom, justice and democracy would have paid a dreadful forfeit'.[41] Nevertheless, as Kissinger wrote, 'it is the temptation of war to punish: it is the task of policy to construct'.[42] It is not a matter of suggesting, as Hastings does, that one side did a better job than the other may have done, but an opportunity for peace was missed, making the ground fertile for war. Despite the sense of concern about what was happening in Germany, there was a feeling of guilt in Britain about the Treaty which was not shared in France. Even Lloyd George who added the thought, often taken up by Hitler, that the victorious Allies had not met their part of the agreement by reducing their military powers. These views raise the question as to whether for some people this feeling of guilt played a part in the demand for appeasement with the old enemy.

A significant visitor to Germany was the Liberal politician the Marquess of Lothian who was known to detest Nazism, but after his visit returned convinced of Hitler's sincerity and stressing the need for Anglo-German friendship. The same scenario was repeated when the Labour peer Lord Allen made a visit, coming back and claiming it was like meeting a Cromwell, and also accepted Hitler's peace overtures as genuine. On the more right-wing of the Conservatives was the newspaper magnate Lord Rothermere, and because his press was capable of influencing British public opinion, he was a welcome visitor to Germany, where he was royally entertained by Hitler and his henchmen. When he returned, he was announcing himself as a friend of the regime, but soon admitted to Churchill that he had his doubts over Hitler's ambitions in terms of his foreign policy, and he launched a newspaper effort to encourage rearmament. Paul Schmidt (Hitler's interpreter) recalled the many social visits Lord Londonderry made to Göring as they both enjoyed hunting, and often, according to Schmidt, discussed politics but always in a cheerful way.[43] Londonderry even met Hitler in the Reich Chancellery where the dictator controlled the political conversation. Schmidt witnessed the time David Lloyd George met and talked at the Berghof, finding a mutual subject of interest in the First World War. When they discussed politics Lloyd George warned that alliances were dangerous, and had it not been for them the First World War might not have occurred.[44] This would have confirmed many of Hitler's views. It was apparent that the two got along like a house on fire, until Lloyd George turned down an invitation to a Nuremberg Rally as it was against his government's advice. Some visitors such as Maurice Hankey were impressed by the cleanliness of the streets and the lack of beggars, not asking themselves the question as to where they had gone. Many returned full of praise for the drama of the Nuremberg Rallies, the discipline of the Hitler Youth, the decrease of unemployment, the sense of orderliness and the popular support the regime had produced. It is easy to pass judgement with the benefit of hindsight, but on high level visits when greeted with a sense of friendliness it would have been difficult to reject such emotions. Ambassador Phipps was worried at the time that casual British visitors, coming for a brief time, were leaving not only with the wrong impressions, but they were carrying back the messages that the Nazis wanted conveyed at this time. These visits to the rallies attracted a wide foreign audience from all occupations and social strata. When Schmidt (Hitler's interpreter) was staying in the Grand Hotel, he wrote that it 'was full of British and French guests who could hardly contain themselves in their enthusiasm for Hitler', and 'I saw British and French people almost moved to tears by these passionate scenes, and even some hard-boiled journalists were groggy' which raises the eyebrows in terms of hindsight.[45]

However, the collapse of the Weimar Republic and democracy had not only shocked the West, but the violent behaviour of the Nazis produced greater tremors in the corridors of power, and a visit by Alfred Rosenberg to London with his racial atavistic outlook had not helped. To try and ease matters there was even a suggestion that Hitler should be invited to England as a guest, but this was soon forgotten. The Night of the Long Knives and the murder of Engelbert Dollfuss when reported came as no surprise to those who had recognised Nazi barbarity, but it disturbed others. Some English papers even suggested that the murder of over 80 people in the Ernst Röhm affair was only Hitler crushing a plot, while Chamberlain referred to the Engelbert Dollfuss as 'an ominous tragedy' when it was simply downright murder.

To the consternation of the British Ambassador Phipps a variety of British visitors continued to visit Nazi Germany, some more important than others, and many taken in by the show-picture of Germany, the uniforms, the sense of discipline, the seeming law and order, the mystical type rallies, all bolstered by the work of the propaganda minister Goebbels and the general Nazi effort to appear as a friendly all-welcoming country of decent folk. Many admired the idea of strong unquestionable leadership, saw Nazism as a bulwark against the feared Bolshevists, and much of this was a trait of the upper crust of society. This was epitomised by King Edward VIII who abdicated, but who appeared to admire the Nazi culture. It has been suggested that the abdication, although causing major concern at the time, was a relief because of the King's attitudes towards Nazism, as well as his immature and naïve attitudes, especially towards the British constitution. Edward VIII and later as an ex-king was a walking talking misjudgement, and perhaps Churchill compounded this by being too kind, when the Duke of Windsor should have been under stricter control, to stop him feeding the Nazi regime, giving them the impression that they had a sympathiser in the highest echelons of British society. Henry 'Chips' Channon had noted in his diary as early as 9 June 1935, there had been 'much gossip about the Prince of Wales's alleged leanings…he has just made an extraordinary speech to the British Legion advocating friendship with Germany; it is only a gesture, but a gesture that may be taken seriously in Germany and elsewhere', which it was.[46]

After the abdication, the Duke of Windsor and his wife visited Germany and met Hitler, where the dictator was praised for the welfare arrangements but apparently politics were not discussed.[47] Ribbentrop exploited the abdication by explaining to the Nazi regime that Edward had been removed because the traditional upper-crust British opposed his friendship with Britain.

Both Phipps and his predecessor Rumbold were concerned about the tourist element who only saw what they wanted to see. The persecution of Jews was halted for a time because the Nazis used the 1936 Berlin Olympic Games as a show piece of the new Germany. There was lavish entertainment provided by leading figures such as Goebbels and Göring, and well over 130,000 foreign visitors poured into Berlin ready to be impressed. The German interpreter Schmidt was impressed but added the incisive lines that only later 'did I realise that stagecraft and statecraft are wholly different'.[48]

In 1937 Ambassador Phipps was sent to Paris as he was probably considered too anti-Nazi to make progress in happier circumstances with the Nazi regime. Sir Nevile Henderson replaced him in the hope that his history of collaborating with despots and dictators might bear more fruit. His two predecessors Rumbold and Phipps had no taste for the Third Reich, and Henderson was undoubtedly instructed to make the Nazis his friends. This appointment concerned Eden, who found it objectionable that the new ambassador saw the proposed annexation of Austria as a natural development, and let it be known that he intended to attend a Nazi Rally which most diplomats and ambassadors avoided. His sympathy for the Nazi regime was a stark contrast with his predecessors, and he was seen by many critics as pro-Nazi. There may have been some justification in this accusation, but he was, on the other hand, following not the dictates of the Foreign Office and Eden, but the demands of Chamberlain who remained convinced that peace by appeasement was the only safe way forward. The journalist William Shirer once wrote Henderson was pro-German, implying he had some sympathy for the Nazi regime. Despite the earlier crisis many were convinced that the issue would not be resolved until Hitler had his own way, and Ambassador Henderson reminded the government of this within his diplomatic messages. Many at the time and to this day regarded Henderson as the wrong appointment for an ambassador in Germany. He had been given instructions to keep Hitler onside, but his critics felt he became a friend of the Nazis. For some, including Eden who had originally offered him the post it appeared to have been a major disaster. Eden later wrote that Henderson 'so far from warning the Nazis, was constantly making excuses for them, often in their company'.[49] Henderson was selected as a believer in appeasement and believed the Versailles Treaty had been a misjudgement, a view he had long held. However, it was soon realised that Henderson was overly fond of the Nazi regime, even breaking diplomatic guidelines by attending a Nuremberg Rally. He thought the Nazi regime with their labour camps and work with the Hitler Youth was good, failing to see the Nazi indoctrination and militarising of the young was the main purpose for such apparent social movements. As far as Henderson was concerned the Czech President Edvard Beneš was dangerous and reckless which was way off target.[50] He seemed to turn against the Slavs, writing to Halifax in August 1938 that 'the Teuton and the Slav are irreconcilable – just as are the Briton and the Slav', indicating similar racial attitudes as Hitler.[51] Later Henderson would support Germany in the Danzig Crisis, and it was no surprise this was the end of his diplomatic career when he returned home, where he wrote his own account, *Failure of a Mission: Berlin 1937–1939* published in 1940.[52]

Munich, Round One, Berchtesgaden

The well-known Munich crisis was more complex than is often portrayed. Before it occurred, it had been brought to the attention of Chamberlain by the British Military attaché in Berlin that it was more than rumoured that Hitler was demanding military preparation against Czechoslovakia. This was mainly because Hitler was convinced there would be no international intervention. Vansittart had an anti-Nazi visitor from Germany sent by Admiral Canaris also at this stage suspected of being suspicious of Hitler, as was General von Beck who had resigned because of Hitler's aggressive plans. The message was asking that Britain and France militarily intervene as it would stop Hitler and even present a chance of overthrowing him. Chamberlain ignored the request, overlooking or ignoring the possibility of a military rebellion against Hitler, which might speculatively have worked at this stage. There was German resistance to the Nazi regime from 1933 to 1944 but the British, not just Chamberlain, were always sceptical about the possibility of a coup, and little was known about the possibility of German resistance until it was too late. Even in 1940 Pope Pius XII had told the British Ambassador Osborne that he had met some German generals, including Ludwig Beck who were prepared to overthrow Hitler, all they sought was an honourable peace settlement. This was conveyed to Halifax and Chamberlain, but his response 'was characteristically cautious, insipid and unimaginative – the response of a glorified clerk to schemes of some boldness'.[53] However, Chamberlain may have been right as their proposed peace settlement was asking too much, and by this time it was far from easy to depose of Hitler and the regime, as would be seen in the 20 July 1944 Plot.

It has often been suggested that before Munich there was major support for appeasement which was far from the truth. Duff Cooper later recalled 'we were being advised on all sides to do the same thing – to make plain to Germany that we would fight. This advice came from the press, from the Opposition, from Winston Churchill, from the French and United States governments, and even from the Vatican: this advice supported by such an overwhelming weight of opinion we were rejecting on the counter-advice of one man, the hysterical Henderson'.[54] Chamberlain has often been accused of being indecisive and hesitant, but he was determined to move in his own way towards peace. He was devising in his own mind what he called Plan-Z when, if necessary, he would be prepared to go on a form of shuffle diplomacy and talk to Hitler personally to influence him in the right direction.

What caused the well-known indecisiveness was that he could not carry the whole of the Commons or the public with him, as there was growing uncertainty about Nazi Germany, and in this Munich period he was personally determined to be proved right. There was ongoing tension with the French question of their coming to the aid of Czechoslovakia even though both countries realised it might provoke a major war. Chamberlain at the end of August 1938 called an emergency Cabinet meeting to discuss the crisis. To declare war was mooted, but not under Chamberlain who had long believed that no one wanted a war. Various views were aired, but no conclusion reached at this junction, with some suggestions that if France and Britain would tell Hitler they would wage war it would deter him, but Chamberlain had long been thinking of a plan to meet Hitler and persuade him from using force.

Churchill was furious and wanted to gain the help of the Soviet Union, who had agreed to join the fray, but France had to react first (as stated in their pact with Russia) otherwise they would only be onlookers. This could have been a two-front war, and Churchill suggested this was worth considering, but he was once again ignored. Henderson had been recalled to London, but he was unable to give a balanced view as he was as keen on appeasement as Chamberlain, and as noted above, sympathetic to German demands. Beneš had made an offer to Henlein, but Hitler had turned it down. Runciman in

Prague had found no solution, and some British newspapers, including *The Times*, caused governmental anger by claiming Czechoslovakia was prepared to cede territory, and it was no surprise that confusion reigned throughout Britain, France, and Czechoslovakia. There were many who believed that Hitler's demands were justified in demanding back lost German territory full of German speakers, and Chamberlain was convinced that after this Hitler would have no other demands. As noted throughout this study Hitler's personality and foreign policy had been forecast in his diatribe *Mein Kampf*, and those who should have read it with care had failed. Hore-Belisha, the Secretary of State for War had read the work, he had warned that Hitler was following the lines of action that he had outlined in this political autobiography, and he was ignored. Halifax was toying with the idea of issuing a warning to Hitler of military action, asking Henderson, who was attending a Nuremberg Rally, to warn Hitler that even the Labour Party was moving along the same lines of thought, but Henderson sent warnings home that this would be an error of judgement, so the threat was dropped.

The Cabinet met again on 12 September to review the situation, and they were faced with opinions from many quarters, not least Churchill and his adherents demanding action in terms of rapid military preparation. For those supporting Hitler, many wanted the issue dropped, to leave it alone as Czechoslovakia was not worth the efforts or provoking the dangers of war. There was the added complexity of how to work or not work with the French which might involve the Soviet Union, but Chamberlain in his lead role as prime minister remained determined and immoveable in his insistence he could reason with Hitler.

The dictator in Germany was holding forth in his usual way about the way Germans in Sudetenland were being treated, encouraging listeners to doubt or distrust the Czechs, which had even worked on the British Ambassador Henderson. It had been hoped by the anti-appeasement lobby that Eden would take the lead, but he had clearly indicated after his resignation that he intended to keep a low profile, so there was a growing tendency to turn towards Churchill (who had hitherto been sidelined as being too bellicose) including members of the Labour Party. Eden found, somewhat to his surprise, much public support in his action of resignation, also noting that 'many Italian newspapers correctly hailed my resignation as a victory for *Il Duce*, who had been proclaiming in his press that there would be no progress in negotiations while I was at the Foreign Office', but at this stage Eden proved somewhat ineffective.[55]

Chamberlain announced his plans to meet personally with Hitler which created a sense of hope and was greeted with enthusiasm, but still doubts that it would work. In his diary Galeazzo Ciano, Mussolini's foreign secretary and son-in-law wrote in his diary 'that the wave of optimism created by the news of Chamberlain's trip has been dampened by the confusing pileup of information coming from Prague and Berlin regarding the civil war in the Sudetenland'.[56] Ciano was right that there were problems in Czechoslovakia, mainly caused by Hitler's orders to Henlein and grossly exaggerated by Goebbels in his propaganda broadcasts and news-sheets. Nevertheless, many people had now come to anticipate war, but Chamberlain was offering hope.

When Chamberlain arrived, he was greeted by massive crowds, with the interpreter Schmidt writing that 'we drove through Munich to the railway station in open cars, the people greeted Chamberlain very warmly – considerably more so, it seemed to me, than they had for Mussolini the year before'.[57] Chamberlain was then taken to Berchtesgaden where he was somewhat bemused by Hitler's appearance and strange dress, but eventually sat with him alone as he had requested, with only the interpreter with them. According to Schmidt this had been previously organised to keep Ribbentrop out of the room. Hitler spoke of his anger over the way the Sudeten Germans were being treated, and even expounded his views on his racial theories. Chamberlain was far from happy, suggesting that if Hitler were that intent on war, he would not have accepted Chamberlain's offer to travel to Germany. Schmidt wrote the conversation 'was not conducted in an exactly serene atmosphere and became occasionally stormy' as Chamberlain and Hitler discussed the ways Sudetenland could be achieved without force to the Germans, but Hitler wanted it accomplished at once.[58] At one stage Chamberlain said there was no point in taking the discussion further because Hitler was intent on using force whatever was said, and Schmidt noted that Hitler then became calmer and more polite, and in Schmidt's own words 'Hitler recoiled'.[59] Chamberlain explained he would need to return to London to discuss matters with his Cabinet, and asked Hitler to promise he would not take further action in the meantime, with which Hitler agreed, unless matters became out of control. This alone gave Chamberlain some hope that Hitler seemed prepared to talk.

On his return he met Runciman back from Prague who informed him that it was his opinion that the Czechs and Sudeten Germans would never co-exist together. In the Cabinet it was decided this was the only way forward, as Germany was now a formidable military power, and Halifax and other major figures decided that the giving back of this territory was essential to avoid a major war. It was a delicate situation because the French had not been involved in the meeting, and they were as divided as the British. Chamberlain was also aware that if anyone could convince the Czechs that they needed to yield the territory for world peace, it had to be the French. As this development of negotiations evolved it was no surprise that Beneš and his colleagues were in a state of confusion and despair, not least because the Czechs knew it was impossible to face a German onslaught alone.

Munich, Round Two, Bad Godesberg

Chamberlain's next visit to Hitler was at Bad Godesberg (near Bonn) on 22 September 1938, but this time he travelled knowing from press reports the divisions between those seeking peace and those demanding preparation for war were increasing in temperature. Between those who could see no sense in defending a distant country of only a few years' standing, to those who saw defending a tiny democracy as a moral demand, were those who believed that Hitler had to be promptly challenged over his remorseless demands. Many hoped or thought that at Godesberg Hitler would come to the party as his demands were reaching sympathetic ears. There was also the concern that Hitler should not support or involve Hungary and Poland who were making similar demands for the return of territory (Irredentist Nationalism). The British visitors were given lavish rooms in a hotel overlooking the Rhine and Hitler was in the Hotel Dreesen, where he had planned the Night of the Long Knives, which with the benefit of hindsight was ironic.[60] Chamberlain carefully read out the arrangements they had agreed with the Czechs, and Schmidt described him as leaning back in his chair 'with an expression of satisfaction, as much as to say "Haven't I worked splendidly these five days"', but Hitler suddenly said it was not good enough, which visibly shook Chamberlain.[61] As far as Hitler was concerned, the arrangements would take too long and they had not considered the claims of Hungary and Poland, and he wanted it dealt with in a few days. After looking at a map which Hitler produced, Chamberlain decided to retire to his hotel, the meeting having ended in some discord. He first explained to Hitler the efforts he had made, even putting his political career at stake, as if that would concern Hitler, who was only interested in immediate action by the occupation of Czech territory. In Britain the anti-appeasers around Churchill were growing in strength and were having frequent meetings, now supported by Clement Attlee because the Labour Party was now prepared to join them. This offered some justification to Chamberlain's plea to Hitler that his political career was in jeopardy. There was also a growing interest in the public arena, a growing number supporting the anti-appeasement lobby. Chamberlain was on the point of wondering whether another talk with Hitler was worthwhile, but decided to send him a note which asked that Hitler clearly outline his demands. Hitler agreed and next day read out his demand that the Czechs moved out of the Sudetenland on 26 April (only three days away) and three days later the Germans would move in. Suddenly a note was passed to Hitler who showed it to the gathering as it announced the Czechs had started to mobilise. Given what is now known about Hitler, it causes any observer today to wonder whether this note was intended at this juncture and had been previously arranged. The meeting became tense, but to most people's surprise Hitler announced that under the circumstances he would advance his proposed date to 1 October. Chamberlain promised to relay the terms to the Czechs and to all sense and purposes appeared to agree with what would be known as the Godesberg terms. Later Chamberlain sent Horace Wilson to Berlin with notes on what Chamberlain was trying to do, amongst which was the Czech reply that they found it all unacceptable. Schmidt described the meeting as one of the worst diplomatic meetings he had ever attended, with Hitler throwing a tantrum and going to the exit door but changing his mind.[62] Horace Wilson was dumbfounded, never having had to face a tirade like that before in his life. It may well have enlightened him to the sort of person Hitler was, but the dictator through Schmidt sent a calmer letter to Chamberlain. It was probably the case that Horace Wilson was a Civil Servant which Hitler felt was an insult to his position as Chancellor, who would normally only speak to heads of government.

At home in Britain many were astonished by what was happening, not least Halifax who was rapidly developing sympathy with the anti-appeasers to Chamberlain's later shock, and others followed him. Britain, as in France remained divided on this major issue but Chamberlain, determined as ever, realised he was in a difficult spot, as he was only just beginning to realise the nature of Hitler's warped personality. It was soon known from Intelligence in Berlin that *Case Green*, the code for the occupation of Czech territory was fermenting. In a speech in the Sportpalast Hitler, in one of his typical frenzied speeches, had denounced the Czechs pledging that the Sudeten Germans would soon be free. There was a growing feeling about the inevitability of a major war developing. In Britain, gas masks were being distributed, trenches dug, and evacuation plans were being prepared. The news also arrived that Beneš had ceded the province of Těšín to Poland based on the grounds they would remain neutral in any conflict. Chamberlain, aware that personal support was diminishing, battled on demanding peace was the objective, and encouraged by a supportive message from Roosevelt. He wrote again to Hitler for another meeting this time with representatives from France and Italy, and he received a positive reply offering some hope in the House of Commons. For Chamberlain the news could not have come with better timing.

Munich, Final Round

This time at the airport Chamberlain was farewelled by most of his Cabinet, and some of the Dominions High Commissioners and many others, which must have impressed on Chamberlain the strength of feeling of the hope for peace which he had pursued for years. He must have known this was his last opportunity, and the task ahead would be difficult, not least knowing that the Czechs were not permitted to be there, and although France was coming there had been no opportunity for appropriate discussion with them. The French, led by Daladier, were in a continued state of complexity about where they stood, not least because of their pact with Czechoslovakia, and as in Britain had produced even more divided opinions at the political and public level. There had been no appropriate discussions with the British, but Daladier had told his accompanying group that they would follow Britain's lead as this was their initiative to keep peace in Europe. For Hitler it was sheer propaganda which he relished, knowing the British Prime Minister had already been twice, and on this 'occasion had hurried across Europe with the heads of the French and Italian governments to meet him at the shortest possible notice, which constituted a personal triumph for Hitler'.⁶³ For his part Chamberlain was also now more aware of Hitler's strange proclivities, not least his mood swings, impatience, and the need to have his own way. The Soviet Union was missing as being unwelcome in Germany, and although distrusted in the West had signed a pact with France, and they remained a critical component in the delicate balance of power. It amounted to a strange conglomeration brought about by Hitler's threats and the understandable desire to live in peace.

In Munich the conference was held at Hitler's headquarters on the Königsplatz where red carpets were out and a reception organised, all to boost and boast of Nazi grandeur. Hitler, who at this stage had some admiration for Mussolini, had met him at the border and outlined his plans as they travelled together on Hitler's special train. Ciano, who accompanied Mussolini, recorded in his diary that Hitler told the Italian dictator that the 'time will come when united we will have to fight against France and England', but Ciano added that in Munich there 'was an atmosphere of agreement'.⁶⁴ It amounted to a matter of Hitler wanting his own way for his own plans projected as outlined in *Mein Kampf*, and before discussions had started, Hitler had dropped major hints of the future as he perceived it to Mussolini. Hitler, who had devised his own plans for taking over the Czech territory, shared this with the Italians to encourage them onboard. As in a game of chess, Hitler was offering a gambit to ensure his long-term strategy would be successful, and Ciano realised that Hitler's move was to enable him 'to liquidate Czechoslovakia as it is now', in other words the whole country.

As the various diplomatic parties came together it was not a matter of joy, but nervous anticipation pervaded by a sense of all-round suspicion. Mussolini was enjoying his self-importance by being there, Göring was wandering around like the 'grand I am', Daladier was depressed, Chamberlain was deeply anxious, and a self-assured Hitler determined to appear as the great leader even with his proneness to behave like a spoilt child. The only two Czech representatives had been locked in their room under police supervision. Each country in turn offered their thoughts, with the interpreter Schmidt later writing that they were all against force and looking for a stable solution, 'even Hitler emphasising that he was all for a peaceful settlement', only becoming intemperate when 'raging against Beneš', and he described

Daladier as 'clearly disturbed' by the discussion.⁶⁵ Schmidt noted that Hitler appeared happier with Daladier because they had both fought in the First World War, which as Eden had discovered was an obsessive fetish with him. When Chamberlain raised the question of compensation for the Czechs, from losing their industry and even their cattle, Hitler became heated, and the subject was put aside.⁶⁶ At this juncture it was apparent that it was simply about appeasing Hitler. After the evening session Hitler invited all to dine with him, but both Daladier and Chamberlain explained they needed to phone their colleagues, so Mussolini and Hitler enjoyed their meal. Afterwards they met again, and others who made their comments, including the so-called legal experts.

The dice had been cast and in the opening hours of 30 September the Munich Agreement was signed, which apart from Hitler's point of view was a matter of joy, a sense of achievement for Chamberlain, it was depressing for Daladier who had felt obligated to sign to keep the peace, and a very upset Czechoslovakia who had felt betrayed by the West. They had been told that they had to accept the agreement, or they would be fighting the all-powerful Germans alone. Beneš said 'we were not defeated by Hitler… but by our friends'.⁶⁷

Chamberlain had requested to have one more meeting with Hitler which was agreed, and during which he convinced the German dictator to sign the famous piece of paper which stated the German and British nations would not wage war against one another, the famous 'Peace in Our Time' statement. An interesting insight into the meeting was provided by the interpreter Schmidt, who wrote that Hitler was 'pale and moody', and Schmidt 'did not share Chamberlain's later claim that Hitler was enthusiastic to sign…showing a degree of reluctance to sign and did so only to please Chamberlain'.⁶⁸ Given that Hitler had already revealed to Mussolini that he anticipated war against France and England it has, with the benefit of hindsight, proved that Hitler was a total liar, which would have shaken a gentleman like Chamberlain as he was soon to discover to his outrage.

As a curious note Schmidt accompanied Chamberlain to the airport through Munich, and he was astonished at the number of Germans lining the streets to greet Chamberlain with noticeable pleasure. They seemed so genuinely pleased that war had been averted and acknowledged Chamberlain's efforts. There were some in the Nazi Party annoyed by such a response from the German public, and Schmidt a fortnight later, heard Hitler give one of his many speeches making the accusations that 'there were some weaklings amongst us'.[69] One of Schmidt's closing prescient remarks, in terms of hindsight, was when he wrote that Chamberlain had meet Hitler three times in a short period, and 'step by step he had allowed Hitler to push him into a solution that contributed very little to the prestige of the Western powers'.[70] Even in Italy, as Mussolini returned, Ciano noted 'from the King to the peasants the *Duce* receives welcomes as I have never seen'.[71] At the time, like many others, Germans, French, Italians, and British, Ciano had hoped it averted war, but Hitler was a man whose corrupted depths few had yet recognised. Hitler, for his part told his SS guard 'that fellow Chamberlain has spoiled my entry into Prague', but he knew it would still happen.[72]

In his diary the German Diplomat Ulrich von Hassell wrote 'then came the great *coup de scène* of Chamberlain's visit…it was another tremendous success for Hitlerian bluff; on the other hand, it amounted to the strongest possible moral pressure by Britain on Germany', which was painfully all too true.[73] There has been some debate over how far Chamberlain knew that peace remained a mere hope and that he was merely buying time, or whether he genuinely thought he had established peace. In the diaries of Alan Lascelles, Private Secretary to King George VI, he noted that a well-known historical academic Keith Feiling was seeking permission to read some of the then deceased Chamberlain's letters, to challenge the then growing belief that Chamberlain had 'bought us a year's respite knowing that war was inevitable. According to Feiling Chamberlain came back from Munich still believing in the possibility of peace, though not at all convinced of its probability'.[74] Feiling may have been right because even the most optimistic appeaser must have had lurking doubts, but this biographer looked to a better portrayal of Chamberlain than most commentators have since.* It has also been argued that Munich bought time for Britain to rearm, but 'the figures show it was in fact Germany that benefitted from the year's peace'.[75] It seems that from whatever angle this aspect from the past is analysed, Chamberlain genuinely believed he had won the day for peace in Europe, and he had no agenda for finding time to rearm.

---

* He wrote the book as the war ended, see, Feiling, Keith, *The Life of Neville Chamberlain* (London: Macmillan, 1946)

In Britain Churchill and his supporters had been doing their best to persuade Chamberlain not to sign, but the prime minister for years had remained determined to keep the peace. On his return to Britain Chamberlain was greeted with joy as he waved the 'Peace in our Time' note in the air like the warrior returning home, and this was enhanced when invited by King George VI to stand with the royalty on Buckingham Palace balcony. In France, Daladier had expected the worst possible reaction, but the vast majority of the deputies were in favour. In London it led to a four-day debate, some objecting to Chamberlain's use of 'peace with honour'. Clement Attlee led the attack pointing out that a democratic country had been sold out to a totalitarian system. However, the congratulations flooded in to Chamberlain's pleasure. The overall picture emerged of a still divided Commons, with some Tory members wondering whether to vote against their government or hold their unity, but in the end just over thirty Tories voted against Chamberlain's efforts, as the Tory Whips were active.

As there had once been a hint earlier of a plot to overthrow Hitler, having been communicated by a visitor sent by Canaris mentioned above, it was later discovered that General Halder (Chief of the General Staff) had been planning a coup had the Western allies not signed, but it remains in the land of speculation as to whether it might have succeeded. Had Britain rearmed earlier and joined with the French and the Soviets, as Churchill had proposed, Hitler would have been confronted with a two-front war. However, the British military were seriously down on manpower and resources, the French were equally undecided, and the Soviet Union would have had to march through other countries to make their challenge, again falling into the 'what-if' speculation game. Intelligence had claimed Germany was not yet prepared for a major war, but with hindsight they were probably much better prepared than Britain, driven by a government which was based on economic issues more than expending money on the military. The Munich Conference had provided time for the Germans to increase their forces, and the Sudetenland now provided them with industrial resources, and their frontier defences were now in the wrong place. It had also enhanced Hitler's views that both England and France were weak and led by ineffective leaders.

Post Munich

Following the Munich crisis the divisions of opinion continued unabated, but for many Chamberlain's efforts swept him forward in a wave of congratulations and popularity. Such was the relief some even thought he was God's help, and the adulation was global, but not in Czechoslovakia and Nazi Germany. The differences of opinion caused rifts not only at the political level, but as in the recent debate over Brexit, families were divided, and old friendships scarred. There were sharp differences between age groups, as younger people wanted to challenge Hitler and more men than women felt this way. There were those who all too well recalled the strife and agony of the First World War, making peace the only way forward, while others were beginning to recognise the dangers of Nazism and Hitler. Within the Tory ranks there were serious divisions, and the Labour Party was rapidly becoming more bellicose towards Nazi Germany. There were serious clashes between Chamberlain and his supporters with the anti-appeasers surrounding Churchill. In his book on the period Tim Bouverie raised the fact that Chamberlain even had a source who had tapped into Churchill's telephone conversations.[76] Generally the conduct in the Commons was gentlemanly but the divisions were deep and at time vociferous.

Opinion for much of the public was driven by newspaper reports, occasional news films in the cinemas and rare broadcasts. Today the on-the-spot television pictures of what is happening in another country has a greater influence on the public mind. As will be explored in the following chapters of this study, the safest way to reach a sound conclusion was by reading essential studies from sources which were revealing about Nazi intentions. This was no easy task for many for several reasons, because at the popular level not only did journalists have their own bigotry, but were often controlled by governments, most especially in Nazi Germany, and even in more liberal countries the press could be influenced by politicians. Other dedicated studies to the subject were often overwhelmingly difficult to read in the popular mind because they were somewhat academic in approach, when many prefer, without being snobbish, a lighter approach which can be more easily read. This is a common human condition which explains today why books written by celebrity sportsmen and chefs, often with a hint of scandal lurking in the background are at the top of a publisher's list, as sales and profit govern such decisions.

The essential ingredient for human interest in scandal or outrage was provided by the Nazis on 9–11 November 1938, with the anti-Semitic attack on *Kristallnacht*. International disgust was widespread and not even Goebbels' propaganda and his attempted control of the foreign press could stop this being known overseas. The events of *Kristallnacht* are now well recorded in history books, and although anti-Semitism was sadly rife in many countries, this destruction of Jewish synagogues, businesses, the loss of life, and the utter humiliation of this racial minority in Germany simply disgusted the outside world, as it tipped the scales into atavistic barbarity. Even Nazi sympathisers such as Lord Londonderry were appalled, President Roosevelt condemned the event, and all this rapidly reduced support in the appeasement lobby in Europe, America, and the large Dominion countries. In America there even developed an almost anti-British view because Chamberlain had led the charge on appeasing Hitler, but it was a relief for the British that the Nazis provoked even more dislike. None of this should have been a surprise for those who had read *Mein Kampf*, or other studies of Nazism produced in the 1930s. It was well-known that Hitler was an extremist, bigoted, psychologically warped and his anti-Semitism knew no bounds, and he had persuaded many (but not all) Germans to his atrocious way of thinking.

The first woman to be an MP was Nancy Astor who married into aristocracy and moved into the ancestral home of Cliveden, and during this period appeared as a supporter of the Nazi regime as solving the world's problems of Jews and Communists. It was generally understood that many from the upper reaches of society would gather at her home, widely known as the Cliveden Set, and following *Kristallnacht* they, and many like them, became a point of derision. The impact of Nazi anti-Semitism was rapidly changing views about Nazi Germany as their attitudes and views had now become public property for scrutiny. Chamberlain, being a man of genuine peace was also unquestionably shocked, but he had no plans at this stage to try and derail his progress with Germany, even though these recent events had sent out a red-warning light about the nature of the Nazi regime. A few weeks later he sent a secret envoy to Hitler in the hope the Munich agreement could be built on by such agreements as aerial warfare, naturally it made no progress. Others, especially MI5, were anxiously aware of this mission making yet more contact with what was now regarded as the potential enemy by many. None of this was helped by Göring's announcement of the growing power of the Luftwaffe, as bombing of cities and towns remained the dominant fear. It was similar to the current fear of a war which involves nuclear weapons, as it was a common belief in the 1930s that one attack by a bomber fleet could destroy a whole city, and the images of Guernica in 1937 did little to assuage this fear. Hitler's intentions were becoming increasingly suspect, and some of the Intelligence had suggested that Ukraine would be his next target.

1939 and War

On 11 January 1939, Chamberlain and Halifax arrived by train in Rome to be met by Mussolini and Ciano which was not only to be a worthless exercise, but one which was much criticised. The British had ratified the treaty mentioned above, but it was known that Mussolini was drawing closer to Hitler. Ciano in his diary on New Year's Day notes having had a conversation with Mussolini in which he had been told of Ribbentrop's proposal 'to transform the anti-Comintern pact into an alliance…seeking a military alignment' which Ciano was authorised to answer in the affirmative.[77] However, a 'good show' was necessary, and the British received a warm welcome from the Italians with Ciano writing in his diary that 'the crowd was good…the old man with the umbrella is quite popular'.[78] It did not seem to cross Ciano's mind that Chamberlain was a man who stood for peace in Europe which would have been music to most ordinary and normal thinking people. There were serious tensions with the French over Mussolini's demand for their lost territories, probably because Mussolini had seen it work with Hitler. This even included Corsica which by then was thoroughly non-Italian as the French had ruled there since 1769. The British visitors were not impressed by the Italians in their copying of the Nazi goose-stepping soldiers as its very action somehow reflected a sense of belligerence. Chamberlain had hoped that he had weakened the possible relationship between the two dictators, but as noted above, Mussolini was already pro-Nazi Germany, linking his hope of Roman grandeur with the support of Germany. Mussolini told Ciano his views on the British visitors, stating that 'these men are not made of the same stuff as the Francis Drakes and the other magnificent adventurers who created the empire. These, are, after all, the tired sons of a long line of rich men and they will lose their empire'.[79] In his hopes for a Mediterranean Empire, Mussolini would be disillusioned by the war in North Africa against British and Dominion troops, but he was right about the loss of empire for the British, but in a more civilised fashion than he would have anticipated, and it occurred postwar.

At home in Britain rumours were circulating from German sources that the Netherlands was Hitler's next target, which was misleading information. It had percolated through because some anti-Nazi Germans such as Admiral Canaris were attempting to stimulate the Western powers to act. It worked to a degree as Chamberlain confirmed if France were attacked then Britain would have to act, but in the meantime, he stuck to his belief that the Germans could be persuaded to keep the peace. Halifax, who was no longer an appeaser, was pushing for a build-up of the military, and Hore-Belisha was demanding a new office of Ministry of Supply, but Chamberlain, concerned about the economics of the country which he claimed could not be put aside, ignored their advice. However, the pressure was mounting, and the army was prepared for mobile divisions to be sent abroad, but by September 1939, it only amounted to two Divisions. Ambassador Henderson sent a message to London denying that Hitler had further aggressive intentions, probably basing this advice on one of Hitler's recent speeches where he had not mentioned further plans, and his only threat was in the event of conflict the Jewish race would be annihilated; itself a major red alert.

When the German army marched into Prague taking over the whole of Czechoslovakia (March 1939) there had already been hints from the Intelligence services, but it still came as a shock in the Western corridors of power. In Italy Mussolini was informed that Hitler had 'acted this way because the Czechs would not demobilise their military forces...and keeping up contacts with Russia and because they mistreated Germans', with Ciano adding the thought that 'such pretexts may be good, for Goebbels' propaganda, but they should not use them when talking with us, who are guilty only of dealing too loyally with the Germans'.[80] This was an indicator that Ciano was having second thoughts about the Nazi regime. There had been understandable tensions in Czechoslovakia where Emil Hácha who had taken over from Beneš had blocked the Slovakian Cabinet, and they had locked up Father Jozef Tiso their prime minister, providing Hitler with a flimsy excuse. Hácha had been invited to Berlin where he was literally bullied and intimidated to such an extent that he passed out, creating a fear amongst the Nazi elite they might be accused of murdering him. It had, as Schmidt noted, occurred when Göring was speaking to Hácha, and given that the apparently affable Göring was also known to be an aggressive bully it was no surprise.[81]

Whatever excuses or reason were sent out to the wider world it was, nevertheless, a clear indicator that Hitler had passed from irredentist nationalism to the aggressive version demanding expansion of his Reich into other sovereign lands. It was a scandalous breach of the Munich agreement not only creating anger in the West, but for many raising the spectre of the need for war. Hitler had broken his public promises, and the appeasement lobbies were stunned. According to one source Hitler was surprised and sarcastically said 'I don't understand why London is so amazed. They must have known it was going to happen'.[82] The British were stunned because Chamberlain and most others were unaware of what sort of person Hitler was, and ignorant about his driving passions.

Daladier said war was likely and emergency powers were announced. In Britain, Chamberlain, although shaken, shook most people when he announced in the Commons that he would still pursue his policy of appeasement. Chamberlain explained to the Commons that the 'action of the Slovaks, before the Germans marched in, was the reason why Great Britain could no longer be bound by any obligation to guarantee the frontiers of Czechoslovakia'.[83]

The criticism of his attitude mounted by the minute, and realising this, he took a slightly harder line in a speech in his old hunting ground of Birmingham, even proposing that Britain may have to go to war. Any modicum of trust Chamberlain had in Hitler was totally destroyed. Later, when Hitler wanted to talk again, even offering later peace proposals, they were treated with contempt. The Civil Servant Colville noting in his Downing Street diaries on such a peace offer that 'Chamberlain, to whom the very thought of war was abhorrent, would have gone further…but nothing would induce him to deal with Hitler.'[84]

Discussions started to take place about various alliances to act as a threat and defence against further German aggression, and the Western powers of Britain and France first looked to Russia and Poland, but the Poles distrusted the communists and Chamberlain tended to agree. Only Sir Samuel Hoare objected as did Lloyd George who warned against overlooking the Soviet Union, but the rest remained stubbornly opposed. As such the Soviet Union was ignored, a possible factor which may have encouraged them to soon look to an agreement with Nazi Germany. Various possible Nazi threats circulated, some, with the benefit of hindsight, were more critical than others such as Romania and Poland.

Chamberlain was dismissive of the rumours, but he accepted the temperature was rising, and there was now the news that Mussolini had invaded Albania, with the intention of occupying the Balkans including Greece, with rumours that Corfu was on the waiting list. He announced to the House of Commons that Britain and France had agreed to support Poland if that country were attacked. It was a mere political promise as both Britain and France were inadequately prepared in military terms as was proved within the year, but it was anticipated that it would deter Hitler from attacking. John Colville noted in his diary 'the Poles knew we could not give them effective help and realised that we could only save them in the long run when Germany has been defeated'.[85] His view reflected the political machinations of the day, and after the Second World War Poland became part of the Soviet bloc. It was all a forlorn hope as the lack of awareness of Hitler's warped personality and his obsessions had not been fully understood. The political machinations appeared seemingly dishonest, as the French and British had 'decided not to launch an independent attack on Germany if Poland was invaded, though this agreement had left the Poles under the impression that they would come to their aid'.[86] Chamberlain was aware that the Chiefs of Staff had advised that neither Britain nor France could support Poland and Romania, and they felt that support from the Soviets was indispensable if the guarantees were to be meaningful.[87]

However, these fraught months all increased the much-needed sense of urgency. Chamberlain authorised the suggested Ministry of Supply, the Territorial Army was increased, and the much-feared conscription was back on the books, but all very much in a mild form. There was a growing sense of urgency amongst many, growing the military forces was becoming a focus of interest, but in August 1939, as mentioned, the British had only two divisions to be sent across the channel to France. Chamberlain, who was not in a sense of panic, did not appoint Churchill as Minister for Supply which most had anticipated. Despite the increasing tempo in international affairs, he remained convinced that Hitler could still be reasoned with and even bribed. Chamberlain must have known that times were rapidly changing and his support for appeasement was dwindling apart from some extreme right-wing groups, mainly from the upper echelons of British society who appeared to appreciate the Nazi movement for a variety of misread reasons. Unknown to Chamberlain, in April 1939 Hitler had directed orders for *Case White*, the invasion of Poland. Schmidt meanwhile recorded that on 22 May 1939, the Pact of Steel was signed and 'it represented Hitler's aggressive reply to the defensive Anglo-French guarantees to Poland and Romania'.[88] Public reaction was becoming unified, a Gallup poll in April indicated that 87 per cent in Britain favoured an alliance with Russia and France, but Poland remained against any help from Russia based on their previous fraught history. It has been noted that the guarantee to Poland, for what it was worth, bound 'Britain's destiny to that of a regime that was every bit as undemocratic and anti-Semitic as that of Germany'.[89]

The main issue was that Britain and France having promised their support to Poland needed a wider pact to contain the Nazi-Germany menace, and many still felt that they should involve Russia. In April, Halifax asked William Seeds the British Ambassador, to ask their Foreign Secretary Litvinov if they would support her neighbours on their western front, but who intimated he preferred some form of a wider Pact. The history of Russia and Poland had long been one of mutual antagonism, and Poland had many times been partitioned. Furthermore, Russia was a communist state, and the Western powers remained fearful of the spread of Bolshevism. Litvinov had in many ways been a strand of hope, but he was dismissed by Stalin and replaced with Vyacheslav Molotov who would be known as Stalin's voice-piece. Even in Britain the military chiefs could see some sense in a pact with the Soviet Union, the French had already signed a pact with Russia, but Chamberlain remained suspicious, not least because he thought this might yet create another division in Europe, but few agreed with him, and Chamberlain persisted in thinking appeasement could still work. It has been suggested the Soviets were deeply suspicious of Britain, as they were content if Hitler looked eastwards rather than to the West, and it is known that both Halifax and Cadogan believed Britain could not act as 'the policeman of Europe', acknowledging 'in other words, German political and economic dominance of central and eastern Europe must be accepted'.[90] There were suggestions that talks should be arranged between Germany and Poland, further underlining the main faultline in this delicate geo-political landscape, namely the lack of awareness of Hitler the man who only tended to listen to himself.

In Britain much popular public opinion was rapidly turning towards seeing war as inevitable and under the circumstances as justified, but the division in public opinion, as amongst the leaders, remained divided. In 1935 'voters had returned a questionnaire in the so-called peace ballot; over 10 million favoured non-military sanctions against an aggressor, and nearly 7 million accepted the principle of collective military action if these were not effective', but the situation was rapidly changing.[91]

In terms of morality few wars in history have rarely been justified except in terms of self-defence against an aggressor, which for a growing number of observers could clearly be identified in Hitler and his regime. Chamberlain's efforts were deeply moral and sincere as he was looking for peace, but he was failing to see that Hitler was no normal head of State, but a man who would not even try to keep agreements, prone to lying, and who felt a personal dedication to expansionism to create himself as head of the Third Reich, an empire builder. Chamberlain in his pursuit of peace failed to be aware of Hitler's evil intentions, and despite many calls for Churchill to have a more prominent government position, he still kept him on the back benches. It was not personal animosity to the man who was always challenging him, but it was part of his appeasement policy because he knew that both Hitler and Mussolini were alert and aware of Churchill's views.

The tension was increasing, and Nevile Henderson sent a message from Berlin warning from an overheard conversation that war was inevitable, and later informed Chamberlain there were rumours about Russia and Germany signing a non-aggression pact. Further Intelligence was garnered, suggesting that Hitler intended to attack Poland on about 25 August. There was a period in which, and mainly based on rumour, that Chamberlain still persisted in secret negotiations with Hitler, which even attempted some form of financial bribery. It was even headlines in some of the press, but Chamberlain denied it was true, and historically it is impossible to verify and may well have been mere speculation. Last-ditch efforts were made by trying to talk with Göring through Swedish contacts, but this was a total failure, as were other efforts to try and persuade the fanatical Ribbentrop who was simply Hitler's mouthpiece, and who blamed the British for causing all the problems.

As far as the Western countries were concerned it was all part of Hitler's pan-Germanism and he wanted the return of Danzig (Gdańsk). The large port-city was technically under the control of the League of Nations, but really under the authority of the Poles, however the local population of the city port was mainly Nazi, making it a potential tinderbox. The Ambassador Henderson was of little help here as he appeared to support the Nazi viewpoint. On the other hand, Chamberlain voiced his opinion in the Cabinet that Danzig was a minor issue compared to the possibility that Hitler intended to dominate Europe. Although this was stated in the privacy of the Cabinet it seemed to indicate in the eleventh hour that Chamberlain was becoming more aware of the German dictator's intentions, if drastically late. In an attempt to gain a better understanding of Polish thoughts and intentions, General Ironside was sent to Poland on an investigative mission, he cheered and charmed the Poles with his personality, but they were unhappy with Britain's reluctance to grant them a loan for military equipment.

Nor had the investigative talks gone well with Russia led by Molotov. The British had travelled there by sea and therefore slowly, and they had sent representatives who had no plenipotentiary powers to Molotov's asserted annoyance, nor was he happy with the 'landmine' mention of the League of Nations. The French were desperate for the British to be more cooperative, and although they tried there seemed little hope of success. Chamberlain may well have been relieved because his suspicions about Soviet Russia had not changed. The Soviets, quite naturally, wanted high representatives of the military forces present, and while the French cooperated the British dithered and failed. Again, the familiar crunch line was that in order to give assistance the Russians would have to pass through Romania and into Poland, but the Poles could not be persuaded, by which time, on the immediate horizon the Russians were looking more towards Nazi Germany.

The base truth was that the ill-will towards the Soviet Union had produced mediocre diplomatic relationships, which would not be repaired until Stalin's Russia was attacked in Operation *Barbarossa* when winning became a matter of survival. The Anglo-Soviet discussions would always remain an embarrassment at the political level. The various accounts were kept in a file known as the 'Blue Book', and later in January 1940 it was decided they should be kept secret and the French agreed.[92]

In Britain a local crisis occurred when Chamberlain, to the horror of most people allowed Parliament the usual long summer break, which angered many people even in the government. The world stood on the brink of a major war, and Chamberlain had travelled north to go fishing, even though Intelligence had suggested that Germany was likely to attack Poland in late August. It led to some vociferous and heated debates in the Commons. Chamberlain won the vote, but to his annoyance many of his own side voted against him. Halifax soon asked Chamberlain to return from his fishing holiday to draft a letter to Hitler as a final warning, not that it could possibly do any good, only to hear of the non-aggression pact signed between Russia and Germany. This was appalling news for those who had hoped for a Soviet pact, but what remained under German-Russian wraps were the secret protocols relating to Soviet Russia's agreement to assist the Germans in Poland, and by sharing the Polish territory with yet another partition. Apart from these secret protocols the pact on non-aggression appeared to justify those who had opposed Russia's involvement. Chamberlain was reported as somewhat distressed if not depressed by these developments, but he persisted in his policy, asking Nevile Henderson to talk directly with Hitler. On doing so the ambassador found Hitler in a bellicose mood, claiming that Britain wanted to annihilate Germany and losing his temper, and Henderson at last realising that rational thought was alien to Hitler.

Meanwhile in Britain frantic efforts were being made to build up the forces and call in all the necessary reservists, and there was equal consternation in France where troops were also being mobilised. However, in Germany there was a brief hesitation as Hitler tried to think through the ramifications of war from the West, having believed that what he described as the 'umbrella men' lacked any strength of leadership, which was why he probably disliked Churchill so much. Hitler had called Henderson back for another meeting, during which he announced that he was prepared to make England a generous offer by guaranteeing the British Empire, even by using German forces after a few colonial re-arrangements. In his memoirs Schmidt described how Hitler had arranged for a plane to fly Henderson from Berlin to London (26 August) so Chamberlain could read the offer.[93] It was not that Hitler was changing his mind about attacking

Poland, but simply trying to cajole what he considered the weak umbrella man to put the brakes on declaring war.

Hitler seemed more concerned by warfare with the British than the French, but he was more irritated by Mussolini's refusal to join him in the war on the grounds that Italy was not yet ready for war. The Italian Ambassador Attolico had explained to him that Mussolini felt the Italians were not prepared in terms of their necessary military resources. Hitler promptly asked what supplies were necessary in an offer of help, as he desperately wanted his fellow dictator to be seen by the world as on his side in the growing divide, if only as a deterrence for the Western powers. Ciano recorded in his diary the supply list Hitler had requested, that 'we go over the list. Our needs are gigantic because stockpiles are virtually nil. It's enough to kill a bull – if a bull could read it', later adding that Mussolini wanted immediate delivery and that 'it involves 17,000,000 tons, which require 17,000 train cars to ship them'.[94] Hitler knew this was an impossible demand within the timespan, and so he replied that he wanted Italy to keep its neutrality secret for as long as possible, to continue their military preparations to divert the French and British, and to send manual labourers to Germany. Mussolini agreed and promised a reassessment of their position after the 'first phase', with Ciano cynically wondering what he meant by the 'first phase'.[95] Chamberlain remained convinced that Italy would not enter the war, but the more astute Churchill disagreed.[96] Mussolini wanted to be seen amongst the world leaders, and as late as 3 August he asked Ciano to contact Halifax claiming that if he could offer Danzig to Hitler, he could bring some peace.[97] It was a worthless exercise, and Mussolini was almost seen at this stage as the little boy in the playground who was friendly with the bully but uncertain, and the others simply wanted him to be quiet and stay out of the way and not cause problems.

The British response to Hitler's latest offer, like the French, was to reaffirm their support of Poland. There was chatter from a few determined appeasers for another Munich conference, but by this stage the vast majority recognised the futility of such a policy, and it was already too late. Chamberlain informed the Cabinet of a new hope, announcing that the Swedish person they had used before with Göring, a Birger Dahlerus, had suddenly received a call from Göring who seemed eager to avoid the conflict. Göring had Dahlerus flown to Berlin and met him at the airport, arranging a sudden meeting with Hitler.

All that happened was that Hitler had another now characteristic tantrum haranguing his visitors on how he would deal with Germany's enemies. Having done so he offered Dahlerus the possibility of an alliance with Britain, but he was determined to have the Danzig corridor. When delivered in Britain it was the same message before which had already been shunned.

There appeared a glimmer of hope when it seemed that Hitler had hesitated, Intelligence had picked up the rumour that some top German military commanders were unhappy at the prospect of a major war, and the Swede Dahlerus was appearing hopeful. It was all transient, Henderson met Ribbentrop only to be greeted with anger and abusive language, and he became as angry as Ribbentrop, with Schmidt remarking that 'I found nothing comic in this scene, it was extremely embarrassing for the only spectator. Fortunately, it did not come to fisticuffs'.[98]

The Poles would not budge an inch and ordered a prompt mobilisation of their forces. Dahlerus had started to blame the Poles for being obdurate, and by this time it must have been more than apparent that all the talking was achieving nothing. The trigger for Hitler's excuse was known as the Gleiwitz incident created at the German-Polish border, where the SS dressed as Poles had taken over a radio station and dumped corpses from a concentration camp, with the intention of creating the excuse that the Poles had started the aggression.

In Britain Chamberlain had invited Churchill to become a member of the War Cabinet, and in Italy Mussolini was making the frantic suggestion for another conference as in Munich. There were the usual tensions between the British and French over their timings of declaring war, and in Germany Ribbentrop was in the angriest of black moods as it was dawning on him that his views that Britain and France would remain quiet had been wrong. In Germany when the British and French had declared war Schmidt noted that Hitler 'sat completely still and unmoving', then he looked to Ribbentrop with a savage look asking, 'What now?' … 'implying that his foreign minister had misled him about the probably British reaction'.[99]

The Immediate Aftermath

From September 1939 to May 1940, known as the period of the Phoney War, and despite the air-raid warning following Chamberlain's announcement that war had been declared on Germany, there were no bombing raids except in Poland, where Warsaw was virtually destroyed. Many Poles felt they had been betrayed by the West as the French with the small aid of the BEF merely sat along the French-German borders. The only thing which might have helped Poland was by invading Germany, but neither France nor Britain at this stage felt militarily confident in such a move. Understandably there have been critics who claimed the massive French army may have succeeded, but with the benefit of hindsight this seems unlikely and remains in the area of speculation. The real reasons behind the promises to Poland had been an effort to deter Hitler, which because of the lack of awareness of Hitler's mind and soul, made it sheer flimsy paperwork. Munich and Hitler's betrayal of the treaty had bought time for some buildup of the military, but after 3 September it accelerated rapidly in Britain, now worried about the future. Propaganda leaflets were dropped by the RAF over Germany, called *Wolkiger* [coming from the clouds] *Beobachter* which Colville thought was well done, especially the cartoons.[100] The Phoney War was detrimental to the wellbeing or psychology of the troops, but also gave manufacturing time to support the growing numbers of uniforms, now a common sight on British streets.

At the political level there was growing unrest, but it was still assumed by many appeasers that despite the declaration of war it could still be avoided, and Chamberlain was uncertain as to whether any direct offensives were necessary. Being the man who had lived economics all his life he hoped that Germany, as in 1918, would run out of food and supplies, but right up to the date of Operation *Barbarossa* the Russians stocked Germany with all the essentials. Chamberlain was always placing economics at the top of his priority list which at this stage seemed to indicate he had stepped out of the real world, and it was becoming clear that he was not a natural war leader. Despite the seismic shift to war, in Britain it was politics as usual, with Colville noting that 'the war seems scarcely to have begun, and nothing sufficiently drastic has happened to break the long-established traditions of party intrigue'.[101]

When Hitler made his well-known peace offer (12 October 1939) Colville also noted that 'I am afraid the Foreign Office are more defeatist about the possibility of procuring peace, but the Prime Minister on the other hand, is in favour of a much more encouraging reply, 'but stipulating that Hitler himself shall play no part in the proposed new order', failing to understand the grip Hitler had on Germany, despite some resistance amongst a few German military officers.[102] At least Chamberlain did not accept Hitler's peace offer (12 October 1939), probably because now Hitler had Poland. It was another indicator that Chamberlain and many others remained unaware of Hitler's and his regime's true nature, by suggesting that Germany could still be open to negotiations if Hitler were dismissed. There was even chatter of asking for Czech and Polish restoration under a government led by Göring, which with hindsight beggars belief. Because of Hitler's so-called peace offer many in Britain wondered why they were still fighting. Others pointed out that Britain had gone to war to deter aggression on Germany's attack on Poland, but now the Russians had fought with them, so Britain should oppose both sides.

To be fair on Chamberlain, although his approach had many critics, he was still supported by many others who wanted no war whatever the cost. He received thousands of letters of this nature, and many so-called aristocrats meeting with the Duke of Westminster could not understand why the British and Germans of the same race should be fighting, and ominously included some anti-Semitic themes, and there were even questions as to whether another Munich should be organised. When news was received that Hitler was looking at the Low Countries, Chamberlain sidelined it on the grounds that Hitler would not be looking for a direct confrontation with the West, he had also heard this threat before the war started, but it was becoming clear he lacked the necessary belligerence of a dedicated war-leader.

When at the end of November Stalin invaded Finland, it cast yet more dark shadows across Europe. The French were keen to rush to their help, suffering from the accusation they would do anything to keep the war off French soil. The British were less enthusiastic as the main enemy was Germany. In Germany, Hitler was watching the Russian struggle against Finland, giving him yet more stimulus for his policy of *Lebensraum* in the East, by the apparent Russian military weakness when facing the smaller Finnish army. What was more concerning to the British was Scandinavia, where Sweden's trade of iron-ore to Germany persisted, but being neutral made any attack on that country counter to international law, but Churchill indicated such was the importance that even illegal means might be necessary.[103] He then came up with the idea of mining Norwegian waters from where the iron-ore was transported. To block any British reaction Hitler invaded Norway (and Denmark on the way) but Churchill's persistence was accepted, not least by Chamberlain who persisted in seeing this as an economic war, but the British failed to take the ports back from the occupying Germans and lost many men and much material making it a major failure. There were outcries in the Commons, Chamberlain bravely taking the blame, but he was supported by Churchill who also accepted responsibility, in short Norway was a fiasco, leaving the Commons in turmoil. There were attacks on Chamberlain's premiership, but he maintained his post by a vote, mainly due to the efforts of the Whips. When this had all started Chamberlain had used the expression that 'Hitler had missed the Bus', which came back to haunt him for months after the Norwegian failure. The attacks on the government continued unabated, and especially against Chamberlain who became the butt of many attacks and jokes. It was an ongoing debate, barely controlled by the Whips as members filed through the lobbies to vote, but the government's majority fell rapidly.

Chamberlain did his best to hang on, trying to persuade the Labour Party to make a national government, but two names were persistently emerging to replace him, namely Halifax and Churchill. The Conservative Party preferred the former, but Halifax was not that enthusiastic about the role. On 10 May 1940 as the Germans invaded the Netherlands Churchill became prime minister and over the ensuing war years became one of Britain's most famous and appreciated leaders. Halifax argued for peace terms with the successful Germans in the ensuing weeks, but the hope for this re-emerging appeasement was in the face of potential disaster. Chamberlain had been a determined leader for appeasement, but Churchill was even more determined to win the battle one way or another, leading to a clash between him and Halifax, which Churchill won. Churchill's ability in his broadcasts to the nation won through. In his memoirs John Colville when serving in the Foreign Office had written in his diary on 28 September 1939 that 'Winston Churchill is a national figure but is rather too old' then, a few days later on 1 October, he heard Churchill on the radio, writing 'he certainly gives one confidence and will, I suspect, be Prime Minister before the war is over'.[104] He would have known that Chamberlain was not only older and suffering from gout, and unknown to the prime minister at that time, he was also developing bowel cancer. Nevertheless, in mid-December, in an extremely cold winter he visited the front in France, where General Alan Brooke noted in his diary that I did not feel he had enough clothes on, only a light waterproof over a shabby suit. I hope he did not catch a chill', but his brave effort could have done him little good.[105]

The Different Opinions

After the Second World War the word appeasement virtually became a dirty word because it was seen as the politics seeking peace with a dangerous lunatic who was evil, and stopping the build-up of critical military resources, which led to indecision and weakness when strength was required. Where the accusation could be seen as more justified related to the few misguided people, often from the higher social classes, who believed the Nazi regime was heading in the right direction with strong leadership, even admiring its anti-Semitism and the sense of Germanic power. Many would later regret their stance, and some died fighting the enemy, but after the revelations of the Nuremberg Trials there was not a shred of doubt that the Nazi regime and Hitler were pure evil. This overview, of course, was with the benefit of hindsight but appeasement was a natural and moral way, mainly because no sensible person wants a war unless in self-defence. The First World War had been so gross in its destructive nature, that no one wanted it repeated with even more deadly weapons such as aircraft, tanks and gas. There was an understandably powerful urge to keep the nations at peace, as there still is to this day. Chamberlain had many supporters in this initial drive to seek peace, accepting quite rationally that the Versailles Treaty was partly responsible, and accepting irredentist nationalism as Hitler wanted to reclaim lost German territory. There had been criticisms that this treaty forecast problems in the future, but in any study of history it is critical for the historian to try and understand the feelings of the day and understand why opinions were so divided.

If a local quarrel with a next-door neighbour over a fence line can be resolved by give and take, by settling in court, by payment, or a degree of acquiescence then most normal people would take this route. However, if the neighbour then demands another person's shed and all the lawns and threatens physical force then a different viewpoint is required. The problem for Chamberlain was that he became so determined to maintain peace he refused to accept his prognosis might be wrong, he was unquestionably a man of high moral values which blurred his vision by assuming that a leader of a major nation must hold the same values.

It has been proposed that appeasement was necessary because Britain and France were not prepared, which raises a few question marks. France had the largest army in Europe and a sound air force. Britain had the largest navy, but it failed to rebuild its army and develop its air force, first because of the ten-year rule driven by economic factors, and the hope that appeasement would work. The argument that appeasement was necessary because of the lack of military buildup should be reversed because appeasement was part of the problem as it seemed to assume that peace made expenditure on arms unnecessary. The best solution was to seek peace but build up the military in case it failed. It is easy to write this nearly a century later, but this was the mistake of Chamberlain and the appeasement lobby.

It must not be forgotten in the glaring stage lights of the post Second World War years that those who demanded appeasement and who were condemned in the light of events not only held the moral high ground in terms of human conduct, but they were more realistic than many suggest. The British had much to lose in the event of a major war, as its colonies and Dominions constituted the world's largest empire, Britain's army was alarmingly small and widely spread across the globe, and the Royal Navy was unreasonably stretched. Not only did the larger Dominions now carry greater influence but were critical in terms of exports. Another factor during the interbellum years, and especially after the signing of the Locarno Treaty, was that Britain had become more of an isolationist island in terms of Europe's mainland, with only the old fear that the continent's coastline across the channel was in safe hands. There were unquestionably divisions of political and public opinions, not least gauging the reactions of the major Dominion countries, the so-called British Empire, and these years are marked by the problems of indecision, not least because the few prophets of doom like Churchill were seen at first as belligerent and unpopular because of the understandable pacifist cry for peace.

The major issue both for the politician and public at large is the main thrust of this study, namely the need to be fully 'aware' of the threat, encapsulated in understanding Hitler and the regime he built. Intelligence sources could inform the government of facts, figures, statistics, which were mainly read by politicians, but what was really needed was knowing and being aware of the driving forces within Adolf Hitler. For such public and political knowledge, the rest of this book explores the possibilities of the day, concluding with two works which were either ignored or given little time, but which provided incisive and suggestive insights into Hitler and his regime which should have alerted the world in 1933 and again in 1936–7.

Part II

Literary Efforts to Reveal the Truth

Author's Notes: *Part Two starts with a brief overview of the importance of the press in informing the public of what is happening in places which they cannot see for themselves, well before the time of television news. There is also the warning that the press can influence public views one way or another. In Germany, the press was strictly controlled, and although Liberal governments might boast of the freedom of the press, they often tried to influence the editors. Perhaps the most vital information and views were those who expressed their views as foreign correspondents in Germany. The study turns to William Shirer a well-known American journalist who managed to live and work in Germany through much of the Nazi era, and the early part of the Second World War. His experience and the way he watched the Nazi development is not only fascinating but informative, as he was obviously intelligent and astute. Following the exploration of journalism there follows a very brief survey of available literature of the day, selecting a book by the author Dorothy Woodman for closer scrutiny as it not only detailed Nazi life but offered the military data as if they had been taken from the best Intelligence sources. It was published in 1934 and had it been properly read it would have sounded major alarm bells, as it made the reader fully aware of Nazi intentions.*

Role of Journalism in the 1930s

Journalists and broadcasters are usually the source of information for what is happening overseas, and the main source for any hope of reliability from abroad often comes from those who work and witness the events in another country as they unfold. Today the public relies heavily on television which often shows events and incidents as they happen. In the 1930s the main sources tended to be written journalism in newspapers and magazines, but radio broadcasting was growing and becoming both popular with on-the-spot information. The freedom of the press in democratic countries was a marked feature of that political system, and the cartoonist David Low was constantly producing drawings which ridiculed Hitler and Nazism in general, and many foreign reporters attacked the new German regime. It was a cause of irritation to Goebbels who approached Halifax in the hope the British press stopped what he regarded as puerile nonsense. Halifax explained the free press was allowed in Britain, but he returned home and did his best, but with little success. Halifax met the same problem when talking to Hitler who made some 'bitter complaints about the British press'.[1]

There was often political annoyance at the press during this appeasement era, but the only governmental guidelines the newspapers and broadcasting followed was in wartime when censorship was accepted for the safety of the country. During the appeasement years the press had freely reflected the divided opinions, some papers taking an almost supportive agenda for the Germans, especially *The Times*, under its editor Geoffrey Dawson, and others demanding fierce action, both sides often creating serious annoyance at the political level. Although *The Times* was not a popular newspaper its editorials were read with considerable interest, and 'in Dawson's eyes, it was the moral duty of every British newspaper to promote harmonious relations between Britain and the new Germany'.[2] The newspapers in Britain, as elsewhere, often tried to influence public opinion but often reflected the public mind. In March 1938, when Churchill was demanding that the government should form a grand alliance, *The Economist* 'felt that his view represents the view of the majority of the nation'.[3] Whether the intention of *The Economist* was to influence the government or whether they had carried out their own census may not be known, but that which is printed is read and often believed.

During the meetings with Hitler culminating in the Munich Conference the newspapers were awash with their various versions and viewpoints, which was often a guide to public thinking, as at governmental level much of what was happening was inhouse. However, the reporters who counted were those living and working on the spot, the foreign journalists, but they worked under much more difficult circumstances. Many were expelled such as Ian Colvin a journalist for the *News Chronicle*, who in late March 1939 brought home information about German intentions in Poland, of a possible attack on Lithuania, and even a proposed pact between Russian and Germany. Halifax believed him, but Chamberlain thought it all too fantastical to be true.[4]

William Shirer, known for his knowledge of Nazi Germany, was an American born journalist and live radio broadcaster, who travelled through Germany and much of Europe during the 1930s, often working with another famous and well-known American broadcaster, Ed Murrow. His meanderings around Germany and Europe often proved valuable both at the time and since, and he later recorded his observations in his memoir published later in life. It is the story of one man but with his usual integrity most of what he wrote reflected the reality of what was happening in Europe during this period, but more to the point, he illustrated the difficulties of the nature of his job working in a country being increasingly controlled by the Nazi regime. Later Shirer would transform into a recognised and respected historian of this era, and as soon as he arrived, he researched Hitler, being told that after Hitler had served his prison sentence the British ambassador had believed that Hitler had 'passed into oblivion'.[5]

His reflections on the 1930s were astute, but his memoirs were written postwar, and for this study it is more important to explore the problems he had as a journalist conveying the truth of what he observed. Shirer was warned by a longstanding journalist veteran that 'the Gestapo probably suspected I was an accomplice of Dorothy Thompson, who under police escort had departed the police station an hour or two before we arrived'.[6] She was an outstanding journalist who following an interview with Hitler described him as of 'startling insignificance' which drew her stay in Germany to a rapid closure. This warning to Shirer was on his entry to his new work in Germany, with the glaring evidence that there was no free press in Nazi Germany even for foreign correspondents. When the *Anschluss* had taken place there were many truthful accounts of the events, especially the barbarous treatment of Jews by the Austrian public, but it is a perplexing task to establish how many of these journalists then went to the safety of their home countries because their reports would have been noted in Goebbels' offices.

When Shirer attended his first Nazi rally, he was informed by Dr Ernst Hanfstaengl (a German American businessman and friend of Hitler) that it was one thing to report on the rally but not try to interpret them, warning that only history can evaluate such events.[7] Shirer was learning that anything he wrote would be examined, and this could lead to expulsion if the Nazi censors objected. For a young journalist earning his living this indicated a high degree of caution. Shirer wrote that over the next few years 'many of my colleagues – and they were usually the brightest and best – would get the axe. I myself would be threatened with it'.[8] He was able to listen to the views of people often conveyed by priests and nuns, which gave him many insights, but for their sake and his own safety their views could not be made public. However, he managed to report on the views of Pastor Niemöller, who would later be incarcerated in a concentration camp. Shirer wrote that 'resistance to a totalitarian regime makes news, and we played it up, such as it was'.[9] For the sake of surviving in Germany as a foreign journalist news items had to be carefully and cautiously written. He had seen the persecution of the Jews, he and his wife Tess with others had tried to offer personal support, but all he could do was report on the various decrees of the Nuremberg Race Laws. He knew above everything else the importance of protecting his sources of information. In their offices they had been visited by the Gestapo, and questioned about informants, which exposed that from the moment he had arrived, he had been watched.[10]

When the American Ambassador Dodd had been trying to protect some individual, he had asked the journalists to keep it out of the American press because that would not help his efforts. It was evident that there were pressure points at every conceivable angle for a foreign journalist. When Göring held a press conference, Shirer noted that one 'brave soul' asked if Göring had a hand in the Reichstag fire, with Shirer writing that 'a German reporter, I mused, would be whisked off to a concentration camp for posing such a question'.[11] Shirer was aware that he and all foreign correspondents were always under suspicion. Shirer related the time, when for American money, Göring offered to author some articles, but Shirer decided that Goring 'wanted to impress the Western democracies that he had a moderating influence in Nazi Germany'. Shirer noted that he found it an impossible task to 'get close' to any Nazi official of rank to find out what was happening. He had to tread with care recalling that Norman Ebbutt of the *The Times* who was anti-Nazi was in danger of being expelled. Shirer quoted Geoffrey Dawson the editor of *The Times* who said that 'I can really think of nothing that has been printed now for many months past to which they could possibly take exception as unfair comment' and 'I do my utmost, night after night, to keep out of my paper anything that might hurt their [Nazi Germans] susceptibilities'.[12] Ebbutt, totally frustrated, gave Shirer his information, but it was always a matter of treading delicately because the Nazi regime had much to hide. Later in life Shirer admitted he had underestimated Hitler and his plans, pointing out with some justification that Hitler was fooling his own people and the world at large, especially when he had announced that 'he was determined to keep the peace', and he 'had not the slightest thought of conquering other peoples.'[13] After one speech by Hitler some of Shirer's colleagues, some British and French, including Shirer at the time, believed Hitler's intention was to keep the peace. *The Times* recorded that anyone who read the speech 'cannot doubt the points of policy laid down by Herr Hitler which may fairly constitute the basis of a complete settlement with Germany'.[14] Later Shirer, like so many other journalists, had to admit they had been blinded by Hitler's talk, and when he later spoke to Americans at home he discovered that few of them were aware of Hitler's crimes, even against the Jews , and they thought Shirer to be somewhat sensational and emotional, indicating a lack of interest in what was happening in Europe. Even for a journalist on the spot it proved impossible to make many people aware of the nature of Hitler and the Nazi regime.

In Germany Shirer was finding it increasingly difficult to work with Goebbels in the background, who was always threatening everyone with expulsion, some had already gone, and John Elliott of the *New York Herald-Tribune* had moved himself to Paris. Shirer found himself confronted by one of Goebbels's men (William Bade) ripping into him for some comments he had made on the Berlin Winter Olympics, claiming he was trying to torpedo the event before it started. It probably became a focus because the Americans had threatened to boycott the event if Jews were not allowed to enter, and soon Shirer was being attacked in the Nazi press, which continued for some time. Most disturbing was Shirer's observation that rich American businessmen visiting the winter Olympics were being taken in by the Nazi propaganda, and despite his efforts he could not change their minds. This left Shirer wondering what attracted the wealthy to fascism, whether it was the clean streets and orderly conduct, or whether it was because the Nazis were anti-Communist.

Nevertheless, Shirer often crossed the Nazi line, writing on the subject of the proposed Rhineland takeover that the French could easily have stopped [which many believed, and others that such an effort would have stopped Hitler in his tracks], and that Hitler was facing opposition from the Foreign Office, some generals, and Dr Hjalmar Schacht. German reporters sometimes joined him and his fellow foreign commentators, but such was the climate in Germany they tended to be suspicious of them because they might be spying. He heard from *The Times'* reporter Norman Ebbutt how little 'his distinguished paper was publishing for fear of offending Hitler'.¹⁵ Ebbutt was eventually expelled from Germany in August 1937. It could not have been an easy life for foreign correspondents, because they knew the Gestapo were constantly watching them, with threats from Goebbels, and with editors at home politically worried about publishing their reports.

Relationships with editors were never easy, and Ed Murrow persuaded Shirer to join him as a radio commentator for CBS (American commercial broadcasting) but the problems of working with the Nazi Germans did not change. First, he had to persuade CBS to put him on air, then he had to negotiate facilities for the broadcast, preferably in a place where there was no Nazi interference. He was desperate to report the events surrounding the *Anschluss*, he tried the Austrian Broadcasting Company but received no answer, causing him to wonder whether the Nazis had already taken over. He decided to go to the building itself and found two Austrian friends surrounded by Austrian storm troopers as prisoners. Inside he was met with a blank refusal, and when he argued his case, he found that 'a couple of guards, fingering their revolvers nudged me away'.¹⁶ It was becoming clear that the danger signals were increasing by the week, and he found it difficult to find an aircraft because the Nazis had taken over the airfields. He eventually managed to make his broadcast, but only because he managed to fly to London. As a result of press coverage and broadcasting about the *Anschluss*, Hitler gave a speech from Königsberg which attacked the foreign press. Ed Murrow talked the situation over and decided that Shirer would be better off broadcasting from Geneva. He also travelled to Prague and managed to put Eduard Beneš on air (with Alice Masaryk) and who spoke on relationships with Germany. Shirer found that Beneš was 'exceedingly moderate and reasonable', which given the circumstance of the day, Beneš was being as diplomatic as some of the editors.¹⁷ Before he left Vienna (9 June 1938) he recorded that the 'Gestapo have been here for two days checking over my books and effects' which demonstrated that the country had rapidly become a police state, not the easiest of places to be a foreign broadcaster.¹⁸ Even on the way to Rome by train to make a recording, his sleeping compartment was broken into by the Gestapo, and he was threatened with arrest. Later when the war started to open up, albeit still technically a neutral, his broadcasts were often cut off under Goebbels' orders.

Shirer stayed on in Germany into the war, his wife and child had earlier left Geneva for America, and he followed later having spent 21 years abroad. The job of a journalist and broadcaster is to keep the world informed of unfolding events of importance. This had proved impossible under the Nazi surveillance despite Shirer's obvious courage. Most pertinently he wrote that, 'It was as if President Roosevelt and the Pope and the rulers of the splendid little democracies in the north lived on a different planet from the frenzied Third Reich, and they had no more conception of what was going on in Berlin than they did on Mars. They simply could not conceive of Adolf Hitler as he really was, nor the German people as the Führer had shaped them over six frenetic years'.[19] Shirer was conscious of the lack of awareness about Hitler overseas, which was a critical observation and the basis of this study.

It was clear from Shirer's account that reliable news from Germany was minimal, hampered by a police state's cunning restrictions, cautious editors at home, and a general ignorance prevailing about overseas, and the European wish for peace at any cost. What was needed was a thorough exposure of the man Hitler, his Nazi regime, his intentions, and a recognition of his criminality and immorality brought to light as it was by an Australian academic in 1936, who was also ignored.

There were many other well-known authors who wrote during the interbellum years expressing their views of the current world. George Orwell with his world-famous books *1984*, and *Animal Farm*, explored the dangers of oppression in totalitarian States. Rebecca West wrote on political and social issues not least in exploring the international tensions in Europe. There were many others including Ernest Hemmingway, Virginia Woolf, and even T.S. Eliot whose work *The Waste Land* reflected this period. Another book written was by the journalist Vernon Bartlett who canoed through German rivers observing what was happening in his books *Nazi Germany Explained*. Bartlett was a pacifist, concerned about the anti-Semitism he witnessed, but was convinced that Hitler did not want war.[20] Hitler's ability to convince people he always told the truth is today mind-boggling, however, the trouble is with written works yesterday and today, they are not always widely read unless written by some form of celebrity preferably involved in a personal scandal.

Dorothy Woodman

However, there were two significant books which directly focused on the potential dangers of Hitler and his regime, one called *The House Which Hitler Built* which was so important it will be explored in a later chapter. The second was first published as early as 1934, a book called *Hitler Rearms*, which was published in London and can still be found in bookshops today. It was a book containing considerable German military data, exposed life in Nazi Germany, and it was written with the purpose of proving that Nazi Germany was preparing for war. The author was Dorothy Woodman, though in the book she has put herself down as the editor. She was a journalist and author well-known in the 1930s as a person who was desperate to expose Nazi intentions in the years ahead, by carefully working on the geopolitical landscape during the early 1930s. Because she addressed herself as the editor it was easy to presume that she had a team of investigators making their contributions, but nothing of this possibility has ever become known, and there is no documentation available about her sources. It does not seem unreasonable to assume she had contacts with journalists in Germany, who may have fed her the necessary information, much of which the press editors wanted to avoid at that time. It should also be noted that the 4th Earl of Listowel had written the introduction. He was a Labour Party man who had entered the House of Lords in November 1931, but notably had served as a lieutenant in the Intelligence Corps, and postwar between February and March 1946 he was Minister of Information, but the post was abolished.

There has been considerable historical debate about the accuracy of her information, much of it incredibly complex, but there can be little doubt that Woodman exposed the various avenues through which Nazism was busy rearming, while her opponents accused her of sensationalism. However, it sparked many discussions and raised awareness of the potential dangers in central Europe. Some historians have claimed she raised the alert signals, but others criticised the accuracy of her facts and knowledge. Whether her book had any direct impact on the public or government is unknown and there is no reliable evidence one way or another. Many claimed or assumed the official Intelligence sources were far more accurate, but such information was kept under cover, whereas Woodman's book encouraged public discussion. It has been argued that governmental Intelligence covered a broader range, had greater expertise, but with the benefit of hindsight Woodman was largely correct in her main arguments, and however clever Intelligence may be it was used by politicians who had their own agendas.

Her book suffered many criticisms such as her accuracy being questioned, her limited sources, her lack of expertise, and writing for the sake of sensationalism, yet her book was and remains significant for stirring up necessary discussion, not least because she raised awareness about Nazi Germany. It raised the temperature between those who recognised the danger signals, those who hoped it was a passing phase, and those who wanted peace at any cost.

Nature of the book *Hitler Rearms*

It was primarily a book to raise public attention of the dangers of fascist rule and what was happening in Nazi Germany, most especially the military significance. Her opening chapter pulled no punches as it was entitled *Towards a New World War*. Woodman proposed there was a building up of a 'war psychosis' on her first page. She made no bones about the reasons, looking to the economic problems and the issues surrounding the Treaty of Versailles, and asking the questions 'Is Hitler honest?' and 'What is the Third Reich driving at?'[21]

The second chapter was based on exploring the totalitarian state and its war machine, including the need to increase the birthrate, food supplies, mobilising labour, the need for raw materials, and communication systems for transport all provided in immense detail. A sceptic might point out that this could be seen in most countries, but such was the sense of frenzied activity in Germany and Woodman's detailed analysis of the raw materials, she left no doubt in the mind of her readers that this was preparation for a war machine seeking its necessary materials. She had not neglected to note that during the Weimar years General von Seeckt had clandestinely rebuilt if not remoulded the German army, and that the Nazis had welcomed this development. What she would not have known at the time of writing was that von Seeckt was a traditional German who never trusted Hitler.

Chapter Three is a natural development as she concentrates on the new growing German army, and the way the Germans had camouflaged and circumvented the restrictions of the Versailles Treaty, writing of the problems of conscription which the Nazis were quietly doing in a clandestine fashion. It is with the benefit of hindsight much of what she wrote we now know was uncomfortably true, but trying to convince a reading public who either did not want war, or who regarded what was happening in Germany was German business making it a difficult road to map. She mentioned the labour service were trained under barrack room conditions, and she was correct, but to many this was all simply just Germanic. She argued that the spades used in marching would soon be rifles, and she insisted that it was clear the Nazis were preparing their young men for military conscription. She understandably introduced the role of the SA, who it was early suspected, would soon boost army numbers. It was the same with the Hitler Youth which she described as 'this militarisation of the youth' which few would disagree with had they witnessed this first hand.[22] She also brought into the picture the youth gliding schools and clubs which were used to train pilots for the soon to be Luftwaffe. There were the same permutations in education and schools from the junior level upwards.

In Chapter Four Woodman turned to the training of officers, noting that under von Seeckt that the post-First World War German army restricted to 100,000 was basically the training of officers, the future leaders of a massive army, which had also been noted by Churchill. This was why younger ones needed training which was how the Nazis ran their schools with this in mind, with an emphasis on physical training, and this even applied to theological students, as the swastika and the cross were ordered to be worn side by side as chaplains would enter battle with their flock.[23] There was even a Post Protection Troop for the postal service, and Railway Protection Troop for rail workers for protection against political disturbance. Woodman noted that before the First World War Germany's standing army was 850,000 but during the war had mustered 13,000,000 soldiers, then noting another war would require more.[24]

In Chapter Five Woodman turned towards the aeroplane describing it as the decisive weapon, and it was certainly the most feared weapon as it took the killing from the traditional battlefields into towns and cities. She pointed out that from the moment the Nazis assumed power the aircraft and the necessary armaments under Göring had increased dramatically. She reported the well-known time Göring had so-called foreign planes drop leaflets over Berlin to encourage support for more fighter aircraft. In her usual sensational way, she added that 'today it is leaflets, tomorrow it may be gas or incendiary bombs which means death and destruction'.[25] The training ground she rightly noted was the German Lufthansa, not just for pilots but civilian planes which could be quickly converted for war purposes, despite the German press claiming otherwise. Woodman also noted the rapid expansion of the German aircraft industry, and the way other countries helped if only to make money from the commerce, including Rolls-Royce from London, just trade, but, she added, making the way to war. It was noted by one outstanding historian of this period that 'Ministers soon realised that they had underestimated both the speed and extent of German air rearmament. Indeed, they contributed to this feat by bizarrely agreeing, in February 1934, to the sale of 118 Armstrong Siddeley aero engines to the Germans with a potential order for a further 260'.[26] Woodman also sounded the warning that the German production lines were now capable of producing yet more planes, and faster and bigger ones. Such was the air-momentum she concluded this chapter with the words that 'it proves without fail that Hitler-Germany is preparing for the coming of war'.[27]

Her Sixth chapter was about the German navy demanding supremacy of the Baltic, describing this as the next goal. She noted that Hitler was proposing not to oppose English interests but wanted to run parallel with them. Hitler was a land man, and his real interest was on the continent and not overseas, later only showing interest in the U-boat fleet. She spent pages, as she did with aircraft, with details of the number of craft which were available, noting that the Germans could build their own submarines and how effective they could be, and it would be only a matter of time before they had a full flotilla. She was deep into this military aspect, quoting the French Admiral Darlan when he said that 'without an air force there can no longer be a sea force'.[28] She also pointed out that the training schools for the navy had long been in existence. She concluded this chapter with the warning that 'Germany will do what she wants, without asking for permission'.[29]

Chapter Seven focused on Germany's war industry at home as well as abroad. Woodman started with the clandestine build up by the military and then its increasing size once the Nazis had grasped power, and the way the German press continually denied rearmament. She pointed to other countries who supplied help, naming Switzerland, Netherlands, Denmark, Sweden, and Germany's allies from the Great War, and war material resources from elsewhere. The implication was stressed that this was assisting Germany, when it was probably just capitalistic trade which benefitted all countries. Naturally, and to no surprise she concentrated on the firm Krupp a major German industry, and she dwelt on 'Herr Krupp' as he and his family held the reins of industrial power at this time. She spent many pages on the types of products and firms such as Daimler's armoured cars, and then named many others with the assumed guilt they were preparing Germany for war. Her dedication to proving that Germany was preparing for war in the near future was correct (with the benefit of hindsight), but many of these international industries were needing trade and believed the Germans were building up their defence forces, which was deemed as normal by many foreign politicians. In the early 1930s when she was gathering her evidence very few believed that Germany or any country wanted a repeat of the First World War. Dorothy Woodman may have been regarded as an opportunist sensationalist, but she was proved within a few years to be right, when she finished this chapter with the words, 'plans for this mass production are being made because a war is believed to be inevitable, and in a not-too-distant future'.[30]

Chapter Eight was an extensive survey of Germany preparing for poison and gas warfare. Giving reams of evidence of experiments, the build-up of necessary supplies for this gas weapon probably more dreaded than aircraft, also mentioning bacteriological warfare, perhaps even more feared than gas. Most military developed countries, as today, have research facilities for such weapons, but the terror of being the first to use them was, like nuclear weapons, a hopeful deterrent. Hitler himself had suffered from a gas attack. Ironically, the only time during the Second World War when gas came to light was when Luftwaffe bombers attacked an Allied convoy in the port of Bari hitting a ship packed with American gas shells, which created many deaths for the Allies and Italian civilian population.[31] In terms of bacteriological warfare, Himmler had reacted with the first biological warfare south of Anzio where the Pontine Marshes had been drained by Mussolini for farming. Himmler had the area checked by 'hydrographers and malariologists, who by flooding knew it would revert to a larval nursery for *Anopheles Labranchiae*, which made the place dangerous, and, in many ways, it was probably the first and only example of biological warfare'.³² Dorothy Woodman was right in investigating this possibility, as the combination of dropping gas from planes was a terrifying thought, and soon most governments had made plans for every civilian to carry gasmasks.

Chapter Nine concentrated on the ideological preparation for war in Germany, looking at the destruction of the trade unions, the propaganda of the 'spirit of the front line', the doctrine of the master race, the so-called Aryan. Much of this is widely known today because of history books, but it must be recalled that Woodman was writing this during 1933 and 1934 which for many would have been revealing. She refers to the authoritative racist element in the Nazi regime, (the primer for these thoughts as set out in *Mein Kampf*), the Nazi hatred of Russian communism, the question of necessary *Lebensraum*, the dangers of Alfred Rosenberg's writings, even down to the skulls worn on SS uniforms. She wrote of the control of what people could and could not read, the power of the propaganda ministry, the control of young people's thought processes, where the school had become the drill ground, and the power of biased broadcasting and newspapers, not just at home but in other countries. She spent time on how Hitler dealt with religion manipulating the Protestant Church, the attacks on pacifism and the changing of the rule of law to suit Nazism, mainly based on 'war laws'.

In her final Chapter Ten, Woodman focused on Germany's foreign policy and war, placed at the end of the book to show the possible consequences of her previous nine chapters. She pointed out that Nazi Germany was busy disguising its aims and intentions, which was to dominate in east and south Europe. She knew that Hitler had little interest in the overseas colonies, but mainland Europe, and especially Russia which was his main obsession. This indicated the Nazi desire was for the total abolition of the Treaty of Versailles, even suggesting it meant some form of European alliance against Russia. This meant, Woodman argued, that Germany would not feel chained by the 1918–19 treaty because first Germany meant to recover those territories lost by the treaty, and demanded at least equality in her military and armaments, because National Socialism intended to build up a powerful nation. She noted that the Germans had a population of 100 million but a third lived outside the German borders, and Goebbels with his propaganda was preparing for this based on his belief in ' national psychology'.³³ She noted that this propaganda was expanded beyond the borders, especially in nearby countries which could be annexed. The German police monitored everything, even overseas where they were dispatched with the diplomatic teams. German influence was gathering pace in many areas such as Romania, Hungary, the Baltic States, Denmark, Sweden, and at different levels in many others.

In her conclusion, Dorothy Woodman pulled no punches, pointing out that in Germany 'the dignity of humanity does not triumph today over the corporal's stick', there is 'no manifestation of the spontaneous will of a people but an attempt to organise that will systematically'.[34] She cleverly used the analogy of 'the existence of a powder magazine in the living-room of a house is a danger to the lives of the inmates' and this one was in the 'very midst of the European family of nations'.[35]

Conclusion

When first reading this book some thirty years after the war the current writer recalled having to remind himself it was written in 1934, that it was not a history book, written with the benefit of hindsight. Many people may have been put off reading her book in the 1930s, not because her background was journalism and supposedly wanting to be sensational, but because it was written in an academic style and full of military data, some without reference as to how they were obtained or their veracity. However, the years 1938 to 1945 proved that most of her thinking was all too accurate. When she wrote that Nazi Germany was busy disguising its aims and intentions, this was something which was totally ignored during the 1930s to the detriment of necessary military preparation. The problem for many foreign observers, especially in France and Britain was the fervent hope of no more major wars, and if this meant appeasing Hitler this appeared the only course, and not listen to the rantings of some female journalist being prophetic about the future in a way no one wanted to hear. George Orwell's books on totalitarianism were brilliant, easy to read, but Dorothy Woodman's efforts were focused entirely on Germany, not easy to read, and regarded at the time of those in power as insignificant as she was advocating belligerence. In the Gospel of St Mark, chapter 6 verse 4, Christ said 'a prophet is honoured everywhere except in his own hometown', but in her hometown Dorothy Woodman was mainly ignored.

Part III

Mein Kampf

Author's Notes: *Part Three continues the theme of written works available in the 1930s which if read properly would have informed the world of Hitler's warped personality and his intentions for European domination. This brief appraisal of Hitler's own work 'Mein Kampf' use some of Hitler's own words but with comments to understand Hitler and his intentions which he clearly indicated in this work. It is also an effort to make his book more readable. It covers a wide range of his thinking process, from dwelling on the economic plight of the nation, to prostitution and syphilis. Hitler makes a sinister reference to the problem of what he called defective people, namely, both mentally and physically handicapped. He dwells on the necessary grandeur of German cities, the Party's so-called Philosophy, the use of propaganda, spends time on projecting a unified Germany based on military power. He argues that education should be biased in favour of physical strength and determination looking to future military recruits, and he concludes with his convoluted and cynical views regarding religious belief. The British Ambassador in Germany when Hitler took power was Horace Rumbold, who had read this work and warned the British Government of the sort of person Hitler was, but like 'Mein Kampf' was largely ignored.*

Introduction

Mein Kampf is a boring book, proving tedious to read and study, lacking any finesse in its literary style, full of needless repetition, and often crude in its outlook and expressions. It is a classic example of what has been dubbed 'black' political literature and its main hallmark is not just bad taste, but an attempt to stir up racial hatred and applaud violence to gain political ends.

It was composed in two volumes, the first sub-titled *Eine Abrechnung* (A Reckoning) and the second *Die National-Sozialistische* (The National Socialist Movement), basically a vague autobiography encapsulating Hitler's fermenting political manifesto and views. It was started while Hitler was a prisoner in Landsberg prison following the failed Putsch and the first editor was Emil Maurice, then his deputy Rudolf Hess, and it was first translated into English in 1933.

It could be argued that it was only the product of a paranoid mind obsessed with himself and seeing his views as some form of eternal truth, almost hinting that he had Divine support, and as witnessed in later years when he convinced himself 'Providence' was guiding and protecting him.

As a student in the 1960s and having struggled to find a copy, the writer read only about a third of the content and became blind with sheer boredom and so disgusted with what he read it became part of a garden bonfire. However, after years of historical research and writing it raised a question as to why it was not more widely read and analysed, not so much by curious academics, but by politicians in the wider world who were becoming alert and nervous regarding the dangers of Nazi power in the 1930s. It would have been a boring exercise, and the possible thought may have arisen that the Nazi dictator was simply uneducated, self-obsessed, immoral, and downright stupid. However, by 1934–6 it must have been clear that Germany was growing in strength and that Hitler was not only seemingly popular, but he also held all the strings of government policy, including foreign affairs.

As previously noted, after the First World War there was a powerful desire to keep the world at peace, and although later derided, the appeasers who pleaded for peace had understandable support. It was widely known that under Hitler during the 1930s Germany was rapidly re-arming and the question was being asked as to what purpose, creating a degree of some concern. In Britain there was a degree of nervous anticipation about Hitler in some quarters of parliament, but it was widely held that 'peace in our time' could be maintained. The British military build-up was painfully slow and there was hope placed on the French having the largest army and defence system in Europe, this hope bolstered by the natural barrier of the English Channel. Only a few like Churchill saw the potential German menace and was often derided for raising the issue.

Had *Mein Kampf* been studied with care, it would have caused mental and intellectual indigestion, but above all it would have made foreigners to Germany, and many Germans, much more aware of the man Hitler and his intentions and ambitions. If a reader of *Mein Kampf* in the 1930s had decided, as many did, it was just the ravings of a lunatic, then the same red flags should have been raised, as they were from 1933 dealing with a madman who was the sole leader of a major central European State. It would have transmitted major red-light warnings concerning the mind-set of the man who controlled the growing military power of Germany, and it may well have sent out the necessary signals of potential disaster, by warning that Munich's 'Peace in our Time' was merely pulling the pin out of a hand grenade. When the Russian Foreign Minister Maxim Litvinov in 1938, suggested to some journalists that all countries should be alert to Hitler, it was noted by Tim Bouverie that 'unlike his British counterpart he had read *Mein Kampf*', which further underlined the importance of reading about Hitler's thinking processes.[1]

It was crystal clear that Hitler may well have been psychoneurotic, atavistic, and a ranting lunatic, but he had convinced many followers and destroyed the Weimar parliamentary system to become Germany's dictator. Many leading conservative Germans had managed to convince themselves that Hitler could be controlled, while in other countries it was often believed he could be negotiated with as he was a man who had lifted Germany out of the quagmire of defeat, and resurrected that country from the humiliation of the Treaty of Versailles. Hitler even had supporters in other European countries and overseas who admired him for his energy and determination. If they had read *Mein Kampf* in depth and still supported him then they would have been confirmed racists of the lowest order, lacking any sense of morality, politically unstable, and criminally inclined.

More significantly, had the major international political leaders read it with care, boring and tedious as the effort would have been, it would have opened their eyes not just to the nature of the man Hitler, but his plans and intentions for the future. Many claimed to have read it, and they may well have picked it up for a time, but it was such a boring monologue it can be sensibly speculated it was glimpse-read or ignored after skimping through the text. This can be stated with a degree of certainty because had it been properly analysed the warnings would have been taken more seriously. It offered such insights that it had to be read at a personal level and not just rely on other people's observations. It would have revealed, especially after 1933, that Germany had fallen into the hands of a dangerous misguided criminal who would have made Mafia organisations look like a vicar's tea-party. He was a man who could not be trusted and was a significant danger to peace but who was now leading a growing and powerful nation.

The journalist William Shirer noted the divided opinions on which way the new Third Reich was heading, and which should have posed many questions amongst international leaders. He wrote that 'Hitler had stated unequivocally in *Mein Kampf* what his goal was in the East: *Lebensraum* for Germany, more living space for Germans' but not seeing the implications of this, Shirer later regretted his own 'ignorance', which was shared by 'my journalistic and diplomatic colleagues, not to mention by the governments in London, Paris, and Moscow – was inexcusable'.[2] He later added that 'nothing could have been clearer. But like almost everyone else who had bothered to read the Nazi Bible, I had not taken the aims set down in that hodgepodge of a book seriously' ...and 'I have often thought subsequently that if more persons had digested *Mein Kampf* and not seen it only as a lot of Nazi gibberish, which it was, but as blueprint for action by Adolf Hitler if ever he gained power' 'but *Mein Kampf* was ignored or forgotten or dismissed', and this 'later proved to be a boon to the author'.[3] As it was Hitler was able to fool his 'own people and the rest of the world into believing that he was determined to keep the peace'.[4]

Hitler's book was manipulated at times, and with various translations it must be kept in mind that in places the book was deliberately changed for political reasons. When *Mein Kampf* was produced for American readers in 1933, some of the more violent views such as his hatred for France had been expunged.[5] It was an indicator that Hitler and his regime knew that however *Mein Kampf* was perceived in the new Germany, its views were often regarded as immoral in other countries. It was the same in 1945 when there was a belated and desperate attempt to cover up some of the extermination camps.

This book will reveal in its designated sections Hitler's thought processes, his intentions, and the danger signals for the immediate future. To avoid endless sheets of endnotes this section will place in brackets the page numbers of any quotations from the given text: 'Hitler, Adolf, *Mein Kampf* (London: Pimlico, 1992)', if the reader wishes to check the original texts.

Chapter One

Hitler, the Man and His Views

Hitler's Ability to Convince the Germans

In the preface to his book Hitler wrote that 'every great movement on this earth owes its growth to great orators and not to great writers'. His oratory lacked finesse but his emotional screaming about Germany and the ills it was suffering, appealed to the down-trodden masses, which rarely occurs with such heat even at an election time in most democracies. With his speeches, especially at the infamous Nuremberg Rallies, he managed to convince many (but not all) that here was a leader who would make life better and restore the old Germany. No foreign observer could have missed that this ranting street-talker grabbed people's attention and at times their adoration, the danger of any cult. The foreign observers must have noted that he may not be to their tastes, but he had a major backing in his own German ranks.

It is clear that Hitler, because of his egocentricity needed an audience to applaud him. Later in life, to Goebbels' consternation Hitler refused to have his prepared speech checked for radio broadcasting. Hitler found the silent studio difficult, because he was accustomed to immediate rapturous applause.[1] Goebbels avoided using Hitler on the radio until he had rehearsed him, because the radio lacked his magnetism and force, 'in fact his voice sounded rather unpleasant'.[2] Hitler's self-belief emerges as he related his early life, noting that 'I believe that even then my oratorical talent was being developed in the form of more or less violent argument with my schoolmates'. (p.5)

In his continuous attacks on the democratic systems, he thought that in a parliament a few hundred turned up to collect their attendance fees, whereas in great public meetings there are many more listeners (p.93), which had greater appeal to him, and he was probably correct that the masses liked to be stirred up rather than listen to parliamentary speeches in expected silence.

He returned to the power of his oratory several times in this lengthy book, writing that 'the power which has always started the greatest religious and political avalanches in history rolling has from time immemorial been the magic power of the spoken word, and that alone'…and 'only a storm of passion can turn the destinies of peoples' (p.98). He appealed to the crowd suffering the defeat of the First World War now impoverished, poor, unemployed promising a better future with the expectancy that once the Nazi Party was in power life would immediately change for the better. He was an astute rabble-rouser preying on the needs of his listeners which elevated him in a way which many modern-day politicians would envy.

Later in *Mein Kampf* he spent time on writing how he pressed for greater mass meetings of the Party and how wonderful he was at public speaking (p.323), and the way he appeared as the natural leader. He wrote that 'I gradually transformed myself into a speaker for mass meetings, that I became practised in the pathos and the gestures which a great hall, with its thousands of people, demands' (p.426), and 'a brilliant speaker will be able to write better than a brilliant writer can speak', (p.427). He even explored the best times for speaking believing evening to be best (p.431) comparing it to Churches and incense at evening services (p.432), stating that it takes oratory to persuade the masses (p.432). This element of a quasi-religious atmosphere was picked up by the journalist William Shirer noting that Hitler was 'restoring pageantry to the drab lives of Germans', and in referring to the great Nazi meetings he added 'it had something of the mysticism and religious fervour of an Easter or Christmas Mass in a great Gothic cathedral'.[3]

Several times Hitler alluded to his ability at public speaking, noting how outstanding he was, and at that time in Germany he proved able to pick up what the mass crowds wanted to hear, thereby establishing himself in a charismatic way, and from his point of view as the natural leader, hinting at times he was under the guidance of the Almighty. This aspect naturally leads to the next sub-section about how *Mein Kampf* revealed some personality traits.

Personality

He was from his earliest days overly ambitious, referring to his parents wanting the best for him, he wrote that 'I too, wanted to become something – but on no account a Civil Servant' (p.17). In terms of drawing, his first

Hitler pictured on 1 February 1933 after his appointment as Chancellor. The journalist Dorothy Thompson described Hitler as of 'startling insignificance'. (*Bundesarchiv, Bild 183-1987-0703-506/CC-BY-SA 3.0*)

Neville Chamberlain, a determined man, c.1921.

Ramsay MacDonald, c.1929. (*USA Library of Congress/public domain*)

Stanley Baldwin, c.1920. (*USA Library of Congress/public domain*)

Sir Samuel Hoare. (*Library of Congress/ public domain*)

First British Ambassador to Nazi Germany, Horace Rumbold. (*Library of Congress/public domain*)

Second Ambassador, Eric Phipps.

Third Ambassador, Nevile Henderson, at Croydon Airport before his flight to Berlin.

Édouard Daladier.

Pierre Laval, c.1931. (*Gallica Digital Library/ public domain*)

Léon Blum, c.1927.

In Munich, the Holy Place of Nazidom was the Feldherrnhalle, pictured here in 1933.

The 1935 Nuremberg Rally, which Stephen Roberts attended.

Mussolini and Hitler, Berlin 1937.

Nazi propaganda: *Ein Volk, ein Reich, ein Führer!* (*Stadtarchive Kiel, CC BY-SA 3.0 DE*)

Hitler greeted in Vienna, March 1938. (*Bundesarchiv, Bild 146-1972-028-14*)

Hitler and Göring, 16 March 1938. (*Bundesarchiv, Bild 183-2004-1202-504/ CC-BY-SA 3.0*)

Hitler greets Chamberlain with Paul Schmidt hovering ready to translate and Hitler's guard, 15 September 1938. (*Bundesarchiv, Bild 183-H12478/ Unknown author/CC-BY-SA 3.0*)

Churchill with Lord Halifax, the 'Holy Fox', c.20 September 1938.

Chamberlain, Daladier, Hitler, Mussolini and Ciano pictured before signing the Munich Agreement, 29 September 1938. (*Bundesarchiv, Bild 183-R69173/CC-BY-SA 3.0*)

Hitler signing the Munich Agreement on 30 September 1938. (*Bundesarchiv, Bild 146-1976-033-06/CC-BY-SA 3.0*)

Churchill and Eden at Spencer Wood, the residence of the Lieutenant Governer of Quebec, August 1943. (*Quebec Archives/ public domain*)

(*NARA*)

The Brown House was the headquarters of the Nazi Party, seen here shortly after its opening c.1932 and after its destruction in 1945. (*Sam via Wikimedia Commons/ CC BY-SA 4.0*)

love, he wrote that 'my ability had developed amazingly' (p.18), never being backward in praising himself. When reflecting on his life he noted that 'talented persons retain traces of memory from this period down to advanced old age' (p.29), classifying himself as worthy of being seen as talented. As noted above, he saw himself as called by obscure universal powers believing that 'fate itself became my instructor' (p.43), which led to his belief that Providence guided and protected him. He saw himself as God's man, writing 'hence today I believe that I am acting in accordance with the will of the Almighty creator: by defending myself against the Jew, I am fighting for the work of the Lord' (p.60), but quite how he arrived at this conclusion defies any sensible explanation. It revealed the inbuilt evidence that he believed he was always right and had the backing of the creator of all things. His self-conceit was almost unbelievable, writing 'I think that I studied politics more closely than many other men' (p.63). In his argument against democracy, he wrote 'in world history the man who really rises above the norm of broad average usually announces himself personally' (p.81) which he had been doing and this book was part of the same effort.

While recuperating in hospital from an injury in the First World War, he was shocked by men admitting to cowardice and causing self-injury to survive (p.174). In his book he often refers to cowards and traitors to the nation for many different reasons, allowing no room for human weakness and vulnerability, and painting himself as a dedicated hero. He was sure he was chosen for great power, admitting that when he joined the German Workers' Party, he was reluctant because 'I wanted to establish my own Party' (p.200). It was little wonder he had few personal friends, though later in life when he had grasped power, Hitler was supported by local henchmen who were extremely pleased to follow his demands. Normally a man of such self-conceit is of little interest to others, but because of his rise to the highest level of German political authority his personality needs some scrutiny, as do his views which soon developed into national policies.

Some of Hitler's Views

In his post-First World War analysis, Hitler attacked the Jews and Marxists, describing the postwar years as 'a period of creeping sickness' mainly due to them (p.211), and such was the venom in his attacks the Jews and

Marxists have their own later sections to try and understand where Hitler was coming from.

He correctly noted that after 1918 there was an increasing population with serious food and economic problems emerging (p.212), writing there was a serious weakness in the peasant classes, that money had become the god for many, causing a 'malignant degeneration to set in' (p.213), and it had not been helped by 'doing things in halves', (p.215), an expression he uses several times to underline his attitude of giving orders, which he insinuates should be promptly executed. To illustrate his position, he refers to his continuous worship of Frederick the Great, as he does many times, whom he saw as being supported by Heaven (p.217). His adoration of Frederick the Great continued as his hero's picture was always on his walls, even in the latter-day bunker, a visible verification that he saw himself as the mirror of the great man. The plague of the nation, as he described the postwar years, continued because of the parliamentary institution which he despised but later utilised (p.218), always blaming the press, especially the Jewish owned papers (p.221). He even found time to devote pages to the social problems of prostitution and the widespread issue of syphilis (p.224), noting again that the cure could not be solved with 'half measures' and that 'the most ruthless decisions will have to be made (p.232). Hitler rarely drank alcohol, never smoked, was a vegetarian, and he was always highly judgemental on such issues. It would not take long before his methods of stopping prostitution would become known, but more to the point, he had barely left the subject of syphilis when he wrote that 'defective people should be prevented from propagating… represents the most humane act of mankind', and then adding 'those who are physically and mentally unhealthy and unworthy must not perpetuate their suffering in the body of their children' (p.367). This should have been a stark warning to those German people who had intellectually handicapped children or even physical disabilities, and soon the so-call T4 organisation would be executing many such unfortunate victims. The Euthanasia Decree was known as *Aktion T4*, the *T4* standing for *Tiergartenstraße 4* which was the street address of the Chancellery Department at that time. Hitler's ramblings often focused on such immoral and criminal matters projecting them as humane and good for the nation, and by the early thirties any astute reader may have spotted the dangers contained in his views and sent out warnings of his plans and intentions which some did. He argued that nature makes procreation free 'yet submitting survival to a hard trial, chooses from an excess of individuals the best as worthy of living' (p.121) plus the need to increase productivity of our soil (p.122). He was more than hinting at what has been dubbed neo-Darwinism, the survival of the fittest, a sinister concept. It is easy now with the benefit of hindsight to state this, but the political leaders should perhaps have been more aware of this book, not so much in the mid-1920s, but as soon as Hitler started his rise to power.

Even in his mundane meanderings there are statements which should have been underlined in red. In his text he inveighs against cities which are just blocks of flats, thinking they should have magnificent buildings and be centres of art (p.240ff), which met some personal fruition for him when he welcomed the architect Albert Speer into his inner circle with grand ideas of rebuilding grand Nazi cities. There then followed the sinister note that if his advice was not followed then in the future people would come just to admire the Jewish department stores (p.241), later adding that 'the deepest and ultimate failure of the old Reich lay in its failure to recognise the racial problems and its importance for the historical development of peoples'(p.257). Throughout his general views as to how he perceived Germany's future there are constant references to the danger he projected about the Jew, which apart from being immoral and racist should have raised questions not only about his warped personality but the potential dangers if he rose to power. His one focus was on a Germany with only thorough-bred Germans in control with others to be ejected from German borders. It is in this vein that he wrote that he admired the army which 'trained men in idealism and devotion to the fatherland and its greatness while everywhere else greed and materialism had spread abroad' (p.255), indicating his idealism was potentially dangerous.

Many of his political views were expressed in Volume Two of *Mein Kampf* when he outlined the Party's viewpoints. He noted that millions of Germans wanted some basic changes which was leading to widespread discontent (p.300), pointing out that after 1918, in political terms, people were 'torn into two parts' with intelligentsia tending 'to fight for their ideas with spiritual weapons which are fragmentary and superficial', while the labouring masses were mainly organised by the less radical Marxist movements', adding that 'no resurrection of German people can occur except through the recovery of outward power' (p.301). He had at least understood the frustration for many working-class Germans who as a result of the First World War and the subsequent defeat were suffering serious poverty, unemployment, and hunger, but he utilised these problems to his own ends for becoming seen as the saviour of Germany. He called the Party, the 'young movement' setting their goal of resurrecting the German state with its own sovereignty (p.303). Hitler recognised that 'the idea of outward German liberation seems senseless' without the same wish by the masses (p.304), which demands 'preparations in the sphere of foreign policy from that of technical rearmament or that of battle itself…so we realised that the highest aim is to accomplish the nationalisation of the masses…to do this 'no social sacrifice is too great' (p.305).

Hitler had understood the importance of the masses and their grievances, and he knew the Russian revolution had proved the importance of the proletariat. He wanted the masses to know that his Party would change their lives for the better, which, as usual, he noted cannot be changed with 'half-measures'. He accused the 'professors and intelligentsia' of having only abstract knowledge (p.306), and the 'soul of the people can only be won by destroying their opponents, by heeding the importance of their racial foundation'…otherwise they are like men who would like 'to teach poodles the qualities of greyhounds' (p.307). Hitler continually painted himself as a man of determination and not using half-measures, writing that 'the German worker will not be raised to the framework of the German national community' by feeble means (p.308). It is therefore essential 'to tear these away from the international delusion, to free them from their social distress' and 'lead them to the national community as a valuable united factor' (p.309). He recognised the importance of mass propaganda which must not omit primitiveness of expression, which meant the appeals to the masses had to be made in their language. He claimed that amongst the thousands of speakers there 'is perhaps only a single one who can manage to speak to locksmiths and university professors at the same time', obviously meaning himself (p.310). 'Propaganda' he wrote, 'must be adjusted to the broad masses in content and in form, and its soundness is to be measured exclusively by its effective result', writing the speaker must 'conquer the heart of the masses' (p.311). He explained the new Party was anti-parliamentarian which was a symptom of mankind's decay (p313). Again, with his habitual self-conceit he wrote that 'some idea of genius arises in the brain of a man who feels called upon to transmit his knowledge to the rest of humanity' obviously meaning himself (p.314). He later added the stark warning that 'the future of a movement is conditioned by the fanaticism, yes, the intolerance, with which its adherents uphold it as the sole correct movement' (p.317), when the Jews slander or attack a member of the Party it is a sign of honour (p.319).

He later added that 'the state is a means to an end. Its end lies in the preservation and advancement of a community of physically and psychically homogenous creatures' (p.357), later writing that black people are 'half-apes' (p.391). His racism is appallingly immoral and criminal, but he proclaimed that National Socialism was a philosophy, writing that 'Political parties are inclined to compromise, philosophies never. Political parties even reckon with opponents; philosophies proclaim their infallibility' (p.413), which is why he wrote this book as it would not be a subject for oratory to the masses. He explained this claim that the Party was a philosophy was the reason why the Party could never collaborate with an existing regime (p.414), stating that a philosophy is 'declaration of war against the existing order' (p.414), which, he wrote, was why the Party established 25 guiding principles to make this clear (p.416). He even compared this concept to the catholic church which had survived so long (p.417), arguing that if 'National Socialism wants to conquer it must espouse the truth (p.419).

As *Mein Kampf* unfolds, his reference to the 'young movement' or the 'Young Party' eventually arrives at the name NSDAP and the habit of referring to Germany as the *Völkisch* (Folkish) movement. This was not a Nazi invention, but a German nationalist movement, active from the late 19th century, but for Hitler it was linked to 'blood and soil'. His appeal to the masses frequently focused on his attacks against the Versailles Treaty, especially the Guilt Clause and the other humiliations (p.421ff), which were easy pickings for him, and with some justification. He wrote that 'the NSDAP should not become a constable of public opinion but must dominate all. It must not become a servant of the masses, but their master!' (p.422). It further angered him that 'millions of Germans regarded the peace treaty of Versailles as nothing more than a just retribution' (p.425).

He placed considerable emphasis in explaining his views on the way Germany crumbled after 1918, stating a country needed an army, civil service and monarchy or a significant leader. He was underlining the need for physical strength, writing 'if you want to hold weak, wavering or actually cowardly fellows to their duty, there has at all times been only one possibility: the deserter must know that his desertion brings with it the very thing that he wants to escape. At the front, a man can die, as a deserter he must die' (p.477), ironically Trotsky had expressed the same thought.

In his chapter entitled *Federalism as a Mask*, Hitler looked back to the unifying of the German state, accepting that each area or province could retain its cultural traditions, but the primary need was to assert itself as a single powerful state with a good leader (pp.505ff), unquestioningly implying himself. Some of his atavistic leanings were clearly indicated when he wrote that 'German tribes were quarrelling amongst themselves' (p.507), and 'as early as this period my personal fight against the insane incitement of German tribes against each other began' (p.508). He claimed he was against the 'anti-Prussian agitation' (p.508), stating the Jews were mainly responsible (p.510), and the old federal state worked because of Prussia (p.516). This part of the book consists of convoluted if not confusing arguments lacking any logical process of thought. He eventually writes that 'the state…everything must be subordinated to its sovereign interests' and 'in future the significance of the individual provinces will unquestionably be shifted more to the field of cultural policy' (p.524), while 'the army must be sharply removed from all influence of the individual states' and 'the German army does not exist to be a school for the preservation of tribal peculiarities' (p.525). He was evidently forecasting his plan for a politically united state and a uniformed army in control, all of which happened when he turned Germany into a police state.

To achieve his aims, namely, to gather the masses behind him to help gain the power to transform Germany into this dream of a powerful military state governed by himself, he expressed his unusual and extreme views on the subject of education. He wrote that the state needs the 'breeding of absolutely healthy bodies' (p.371) because 'a decayed body is not made the least more aesthetic by a brilliant mind' and what 'makes the Greek ideal of beauty a model is the wonderful combination of the most magnificent physical beauty with a brilliant mind and noblest soul' (p.371). To achieve this so-called ideal he argued that 'physical training…is a requirement for the self-preservation of the nationality, represented and protected by the state' (pp.372), and that the schools must give this more time, (p.372). He proposed that teaching youngsters to bear hardships…(p.373), that 'self-confidence must be inculcated in the young…his whole education and training must be so ordered as to give him the conviction that he is absolutely superior to others' (p.374). It is noteworthy that most of these dreams focused on boys and not girls, and his later well-known obsession with uniforms comes to the fore at this stage. He demanded that the boy's clothing must reflect this, 'not the nonsense they look to at the moment (p.375), claiming it is essential because today there is no military training (p.375) which there was, but not to the extent he needed with his military ambitions. He was obviously attempting to build up a young generation of strong determined young men which later he would influence with the indoctrination of the Hitler Youth. Young boys were soon to be influenced by Nazi doctrine, instructed to hate Jews, taught to obey orders without question, and to regard Hitler as their demi-god, which became a characteristic of the type of candidate for the SS movement. Hitler argued that 'of the highest importance is the training of will-power and determination' (p.379), 'the plague of our present-day cowardly lack of will and determination is, all in all, mainly the result of our basically faulty education of youth' (p.379). For Hitler primarily came the need to build up physical strength and stamina, the ingredients needed for a soldier. He argued that there was no point in training them in matters which 95 per cent cannot be used and hence soon forgotten (p.380), increasing the time for physical training (p.382), and arguing that there was a need to provide better political history (p.382), while science education should be turned to more practical matters (p.384) to make an 'idealistic national community' (p.385). He attacked 'our era's fear of chauvinism as the sign of its impotence' (p.388), arguing that 'no boy and no girl must leave school without having been led to an ultimate realisation of the necessity and essence of blood quality'(p.389).

He concludes his sally into education by arguing that preparations for the First World War were not adequate 'because the rulers were overeducated men, crammed full of knowledge and intellect, but bereft of any healthy instincts and devoid of all energy and boldness' (p.392). He continued that it was necessary 'to gather and to organise from the ranks of our nation those forces capable of becoming the vanguard fighters for a new philosophy of life' (p.396), leaving no doubt about his views of preparing young boys to become obedient soldiers, if not robots, a warning of the future, which went unheeded because most people saw it as mere ranting. Too many outside observers later ignored the stunning growth of the Hitler Youth, being prepared to see it as a Boy Scout movement, and ignoring the politicising of the young.

His attitude to religion and religious belief is at best confusing, at one time he can sound like an ardent Christian, writing that 'God's will give men their form, their essence, and their abilities. Anyone who destroys His work is declaring war on the Lord's creation, the Divine will' (p.512). He was evidently sensitive to the fact that many of his potential adherents, even those in the military held religious beliefs, and he probably realised that he was skating on thin ice. It later became clear that he had no time for genuine religious belief, but somehow convinced himself that Providence was always supporting him. The word Providence can be interpreted in many ways, ranging from Divine interference to external circumstances, fate, or destiny. Above all he did not want religious interference in his cause (which happened) or involve his followers over matters of religious faith, writing 'I do not hesitate to declare that I regard the men who today draw the folkish movement into the crisis of religious quarrels as worse enemies of my people than any international Communist' (p.513). It was curious that at this stage of writing in the mid-1920s, that he referred to 'my people' almost projecting himself to the time when he would be the dictator. He even mocked the denominations noting that 'Catholics and Protestants wage a merry war with one another, and the mortal enemy [the Jew] of Aryan humanity and all Christendom laughs up his sleeve' (p.511). He decided that 'Protestantism as such is a better defender of Germanism' (p.103) some 'scoundrels have not shunned to make even religion the instrument of their political bargains' (p.105). 'For the political leaders the religious doctrines and institutions of his people must always remain inviolable; or else he has no right to be in politics, he should become a reformer, if he has what it takes' (pp.106–107), indicating a high degree of hypocrisy on the part of the writer.

Later he would interfere in the German protestant Church making a pro-Nazi clergyman Ludwig Müller the Reich Bishop thereby dividing the Lutheran Church. It was more difficult with the global Roman Catholic Church which tended to fear communism more than fascism, and in 1937 Pope Pius XI published two encyclicals, *Mit Brennender Sorge* and *Divini Redemptoris,* which basically stated that both communism and Nazism (not just fascism) were incompatible with Christianity. It resulted in a Concordat with Rome with Hitler wanting the Church out of politics and the Church trying to ensure its safety. Hitler's attitudes and behaviour soon became clear as thousands of clergymen and Christians of all denominations and positions died in the many concentration camps.

Chapter Two

His Special Hatreds

Author's Notes: *This section outlines Hitler's obsessive hatred of Jews, which inundates the entire book to such an extent it clearly indicated to Jews an urgent warning if he should rise to power. It also constituted a stark signal at the international level that this man was warped, was immoral, a criminal, if not psychologically damaged and would be a danger if he grasped power. The second part deals with Hitler's intense hatred of Marxism, and it should be noted that Hitler may well have had some sympathy for opposing communism, but the alert should have been noted in his creation of a paramilitary force, the SA, which was widely used to oppose any opposition to Nazism even against the German civilian population, introducing a sense of fear on everyday streets and shopping centres.*

When as a young man Hitler was aimlessly wandering in Vienna, he claimed he became aware of two significant menaces he did not understand, namely Marxism and Jewry (p.20). Whether this crossed his mind as a lost teenager and casual labourer must be open to some doubt, as it is clear that most seasoned experts in this text have noted he was prone to exaggeration and telling lies. He would soon link Marxism and his anti-Semitism in the same bundle, blaming the growth of Bolshevism on a Jewish conspiracy to bolster his hatreds. He even developed a dislike for the ordinary labourers with whom he had to work in order to feed himself. He wrote that he was horrified by the 'economic misery of the labourers (my companions)' and their 'moral and ethical coarseness…and the low level of their intellectual development' (p.28). For Hitler to use words such as ethics and morality appears somewhat hypocritical for today's reader, but this book was about selling himself, his views, and the need to be recognised as Germany's natural and necessary leader of the future.

Anti-Semitism

In his early recollections Hitler could not remember the word Jew as having any significance, only the memory of a Jewish boy at school whom no one trusted (p.48). He knew there were Jews in Linz, noting they had become 'Europeanised and taken on a human look', also noting that it had nothing to do with their religion, underlining the fact that in Hitler's case it was pure racism. He wrote that if it were a matter of religion there were no problems as a 'splash of baptismal water' would sort that issue out (p.110). He claimed that when he first saw an orthodox Jew with black hair locks, he asked himself 'is this a German' (p.52). As he saw more orthodox Jews, he commented on their 'unclean dress and their generally unheroic appearance', (p.53), writing that he was becoming aware of their influence in the press, art, literature, and theatre. He took some joy in pointing out criminal Jews as if they were the cause of criminality (p.55).

He identified the Jew as being a global threat, writing 'International Jewish world finance needed these lures to enable it to carry out its long-desired plan for destroying Germany (p.136), noting 'the Jews always form a state within the state' (p.138), and 'the Mosaic religion is nothing other than a doctrine for preservation of the Jewish race'. (p.138). His personal hatred knew no bounds or reason, writing 'if the best men were dying at the front, the least we could do was to wipe out the vermin' (p.155) which was written after the First World War as a general attack on Marxism. In the same vein he wrote that 'as regards economic life, things were even worse. Here the Jewish people had become indispensable. The spider was slowly beginning to suck the blood out of the people's pores' (p.175). He proclaimed 'there is no making pacts with Jews; there can only be the hard: either – or. I, for my part, decided to go into politics'. He accused the Jews for the First World War failure (p.207), blaming Germany for a sense of losing its sense of cause (p.208), announcing it was not a military defeat (p.201) and attacked the Marxists who were Jews. The well-known 'stab-in-the-back' theory that the Jews were the cause of the German failure was widespread, and Hitler fastened onto this bizarre issue in a frenzied fashion, even though thousands of German Jewish soldiers had died in the trenches.

In his vitriolic attack on Jews, he referred to the now well-known 'Aryan', writing that 'the mightiest counterpart to the Aryan is represented by the

Jew'. The word Aryan is best traced to an ethnocultural self-description by Indo-Iranians and is now recognised as an ideology of racial supremacy, by the Nazi regime somehow creating the ruse that the ancient Germanic tribes carried this blood in their veins. Hitler used every tool in his limited vocabulary to attack Jewish people and their traditions, writing that in hardly any people in the world is the instinct of self-preservation developed more strongly than in the so-called chosen (p.272). He attempted to debase them by writing that they base their success 'on the very primitive herd instinct' (p.273), making it sound animalistic. Ironically, further on in his *Mein Kampf* (p.360) he criticised the German people for 'lacking that sure herd instinct which is based on unity of blood'.

His attack on Jews occurs on the majority of pages, if only with some passing barb or innuendo. He claimed they were 'led by nothing but the naked egoism of the individual' (p.274), which was more like one of his own defects. He identified the Jews as 'a parasite in the body of other nations and states' (p.277), as always being a 'people with definite racial characteristics and never a religion' (p.278), pointing out that the Talmud was about making a profit (p.278) and even Christ drove them out of the temple (p.278). For one lengthy stretch of his diatribe (pp.280–290) he argued how the 'Jew always slowly takes control of his host environment from arrival and insinuates his way to the top leaders', and 'poisons the blood of others but preserves his own…never marrying a Christian woman' (p.286). He wrote 'it was the Jews who brought the Negroes into the Rhineland' referring to the time when the French used Senegalese troops to occupy that area, later adding that 'the Jew would really devour the peoples of the earth, would become their master' (p.411), ironically the same fear which brought most of the global nations against Hitler in the Second World War.

Hitler hated the Marxists, looked down his nose at Negroes and other races whom he felt were diminutive in stature, but his anti-Semitism was obsessively extreme and deeply personal to the point of excessive sheer hatred, seeing them as vermin, and although with the benefit of hindsight the Holocaust seems a natural consequence, it could not be foretold because it was so unbelievable. Nevertheless, his attacks in *Mein Kampf* should have been a warning of a deadly pogrom against the Jewish people, and a warning to international observers that Hitler was completely warped if not mad, and as soon as he rose to power the warning signals should have been flashing sharp red. It was no surprise that his penultimate sentence in the book reads 'A State which in this age of racial poisoning dedicates itself to the care of its best racial elements must someday become lord of the earth' – namely his great ambition.

Marxism

As mentioned in the previous section it was Hitler's constant belief that Marxism was a Jewish conspiracy, seeing them as 'the founders of the doctrine' (p.59). He claimed that the 'Jewish doctrine of Marxism rejects the aristocratic principle of nature and replaces the eternal privilege of power and strength by the mass of numbers and their dead weight' (p.60). He wrote that if the Jew is successful in his venture of communism 'his crown will be the funeral wreath of humanity', (p.60). Hitler later added that 'it was an unequalled absurdity to identify the German worker with Marxism in the days of August 1914' (p.154) because 'Marxism, whose goal is and remains the destruction of all non-Jewish national states' (p.154), and 'if the best men were dying at the front, the least we could do was to wipe out the vermin' (p.155) as it needs brute force to destroy Marxism (p.158).

He noted that Marxists shrewdly pretended to march with democratic procedures until they gain the support that they need (p.342), which he would emulate later for a brief time if only to overturn democracy. He argued that 'what has won the millions of workers for Marxism is less the literary style of the Marxist church fathers, than the indefatigable and truly enormous propaganda work of tens of thousands of untiring agitators' (p.429). It was clear that Hitler had never read Marx, but he tended to see this political revolution as a personal enemy, and he remained concerned, mainly because in his early days for seeking power it was the one political group which bothered to note and oppose his Party of National Socialism. It was only in Munich that the NSDAP was becoming known by other national parties who were also opposed by the Marxists (p.435).

Hitler, probably out of sheer ignorance rarely commented on the nature of original communism, apart from a few insults and sweeping generalisations. For him Marxists were those who opposed him on the streets with the usual mayhem which had been a hallmark of German life after 1918. Hitler described the clashes with Marxists in their meetings, the way they turned up to disrupt Party gatherings (pp. 437ff) which were therefore never peaceful. Reading between the lines it is easy to gain the impression that Hitler enjoyed fierce meetings, writing it was necessary 'to introduce 'blind discipline in our meetings and absolutely to guarantee the authority of the committee in charge' (p.439).

He noted that because of the big rowdy meetings 'I began the organisation of a house guard in the form of a monitor service' (p.446). These 'monitors' as he first described them were the first signs of the *Sturmabteilung*, the SA, more commonly known as the Brownshirts, making it in his words 'not a debating club but a combat group' which 'like a swarm of hornets would swoop down on the disturbers of our meetings' (p.447). It was not long after this development of watching the Marxist fly their red banners, that as a counter the Nazi swastika flag was introduced, (the swastika supposed to have Aryan origins). He called them the monitor troops and worried about their abilities when they held a massive meeting in a large space known as 'The Circus', (perhaps appropriately) but he proudly noted they worked well against the Marxist protesters (p.454), noting the storm troopers soon sorted out the problems (p.460). Later, after explaining the nature of the SA, he wrote 'we must teach the Marxists that the future master of the streets is National Socialism, just as it will someday be the master of the state' (p.494), which was another significant warning signal. Following his release from Landsberg prison (December 1924) the NSDAP founded itself on 27 February 1925 determined to train and set up the SA according to Hitler's policies, with Hitler noting 'it must not suffer the SA to degenerate into a kind of combat league nor into a secret organisation…but it must train as a guard and number hundreds or thousands of men' (p.504). There were many international observers, including elements within the Catholic hierarchy who would not have disapproved of Hitler's policy of opposing Marxism. However, as a means of combatting the foe, Hitler had introduced the SA which was a political para-military force, which in a fleeting time became extremely brutal, not just against Marxists but any form of opposition to the NSDAP. The Nazi willingness to develop its own army to use on civilians should have been yet another red warning about the rising figure of Hitler.

France and Russia

Hitler's views on international relationships will be explored more fully in a later part of this summary in dealing with foreign affairs. Nevertheless, when Hitler was composing *Mein Kampf* in the early 1920s, he had already developed a significant hatred of two countries in particular. One can be passed over without much necessary comment, as Russia was now the home of the hated Jewish Marxist. His attitude towards France was one of intense loathing, and he wrote that he was angry with the 'loathsome cult for France' he had seen in the newspapers, describing it as 'this wretched licking of France's boots' (p.51). He had noted that 'by the winter of 1922–23, at the latest, it should have been generally understood that even after the conclusion of peace France was still endeavouring with iron logic to achieve the war aim, she had originally had in mind' (p.613). He then added that 'not only did the English possess no interest in the total extermination of the German state; they even had every reason to desire a rival against France in Europe for the future' (p.614), and from the standpoint of foreign relations, the occupation of the Ruhr for the first time alienated England from France (p.617).

As will become clearer later in his book his attitude towards France was one of bitter anger, not least because of France being amongst the victors of the First World War, but their powerful demands for recompense from the agreement of the Versailles Treaty, but also because they had the largest army in Europe and appeared at that time as a formidable opponent to Hitler's wish for an all-powerful Reich. This probably explained Hitler's later childish and rapturous joy when France fell so swiftly in 1940. Amongst others, French observers should have noted these embryonic feelings as early as possible. His pact with Stalin to invade Poland followed by Operation *Barbarossa* was unpredictable unless one had read in *Mein Kampf* of Hitler's deviousness and determination to attack Russia. Hindsight can unfold past mysteries and events, but a minimal amount of foresight which can be gleaned from *Mein Kampf* would have given better preparation against the Nazi onslaught after Hitler had been in power for a few years.

Chapter Three

Pan-Germanism

Author's Notes: *This section relates to Hitler's obsession of defining a country by the race of the inhabitants, in Germany's case the ubiquitous Aryan, and his belief that people of the same blood should form one nation, pan-Germanism. He despised the old rulers of his homeland of Austria for making it what we would today call a multicultural society. Strangely he drops his first hints of seeing England as an ally and the hint of finding more space for Germans, the policy of Lebensraum.*

In his opening pages of *Mein Kampf*, in raising the subject of the projected nation as he saw it, Hitler throws the loss of German colonies aside as in his belief that the first fight must be for a unified German state (p.3). He mentions his policy of pan-Germanism that wherever there are German speakers that must therefore be German territory. Time and time again he raised this concept of pan-Germanism and implies that territories taken by the Versailles Treaty had to be returned, a form of irredentist nationalism (the return of former lands) dressed up as a holy crusade, and he acknowledged it would probably have to be by force of arms. This was how he interpreted the often-misused word of Nationalism, writing 'I can fight only for something that I love, love only what I respect, and respect only what I at least know' (p.31), thereby indicating his starting base was limited by his own limited experience of the world. Pan-Germanism, he argued arose in Austria because of the glorious love of fatherland (p.89), but it failed because of its unclear conception and too many social problems (p.93). In Austria he thought they had sold their soul to parliament (pp.96–7). However, he believed Pan-German movement was right in its theoretical view about German reincarnation, it was nationalistic, stating that 'its anti-Semitism was based on a correct understanding of the racial problem, and not on religious ideas (p.111). Hitler was an Austrian by birth but obsessed with Germany. When the First World War was declared he wrote 'I fell down on my knees and thanked Heaven from an overflowing heart for granting me the good fortune of being able to live at this time' (p.148), and he instantly sought permission to join a Bavarian regiment. In his adoration of Germany, he wrote that 'the German Reich as a state embraces all Germans and has the task, not only of assembling and preserving the most valuable stocks of basic racial elements in the people, but slowly and surely of raising them to a dominant position' (p.362), and the folkish state 'must set race in the centre of all life' (p367).

Nation and Race

According to Hitler, nature has made all creatures to keep to themselves and not breed with others (p.258), what he describes as a natural segregation. From this viewpoint he then jumps to human beings, as if it were pure logic, writing that when two different people have a child, they produce a medium of themselves, the child would be taller than the 'racially lower' parent and not as tall as the other, and so succumbs from being of the higher level (pp.258–9), noting that the stronger must always dominate, explaining 'the fox is always a fox and a goose always a goose' (p.259). From this he deduced that interbreeding leads to the lowering of the race (p.260), adding that 'pacifist-humane idea is perfectly all right perhaps when the highest type of man has previously conquered' all (p.261), which for him was the Aryan. Nothing could be more bizarre and reflect a perverted way of thinking, and yet dressed up as if he knew it was correct, assuming the pose of being a leading authority in such matters.

He hammers away at the importance of the Aryan, noting that 'All the human culture, all the results of art, science, and technology that we see before us today, are almost exclusively the creative product of the Aryan' (p.263), which was not only totally ridiculous but severely racist. Despite not being a scientist of the natural order, he pontificates that the Ayran is seen in the lighter skin colour (p.265). If the original Aryan had ever existed, he and she would not have had fair skin. He continues with his obnoxious thinking stating that 'Aryans had to use lower human beings to make progress', but 'growing technology means we can do without these beasts', and he quotes the old saying that 'the Moor has worked off his debt, and the Moor can go' (p.267). He pursues this by writing that the 'pacifist fools' are now no longer needed (p.268). He looked back on early history, again as if an expert, writing that 'hence it is no accident that the first cultures arose in places where the Aryan, in his encounters with lower peoples, subjugated them and bent them to his will' (p.268). As far as Hitler was concerned, the nation is defined by race, and 'all who are not of good race in this world are chaff' (p.269). He noted the main characteristic of the Aryan, which was, he projected as if an expert, a matter of putting all his efforts into his community (p.270). He also added that 'In giving one's life for the existence of the community lies the crown of all sense of sacrifice' (p.271). He quoted the German word *Pflichterfüllung* (fulfilment of duty) about sacrificing oneself for the community, as if it were a natural German feeling (p.271). He naturally raised the Jew who opposed this concept, and as if proving his point, he declared how Aryans had conquered America (p.276), remarking that a Race does not lie in the language but exclusively in the blood (p.283).

To enhance his argument, he wrote that 'it is a scarcely conceivable fallacy of thought to believe that a Negro or a Chinese, let us say, will turn into a German because he learns German' (p.353).* He then added the vicious comment that 'surely no one will call the purely external fact that most of this lice-ridden migration from the East speaks German a proof of their German origin and nationality' (p.355).

He wrote that the state recognises two types of people, the citizen, and the foreigner, and between these two the stateless. He wrote that a 'Negro, who formerly lived in the German protectorate, and now has residence in Germany, gives birth to a German citizen in the person of a child' (adding the same applied to Jews, Poles, and the Asiatic) that in the current climate 'racial objections play no role whatsoever in this' (p.399). He argued that 'a simple dab of the pen and a Mongolian Wenceslaus has suddenly become a regular German' nor does the state pay attention to their regular health… citizenship laws are 'hair-brained', obviously intending to change the system, and supporting his views by adding that even in America immigrants are checked for health, evidently aware of the USA Immigration Acts of 1921 and 1924 (p.400). Hitler concluded by noting that 'it must be a greater honour to be a street-cleaner and citizen of this Reich than a king in a foreign country'(p.401), adding that 'in general I must evaluate peoples differently on the basis of the race they belong to, and the same applies to the individual men within a national community' (p.402).

---

* When discussing this with some students during a football match with Germany one amusingly asked how Hitler would have felt about the German national team having three or more coloured players.

Hitler and His Homeland Austria

Hitler was not born in Germany, but in *Mein Kampf* he spent an inordinate amount of time attacking his homeland of Austria under the Hapsburgs, noting that 'Germanism could be safeguarded only by the destruction of Austria'…and 'that the House of Hapsburg was destined to be the misfortune of the German nation' (p.15). From this early comment it is possible to detect his later plans for the *Anschluss*. He developed among his many hatreds an intense animosity to the Hapsburg regime, claiming the 'Austrian Empire could never be preserved except by victimising its German elements' (p.35). He later added that 'old Austria more than any other state depended on the greatness of her leaders…the foundation was lacking for a national state, which in its national basis always possess the power of survival' (p.67) almost returning to a state of tribalism.

He wrote that 'the longer I lived in this city, the more my hatred grew for the foreign mixture of peoples which had begun to corrode the old site German culture' revealing his inbuilt racism (p.113), and the concept of a multi-cultural society would have been a nightmare for him. It is clear from his passion that this was deeply personal to Hitler, who wrote 'my most ardent and heartfelt wish…the union of my beloved homeland with the common fatherland, the German Reich' (p.114). He was happier when he moved to Munich (p.116), writing 'what a difference from Vienna! I grew sick to my stomach when I even thought about this Babylon of races' (p.116), adding that 'Austria had long ceased to be a German State' (p.117). For Hitler his concept of a nation was not an organised state with built in rules and constitution, but a race of people, clearly indicating his atavistic attitudes as he based his thinking on traditional tribalism.

Democracy

For Hitler, a nation needed a significant leader, arguing that the Austrians made a mistake by creating a form of parliamentary representation without a state language (p.68), and they had taken their ideas from England, the land of 'classical democracy'. Strangely he appeared to be more supportive of the English system (p.69) and blamed the various nationalities encompassed by the Austrians (p.69), but he added that 'my instinct of national self-preservation caused me even in those days to have little love for a representative body in which Germans were always misrepresented' (p.70). 'The Western democracy of today is the forerunner of Marxism' (p.72), … 'what gave me most food for thought was the obvious absence of any responsibility in a single person' (p.73), adding 'can a fluctuating majority of people ever be made responsible in any case?' (p.73). Democracy has grown because of the 'cowardness of a great part of our so-called leadership' (p.75), 'a body of let us say, five hundred men, or in recent times even women, is chosen and entrusted with making the ultimate decision in any and all matters' (p.80), 'altogether we cannot be too sharp in condemning the absurd notion that geniuses can be born from general elections' (p.80). He was obviously thinking of himself as the born leader, noting that on the other hand 'truly Germanic democracy characterised by the free election of a leader and his obligation fully to assume all responsibility for his actions and omissions' (p.83).

England

In his convoluted arguments for a pan-German State his views regarding England are curious, because although among the victors of the First World War, he does not hold that country in the same degree of hatred as he does France. It could have been his admiration for the British Empire but possibly a matter of race. He knew that Saxons, Jutes and other Germanic tribes had occupied England. He may well have, speculatively, seen the English as Aryan, and several times in his ramblings mentioned that of all countries England could well be Germany's ally. He may have envisaged a form of collaboration with England holding its overseas Empire with its powerful navy, and later in the book states that England and no other should dominate the sub-continent of India (p.601). In talking about how to repair Germany, Hitler wrote 'the English nation will have to be considered the most valuable ally in the world' (p.302). However, he expected Germany to be the main power in mainland Europe.

As a consequence of his newspaper reading as a young man, he felt he had been inoculated with a certain admiration of the British Parliament (p.7) because of its linguistic and cultural bond with America, adding that England cannot be compared to other European states (p.128). When he later turned to the German need (or in his way of thinking 'demand') for more living space (*Lebensraum*) he was thinking of the vast lands controlled by Russia, he wrote, 'for such a policy there was but one ally in Europe: England' (p.129). He then continued that 'consequently, no sacrifice should have been too great for winning England's willingness' (p.129). Later he ruminated on the past, writing that 'when from time-to-time incomprehensible threats came over from England; therefore, we decided to build a fleet, though not to attack and destroy England, but for the defence of our old friend world peace and peaceful conquest of the world' (pp.131–132). He then added what for him was praise by writing that England has used great brutality for its economic conquests with the sword (p.133).

He had even admired Lloyd George's speeches more than Bethmann-Hollweg (p.433), adding that 'even in the pre-war period, I would have thought it sounder if Germany renounced her senseless colonial policy and also her merchant marine and war fleet, had concluded an alliance with England against Russia' (p.606), adding that 'see to it that the strength of our nation is founded, not on colonies, but on the soil of our European homeland' (p.607).

Lebensraum

In referring to the growth of the German population and lack of food he pointed out that there were yet immense areas not used, and 'nature has not reserved this soil for the future possession of any particular nation or race; on the contrary, this soil exists for the people which possesses the force to take and the industry to cultivate it' (p.123). He argued there is a need to find new soil (p.125) and the size of one's territory is also the best means of defence (p.125), adding the encouragement that new soil also adds to better employment (p.126). He pointed out that this ideal cannot be fulfilled in the Cameroons (p.127), but we need this in Europe, 'let us be given the soil we need for our livelihood' (p127), because our forefathers did not rely on some 'pacifistic nonsense' (p.127). 'If land were desired in Europe, it could be obtained by and large only at the expense of Russia' (p.128). If Stalin and his inner circle had read *Mein Kampf* in depth then Operation *Barbarossa* would not have been such a surprise, and a warning to others that this book may have appeared like the ramblings of a stupid young politician, but once in power it needed a closer scrutiny and not just sweeping views.

Chapter Four

Idealism and Foreign Affairs

Author's Notes: *This concluding section reflects the many pages Hitler devoted to singing the praises of National Socialism, which are evidently his own thought processes and ambitions. It then moves onto his views regarding German Foreign Policy in which he refers to his hatred of France and Russia while once again seeing England and Italy as natural allies. In terms of Russia he ironically refers to the country as run by criminals, with the pot calling the kettle black. He makes it abundantly clear that Germany needed to occupy much of Russia as if by natural right.*

Hitler's Idealism

Hitler wrote that when a man fights for economic reasons, he wants to live to enjoy the results, but it is different when you are fighting for a political ideal (p.140). He wrote that 'Germany above all other countries is a marvellous example of an empire which had risen from foundations of pure political power…Prussia, the germ-cell of the Empire came into being through resplendent heroism' (p.141). Political power dominated Hitler's thought process all his life, and his admiration for Prussia indicated that his type of political power should have a military foundation with 'heroic' eyes on expansion. He quoted General Moltke who said that war lies in the brevity of the operation, so Hitler added 'that means that the most aggressive fighting technique is the most humane' (p.163), clearly indicating that he wanted Germany restored to greatness, and he would not hesitate to use the military and war to achieve his ends. Only his warped way of thinking could claim aggressive fighting could be considered 'humane'.

As such Hitler knew that his ideal world needed to be influenced if not controlled by propaganda, not so much for the intelligentsia, but it 'must be addressed always and exclusively to the masses' (p.163). He continued to write that 'the receptivity of the great mass is very limited, their intelligence is small, but their power of forgetting is enormous' (p.165). He added that 'the people in their overwhelming majority are so feminine by nature and attitude that sober reasoning determines their thoughts and actions far less than emotion and feeling' (p.167). He also attacked the 'bourgeoise suffering from mental senility' (p.198). His ideal was to persuade the masses for his own support. Later many Germans purchased *Mein Kampf*, often for safety reasons, and Hitler's evaluations of the various strands of society were almost insulting. Perhaps, like many on the international stage it was such a boring monologue most gave up attempting to read his literary effort.

He saw himself as the master of propaganda in the early days (p.527) adding 'moreover, I am an enemy of too rapid and too pedantic organising' (p.537). However, according to many observers (including Stephen Roberts later in this study) the Nazi machine was a state within a state, and its administration was overwhelmingly complex and massive. He knew that 'the function of propaganda was to attract supporters, the function of an organisation was to win members' (p.529), adding that 'propaganda tries to force a doctrine on the whole people' (p.529).

He was from the very start fixated on dictatorship for himself, and he was opposed to any form of electoral system unless it was there to support him and his policies. He wrote that 'in any case a movement that wants to combat the parliamentary madness must itself be free of it. Only on such a basis can it win the strength for its struggle' (p.536). He wrote that 'a movement which in a time of majority rule orientates itself in all things on the principle of the leader idea and the responsibility conditioned by it will one day with mathematical certainty overcome the existing state of affairs and emerge victorious' (p.537), which if read by concerned people must have stood as a stark warning of things to come.

On the question of Trade Unions Hitler raised four questions: 1) are they necessary, 2) should the NSDAP engage with them, 3) the nature of a National Socialist trade union, 4) and how shall we arrive at such unions (p.546). He admitted that Trade Unions were necessary and were a form of economic parliament, and because they are important the NSDAP should take a stand on them (p.546). In his ideal world he claimed the NSDAP did not recognise classes and that workers and employers are 'both servants and guardians of the national community' (p.549). Finally, he stated that there should be one form of Union, namely the NSDAP union which should tackle the Marxist ones (p.550). Trade Unions accustomed to looking after their workers based on the nature of the work. Normally, the Postal Union would differ from the Teachers' Union which would also be different from the Dock Labourers' Union. Under Hitler's ideal world the NSDAP would be the one union with both the employers and workers as servants of the State, and later strikes and walkouts would be regarded as a form of treason. All Hitler's idealism revolved around one single factor, the new Germany would be governed by him as dictator and his views would always be followed without question. In short, he hoodwinked many by offering employment, and the organisation of 'Strength through Joy', (*Kraft durch Freude* [KdF]), established through Robert Ley in November 1933, offering cheap holidays even cruises, and the production of an affordable car, the still popular Volkswagen.

Hitler's idealism focused on himself as the potential saviour of Germany, and its growth as a leading if not the leading nation. This is basically what he meant by the idealism of the National Socialists; it emerges with considerable clarity raising the question of how many German workers read his only written work.

Foreign Affairs

Hitler in his politically belligerent approach wrote that 'only the elimination of the causes of our collapse, [meaning 1918] as well as the destruction of its beneficiaries, can create the premise for our outward fight for freedom' (p.555). Hitler claimed that 'Foreign policy is only a means to an end', and all foreign policy must proceed from the following, namely, asking whether 'it benefits our nationality now or in the future, or will it be injurious to it' (p.556). He added that for us it 'must be the preparation for the reconquest of freedom for tomorrow' adding it can also prepare for the military fight for freedom'. He enlarges this as 'a question of regaining lost sections of a people's and State's territory is always a primary question', 'for the liberation of oppressed, separated splinters of a nationality' (p.557). There was no need for him to name the areas, but unquestionably it would have been understood he intended to overturn the Treaty of Versailles agreement. This is known as irredentist nationalism – the re-claiming of lost territory – and would have met full support in Germany and even some sympathy overseas.

At a more sinister level he wrote of the necessary acquisition of land in Europe which had been neglected, blaming it on our 'old leaders who had turned to colonialism and sacrificed the alliance with England, who had always sought protection from the rear looking to interlocking relations of power [balance of power] (p.559). He argued that England never wanted the rise of a single great power in Europe, giving his brief historical view to justify this claim (p.560). He suggested England had always sought world domination, but since 1918 'England has had no further interest in the complete effacement of Germany from the map of Europe (p.561), yet another reference to his conciliatory attitude to that country. Hitler noted that in 1914 'Germany as a military state was wedged in between two countries one of which disposed of an equal strength, and the other of superior power. In addition, came the superior sea power of England' (p.562). On the other hand, he wrote that 'France today is different: the first military power, without a serious rival on the continent', and while 'England's desire is and remains the prevention of the rise of a continental power to world-political importance', France's desire remains the prevention of the formation of a unified power in Germany (p.563). Hitler wrote that 'National destinies are firmly forged together only by the prospect of a common success in the sense of common gains, conquests; in short of a mutual extension of power', which 'is never based on mutual respect, let alone affection, but on the prospect of expediency for both contacting parties' (p.564). This would certainly explain why he accepted a pact with Stalin to invade Poland, a pact with the Bolshevists whom he hated.

It was also clear about how Hitler viewed France, making it abundantly obvious when he wrote 'the inexorable mortal enemy of the German people is and remains France', referring to their occupation of the Rhineland, and noting that 'England desires no Germany as a world power, but France wishes no power at all for Germany', and 'if we look about us for European allies from this standpoint, there remain only two states: England and Italy' (p.565). He observed that few nations wanted any alliance with Germany today because Germany cannot defend itself, recalling that enemy propaganda had taken its toll addressing 'Germans as Huns, Robbers, Vandals etc', adding it had not been helped by the Jewish stock exchange (p.567). He was back on his old horse stating that the 'Jew today is the great agitator for the complete destruction of Germany' (p.568), especially in France and 'for this very reason, France is and remains by far the most terrible enemy', not least because of 'the contamination by Negro blood on the Rhine' (p.569).

Hitler added the ominous warning that 'today I am guided only by the sober realisation that lost territories are not won back by sharp parliamentary big-mouths and their glibness of tongues, but by a sharp sword; in other words, by a bloody fight' (p.574). He swiftly added that 'what must guide us today is again and again the basic insight that the reconquest of a Reich's lost territories is primarily the question of regaining the political independence and power of the motherland'(p.574). In the early 1920s this could have been regarded as mere angry ranting, but by the time he was coming to power it was a serious red-light warning.

Eastern Policy

Hitler devoted another section to what he termed the Eastern Policy by which he meant Russia, writing that 'Russians tend to look down on other people, and 'the folkish state' needs to create 'a healthy, viable natural relation between the nation's population and growth on the one hand and the quantity and quality of its soil on the other hand'. He then argued that 'only an adequately large space on this earth assures a nation of freedom of existence' (p.587), adding that 'the National Socialist movement must strive to eliminate the disproportion between our population and our area – viewing this latter source for food as well as a basis for power politics', and 'we, as guardians of the highest humanity on the earth are bound by the highest obligation' (p.590) 'to bring the soil into harmony with the population' (p.593).

He was forecasting his deadly policy for the right of *Lebensraum* in such a deliberate and determined way that it could hardly be missed. He was very clear as to how he saw German policy, writing 'we must hold unflinchingly to our aim in foreign policy, namely, to secure for the German people the land and soil to which they are entitled on this earth', and pen-pushers cannot say otherwise, noting that 'State boundaries are made by man and changed by man' (p.596). He further argued that 'the right to possess soil can become a duty if without extension of its soil a great nation seems doomed to destruction', adding that 'Germany will either be a world power or there will be no Germany' (p.597), and 'if we speak of soil in Europe today, we can primarily have in mind only Russia and her vassal border states' (p.598).

Even by Hitler's standards it was a strong warning about how he saw the future. He wrote that between Russia and Germany is Poland, which he claimed was entirely in French hands, and warning 'never to forget that the rulers of present-day Russia are common blood-stained criminals' and 'they are dominated by the international Jew', noting 'the danger to which Russia succumbed is always present for Germany' (p.604) and 'you cannot drive out the Devil with Beelzebub' (p.605).

Final Observations on *Mein Kampf*

Mein Kampf was a book not widely read and mainly ignored for several reasons. It was all too easy for the reader of those days, as to this day, becoming excruciatingly bored as this writer can personally testify. It was a lengthy book full of repetition, poorly expressed which is even reflected in the English translations, and for many would appear as the mere rantings of a naïve romantic deluded fool. It was started by its author while in prison for what many saw as the stupid behaviour during the Munich Putsch of a person behind bars who was of no consequence. However, in 1933 it was translated into English, and at the same time Hitler was the sole leader of the powerful German State. International leaders were becoming aware if not sensitive about what was happening in Germany.

The rise of fascism in Italy had happened and the Western countries had believed, despite being horrified by the lack of democracy, that they could work with Mussolini. Later the Spanish Civil War brought another dictator to power, but Franco, apart from greedily wondering about expansion in North Africa, seemed content to stay within his own frontiers, and he was not regarded as an international threat. Russia and its form of communism (although by now Stalin was becoming a totalitarian despot) created the greatest fear in the West because of its cry for international communism, and each and every country had small gatherings of communists. Even the international Roman Catholic Church felt Mussolini was controllable in Catholic Italy and were supportive of Franco in Spain, mainly because they also feared communism.

Nevertheless, only a few of the more astute national leaders saw Hitler as an imminent danger, many others feeling that Hitler was improving matters in Germany and a few almost admired him. In addition to these factors was the shadow of the immense destruction of human life in the First World War. Such was the appalling loss of life in this industrial war with gas, machine guns, the first warplanes, and a myriad of other weapons, peace seemed essential even after centuries of international conflict. Many wanted peace at any cost, and it seemed for some inconceivable that any single individual would ever again want a repeat of the First World War as the lessons were so appalling. The final factor in not bothering to understand or be aware of who Hitler was, and the belief he could be reasoned with, a fault which was evident even in Germany where the old hierarchy had believed they could keep hold of the reins. Even at the Munich Conference the British Prime Minister Neville Chamberlain thought that 'peace in our time' had resolved the German issue.

By 1933 with Hitler in power and *Mein Kampf* translated from the German was the time to suffer the problem of reading this book if only to try and understand the personal nature of Hitler, who he was, and his plans for the future. In 1939 the Queen of England sent a copy to Lord Halifax advising him to skip through it because it would give him an innovative idea of Hitler's mentality, which was sound advice albeit by this stage somewhat late.

Had it been studied in depth it would have revealed what any semi-civilised person would have considered the ravings of a small-minded freak lacking any sense of humanity, having moral standards with a leaning towards criminality. The problem would be enlarged by knowing that Hitler was popular in Germany and had total control of that country and had built up a considerable military force, especially with Göring's Luftwaffe.

Mein Kampf would have outlined for any reader his perceived policies, and even his educational views on physical training taking priority in the curriculum, and by 1933 the obvious warning the Hitler Youth was emerging as potential robots for conscription. This may well have been in Hitler's mind as he condemned mentally and physically disabled children, obviously of no use to the military, and Hitler suggesting it was humane to stop them breeding more. By the mid-1930s people knew such people were being exterminated. This alone should have underlined that Hitler was not only criminal and immoral, but by ordinary standards psychologically damaged and in layman's terms, dangerously warped.

Across Europe there were and had been for some time an inexplicable and irrational degree of anti-Semitism, there had been pogroms in Eastern

Europe, the Alfred Dreyfus affair in France had its ramifications, and in Britain social snubs with Jews not permitted in some golfing clubs. There is hardly a section of Hitler's book which does not attack Jews with a senseless hatred, and major hints that Hitler would rid the country of 'these vermin'. This was not only a stark warning to the Jews but to others about this man's mindset. The more astute Jews left the country when able, many thought the stupidity would pass, and then it was too late, and the Holocaust occurred which shook the world.

Many international leaders would not have been overly disturbed by Hitler's attack on the Marxists, but to combat them he introduced the SA. For any politician to form his own paramilitary force, especially as it developed into bringing terror on the streets to any civilian, Aryan or otherwise, who opposed him, drew an even sharper picture of Hitler as a dominating and dangerous force.

His racist views were not restricted to his anti-Semitism, he was ruthlessly crude about coloured people, and in his concept of pan-Germanism based his theory of a nation based on race only, a matter of the right German blood. A fixation which at one level was laughable, but which brought death and mayhem to many millions, and this damaged philosophy is all too clear in *Mein Kampf*.

Near the end of his literary rantings came the clearest warnings of the future, with his animosity to France almost brimming as high as his hatred of Russia. He makes two things abundantly clear, the call for the return of lands taken after the Versailles Treaty, underlining that force would be the only way. In addition to this he attacked Russia making his claim of justification based on *Lebensraum* that the Germans need more soil.

His type of personality, his racism, his desire for personal power to lead Germany to dominate Europe, his hatreds, his vindictiveness, his sense of revenge, and his instability as apparent in *Mein Kampf*, should have made everyone, especially national leaders, aware of the sort of leader they were facing.

There is no doubt that concerned countries were watching Germany's military growth, and their diplomats and top military men who met their German counterparts found their opposite numbers pleasant and polite. Few of them at the time had not realised that behind them was a dangerous dictator who would be obeyed for a variety of reasons, ranging from hero worship, the Prussian-German belief in obeying orders without question, and later from fear of not towing the Hitler line because of repercussions, to some younger people virtually seeing him as a demi-god. Hindsight is easier than foresight, but national leaders often failed to read Hitler's work and badly underestimated the warped and dangerous criminal they faced. Had they read *Mein Kampf* then the world outside Germany may have been better prepared for the hurricane of war which engulfed them for the years 1939–1945.

Part IV

The Man Who Was Ignored

Roberts, Stephen H., *The House that Hitler Built* (London: Methuen Publishers, 1937)

Author's Notes*: Part Four is a close study of a book published in early 1937 written by an Australian academic travelling through 1936 Germany. It was widely appreciated by some, and the findings dismissed by Chamberlain and ignored by others. In places his almost prophetic forecasts arising from what he saw reads almost like a postwar analysis of the situation in Germany in the 1930s. It unquestionably makes the reader aware of Hitler and his regime and warns of the imminence of war. It was written in an easy style of English, not tedious like 'Mein Kampf' nor overly academic like Dorothy Woodman's book, and unlike many journalists, he was not writing this under the beady eye of Goebbels or for a biased newspaper editor. He covered every aspect of the Nazi State, from Hitler and his henchmen, and the rise of the Nazi Party to government. He studied the political para-military brown and blacks (SA and SS), the German Army and attended a Nuremberg rally. He spent time on Germany's economic efforts seeing war as the only outcome, rarely mentioned by some historians. He saw for himself the indoctrination of Nazism from the schools to Hitler Youth, children to teenagers, to young men in the labour service all being trained in a form of military discipline and life. The way the public mind was captured and controlled, and the laws changed to suit the Party, even to military chaplains being obliged to wear their cross insignia alongside the swastika. He concludes his book with a major survey of German foreign policy for the future with the inevitable conclusion it could only result in war.*

The author's father purchased this book in 1937 and often wondered why it was never read as he believed it predicted the near future. Had this book been properly read and believed it may have changed the course of history for the better. Had Mein Kampf been read first, then Roberts's book would have confirmed that the plans and thoughts of Hitler were already taking shape. For the student of history this booked is presented here in précis but with comments, a form of critique. For this historian writer, it was unbelievable and explosive that the author was so widely ignored.

Introduction

Stephen Roberts was an Australian academic, a professor, and later Chancellor of Sydney University, known well in academic circles for his interest in colonial history, and a growing curiosity in current affairs. It was on the topic of *The Rising Tide of Dictatorship in Europe* he was heard on the Australian radio as one of the expert commentators, with the broadcast occurring on 30 September 1932. It was possibly because of his academic curiosity as to what was happening that the university Senate granted him one year's leave on full pay to travel to Germany, following Hitler's rise to power. Possibly he would have had a deeper motive because he had a German grandfather, Frederick Wagener.[1] He was provided with a letter of introduction to von Ribbentrop (at the time the German Ambassador in London), which meant he was given full assistance on his arrival, meeting Hitler, Hess, Himmler and Schacht (Hjalmar Schacht, President of the Reichsbank and Minister of Economics) and hearing and seeing many others in the top circle of power, as well as the opportunity to converse with many other German people. He explored Germany in 1936 after Hitler had been in charge for over three years, leaving that country in January 1937. When he returned to London, he met a friend who worked for Methuen Press who suggested he should draft a book on his experiences and observations, which he duly set to, as he travelled home. The book's title was *The House that Hitler Built*, which promptly became a best seller in many languages, but was not taken seriously by those who should have read it with care. In this book he not only wrote about Hitler and his major henchmen, but traced their rise to power, their policies and so-called philosophy, passing intelligent and incisive comments on their growth and various events up until 1936. Professional historians were and still are regarded as only interested in the past, but too many people forget that history provides a remarkable guide for the future.

In this book which is central to this particular study (which will be analysed in this chapter) his observations and conclusions were, with the benefit of hindsight, stunningly accurate. He was always proud that once it was read in Germany, they declared Roberts a *persona non grata* and he was pleased to tell his friends he was on Hitler's wanted list.[2]

In 1938 an aide gave a copy of Roberts' book to the Prime Minister Neville Chamberlain, but 'after reading for some time Chamberlain said, "I don't believe it" and threw it on the floor'.[3] Whether this was an exaggeration or not will remain debatable. In his highly detailed exposition of the appeasement years, Tim Bouverie wrote that Chamberlain read the book, describing it a 'searing analysis of Nazism which argued that Hitlerism cannot achieve its aims without war', and that it would cause him despair if he believed the writer'.[4] On the other hand Anthony Eden recalled that Chamberlain had been impressed and 'even went so far as to suggest that if we could not reach agreement, we might have to aim at the encirclement of Germany and a possible alliance with Russia...[but] the mood did not last...he was the subject of incessant flattery [from the apparent success of the Munich Conference]'.[5] In his memoirs Eden claimed he had read this book written 'by an Australian' without mentioning his profession, stating it contained 'a realistic account of the Nazi regime' but 'it said no more than the Foreign Office had been saying for months'.[6] It was the lack of awareness, which was the main issue, the awareness of the degenerate spirit of Nazism which Roberts had clearly outlined. Intelligence reports, as with Dorothy Woodman's book, could produce facts and figures about Nazi Germany, even quick sketches of their social plans, but not penetrating insights into Hitler's mindset and that of his regime. Roberts' insights and perceptions of how Hitler was indoctrinating youth from schoolchildren to teenagers to young men in the Labour forces was in itself a red-warning alert about the future. Chamberlain, according to Eden, had read *Mein Kampf*, and had read Roberts' exposition which was a profoundly sound analysis of Nazi Germany and Hitler by a gifted academic mind. Unlike *Mein Kampf*, Roberts' book was easily readable, and underlined what was missing in the appeaser's mind, an awareness not just of the psychologically warped dictator and his henchmen, but the way they were constructing a society along their own atavistic way of thinking, and the intentions of becoming the masters of Europe. It may never be known, if the book had been read by the general public in Britain and France, how far it would have changed the minds of those who thought Hitler could be appeased. This writer's father told him that Roberts' book stopped him believing in appeasement and the need to prepare for war. The value of this book was two-fold: it confirmed that *Mein Kampf* had to be taken seriously, and it made the reader more aware of the nature of Hitler and the Nazi regime with its overall intentions.

In Australia Roberts was involved in many broadcasts about the subject and wrote several newspaper articles for the *Sydney Morning Herald*, and during the Second World War became their war correspondent but remained anonymous.[7] In 1948 Churchill as Chancellor of Bristol University awarded Roberts the honorary degree of Doctor of Laws which pleased Roberts as he had, understandably, admired Churchill and his policies long before the war started. Roberts wrote seven books and *The House which Hitler Built* was the last one, the most important one, and today its importance is still not realised. Politicians are often the cause for war, the military fights it when war occurs, and academia is often placed in the distant background unless it is science.

In his book, like any human being, Roberts proves capable of an occasional misjudgement, but most of his material is accurate and his predictions of where Hitler was heading were not only accurate, but the picture he paints of the dictator and his henchmen, and the general aims of the Nazi Party were all stark warnings about the near future. Decades after he wrote this book there were countless historical studies of Hitler and the rise of Nazism, but Roberts was writing at the very time these events were brewing in Germany. Many horse racing punters would like today's results by having a dream of tomorrow's papers, and many politicians would like to read tomorrow's history. Roberts's skill and perceptive abilities was almost providing this gem of future knowledge.

A sound academic like Roberts should have been read by every national leader concerned by the developments in Germany. He had gathered insights much more informed than many diplomats could manage, and he had no seniors above him to demand he be more moderate in his views. There must be a degree of human sympathy for people who gave up reading *Mein Kampf* because it gave them indigestion, but Roberts' book is well written, not repetitive and with no axe to grind except for telling the truth as he perceived it to be.

He divided the book into five parts, the first dealing with an account of the man Hitler and the growth of Nazism, with its so-called philosophy. The second part outlines the Nazi revolution with the rise of the Brownshirts, views on the army, and even described his attendance at a Nuremberg Rally. The third part is a scholarly analysis of the economic struggle of the Nazi State looked at from many angles. Part four provides a major overview of the newly formed Nazi Germany, offering insights into a wide range of their ideas, from their youth movements, Labour Service, public works, their anti-Semitism and the law. The fifth and final part is a study of their general foreign policy, their call for reclaiming their lands lost after the First World War, their demand for *Lebensraum* in the east and other pressure points. His book is approximately in the region of some 130,000 plus words, and there follows a short précis of his book with comments in an attempt to demonstrate its sheer importance. It concludes that with the benefit of hindsight, Roberts' foresight and analysis was at least 90 per cent correct, and it should not have 'been thrown on the floor'.

As with the section dealing with Mein Kampf any direct references to this book, (Roberts, Stephen H. The House that Hitler Built (London: Methuen Publishers, 1937)) are marked in the text in brackets to avoid unnecessary endless pages of endnotes.

Chapter One

The Early Days

In the preface to his book Roberts noted that the Nazi authorities did everything they could to be helpful, even 'though they knew from the outset that my attitude was one of objective criticism'. This would have been no surprise because in the year of his visit the Nazis were trying to gain an image of respectability on the international stage, not as a sign of weakness but as a growing powerhouse which was stable. He was allowed access to many things, but not their banned literature which was the only negative criticism in his opening preface. Wherever he travelled in Germany he found everyone pleasant, and he wrote there was 'a striking eagerness for friendship with Great Britain'. This reflected Hitler's *Mein Kampf* where time and time again Hitler referred to England as a possible ally, which stood in stark contrast to Hitler's views on France and Russia, but Roberts experienced the friendly approach mainly by the German public.

The Man Hitler

Although since the end of the Second World War many biographies and studies of Hitler have been produced, Roberts provided some insights into what he called the 'Riddle of Hitler' as early as 1936–7. He was aware that Hitler was reticent about his family background, and even his real name was confusing. There was a variety of confusing possibilities, as Roberts discovered: it could have been Huttler, Hittler, usually Heidler, and when he joined Drexler's early party he was put down as Adolf Hittler but one 't' was crossed out at his request (p.33). It could have been Schicklgrüber, after his father a cobbler, and Roberts heard 'he was the neurotic child of a neurotic repressed mother' (p.3). At this stage it was clear that few if any knew the background of this man. Roberts even managed to speak to people who had been schoolfriends of Hitler, hearing how they laughed at him as he was always pouring over an atlas, and when asked why, he responded, 'I am wiping out German boundaries and making them larger'. If this reported rumour were true, it indicated an obsessed personality, if it were mere gossip, it reflected a negative attitude towards the Führer by old friends. Apparently, he was 'lonely, dreaming, ignoring facts, living in a world of fancy, and happy in his artificial isolation'. Later Roberts went to a National Socialist Party Day with an eminent neurologist who suspected Hitler of having a dual personality trying to hide his ignorant peasant background, because he was trying to act as 'the demi-god of a great people', seeing 'himself as a crusader' (p.8). These and many other insights that Roberts noted in his book should have provided some sound insights to concerned international observers, making them aware of this 'strange man'.

As a young man Hitler just wandered around in Vienna, which according to *Mein Kampf*, he felt some distaste for because of the mixed races, and he left for Bavaria where he found life better and signed up as a soldier for the duration of the First World War in which he was wounded, gassed, and won some medals but remained a corporal (p.5). Roberts noted that 'neither his fellows nor his officers liked him', and he was noted because he despised Jews and workers and felt 'himself ineffably superior to the rest of mankind' (p.6). According to Roberts the man Hitler was perceived at this time as represented by two popular views which saw him as 'a mere ranting stump-orator, or as a victim of demonical possession'. Roberts was kinder, thinking of him as 'primarily a dreamer, a visionary' (p.7), hoping to save the world from Bolshevism, a romantic using Wagnerian operas as a backdrop. Exceedingly early in his visit, Roberts had picked up that Hitler once spoke about taking Ukraine and Siberia, thereby hinting at German eastern Imperialism with Roberts describing this as Hitler 'wandering off into his own dream world' (p.9). In 1936 such a preposterous idea may have struck observers as a dream world, but as Roberts saw more of the Nazi regime and Hitler it raised serious question marks.

Roberts believed Hitler could only have survived because of the backing of the Party organisation and support of some henchmen, adding he 'wants to be Siegfried and Frederick the Great rolled into one'. He recalled that 'in 1936, I saw pictures of Hitler in the actual silver garments of the Knight of the Grail' but it was soon withdrawn, because, as Roberts thought, they were seen as too close to the 'truth of Hitler's mentality' (p.10). Roberts was evidently correct that Hitler needed considerable backing from Party members, but as the early months and years unfolded, Hitler was soon in charge of his supporting team members.

Roberts noted that 'nobody could claim Hitler is of outstanding mental stature' as he suffers from a confusion caught between good and bad objects, terrified of imaginary persecutors, especially Jews and Communists (p.11). He thought that Hitler 'seems to have a single-track mind' always applying a simple solution to some complex problem. This estimation of Hitler was dangerously accurate as can be seen with the benefit of hindsight, not least when Hitler took over the military command with his insane orders of fighting to the last man, especially at the Battle of Stalingrad, a significant defeat, turning the war against Nazi Germany.

Roberts was not only sounding some alarm bells about the new dictator, but added a reason as to why Hitler was initially so popular. He wrote that 'no one can doubt his sincerity' because he cannot restrain himself, which is why he carries the crowds with him. He knew Hitler was appealing to an impoverished people humiliated by the Treaty of Versailles, adding 'it is not his honesty that is in question; it is his terrific power of self-delusion that introduces such an element of uncertainty into everything he does', thereby basically it was his power as a rabble rouser (p.12). Roberts follows this through by adding that Hitler's 'strength, then, is the unduly assertive characteristics of a man not certain of himself and shunning a real analysis of the problems confronting him'(pp.13–14). Hitler was obsessed with legal rules especially after the 1923 Putsch, so he changed the laws to suit his views with a strong legal department. As a non-German, Roberts thought his speeches were monotonous, and he appeared as if waiting for the next thought to enter his mind (p14). He described Hitler as very temperamental in his speaking, and 'he knows that an uneducated political public wants endless repetition of a few trite phrases' which was especially true at the Nuremberg rallies (p.15). Roberts listened to Hitler's first broadcast after being made Chancellor, which amounted to a rant against Jews and Communists, and Roberts believed Goebbels was the better and more refined speaker (p.16).

As regards Hitler, Roberts thought 'no display of emotionalism is too crude for him' and added the interesting line that when talking with Göring, dressed up in leather pants at the Berchtesgaden, 'they reduce some complicated world problem to a simple discussion, ignoring all the complexities and dealing with it as if they were two peasants talking about the next meeting of the village hall' (p.17).

Roberts knew that Hitler used aircraft travel for stirring up support and noted with evident pleasure that it had almost become a joke, as when asked where Hitler was the usual reply was 'Oh, Adolf is up in the air again'. During the 1936 Olympic Games Hitler had remained expressionless, only relaxing and smiling when a German won, and it was noted he was too tired to meet the negro victors (p.18), his base racism again exposed in this passing comment. Nor, Roberts noted, did Hitler have any interest in women, but added that it was probably not true that his niece committed suicide because of his attentions, pointing out there was no tangible evidence, which remains true to this day. Hitler always appeared uneasy in the presence of women, and he avoided alcohol, smoking and meat, which Roberts speculated may have offered one of the reasons he was unpopular with fellow soldiers (p.19) which made sense. Roberts found Hitler 'a strange man, this Adolf Hitler'. In one historian's account Hitler was nicknamed by his fellow soldiers as the 'white crow' because he was so odd.[1]

Roberts found Hitler infinitely polite and courteous in his interviews but 'gives the appearance of a hunted man' with no real personal contacts (p.21). Roberts also noted the disturbing fact that some Germans thought he had a direct line to God (p.22). He concluded his insights into Hitler by asking himself and the reader as how such a man rose to power. He thought that Hitler might be the 'greatest popular orator' at the moment which was a time of 'political chaos and national depression', and he regarded himself as the crusader who had captured the Holy City, the embodiment of the city, *Der Führer-Gott* (p.23). Hitler in *Mein Kampf* also regarded himself as the greatest orator ever, but with Roberts' qualification of 'might be' and who was speaking at a time of serious national depression. If a group of people are starving with little hope for the future, and a man stands offering hope, then they will listen and follow him. As Roberts wrote, his speeches were monotonous, and he often paused as if wondering what to say next. However, his emotional powers were powerful, and he promised a better future which is why he rose to power, and the insights provided by Roberts would have painted a more accurate picture of Hitler's personality than that of people who had merely heard of him, seen him on films, but not met him or talked to his supporters and the cynics as Roberts had managed.

Hitler's Major Henchmen

Roberts turned his attention to those men closest to Hitler and offering him major support, pointing out that Göring was the 'second most popular' figure (p.24), which was undoubtedly true in the mid-1930s. He described Göring as 'the embodiment of direct force'… 'and if need be insensate brutality'. Even after the war at the Nuremberg trials many found Göring pleasant if not likeable and affable, but Roberts had understood this man, and the journalist William Shirer had felt the same way when he wrote that 'Göring could be affable and even charming, but he was an utterly ruthless man'.[2] Roberts observed that Göring had no fixed opinion but would do anything to make Germany powerful again, preferring 'to solve his difficulties by smashing through them'. He noted that when the people grumbled about food restrictions, he wrote that 'Göring roars at them… look at me! I have lost two stone in the service of my country patting his fat stomach', noting that elementary as his humour appeared, he was shrewd enough to value such tactics because they carried some appeal (p.25). Roberts wrote that the people must be kept in good humour, and Hitler knew that a 'battering-ram like Göring must always have a subtle brain behind it to direct his energy', adding that 'perhaps his belief in a sudden shattering blow against his enemies with his belief in an aggressive aerial war may be justified' (p.26). Roberts was correct in his assessment because Göring's character, built on his role as a fighter pilot in the First World War, made him popular (especially with Hitler at this time), giving him a degree of charisma and popularity in his often-jovial approach. He was also a critically important person for the regime and for foreign observers, because of his passion for developing the Luftwaffe, as planes and their bombing capacity were amongst the greatest fears of other nations, especially Britain, all too uncomfortable with bombers able to cross the English Channel in minutes. There was a genuine fear of bombing, and as soon as war was declared in September 1939 children were instantly evacuated often followed by their mothers and many women. Göring unquestionably at this time was a figure of importance in the new Nazi ranks as he used his personality to boost Nazism, was developing the Luftwaffe, helping to found the dreaded Gestapo, deeply immersed in the politics of the day and soon involved in the economics of the country.

When Roberts turned to Goebbels, the emerging propaganda expert, he described him as having 'a reputation for calculated brutality and a cold precision that took no heed of human values'. He pointed out that 'the word propaganda in a totalitarian State like Germany covers far more fields of activity than it does with us', noting that 'the outstanding feature about Goebbels is his searing contempt for humanity. One feels he despises the human race and looks on the people as so many ants to be managed' (p.27), which given what is now known about Goebbels was a shrewd observation, because with the benefit of hindsight Goebbels was an immoral and dangerous component in the regime.

Roberts observed that Goebbels's constant repetition in the press 'wears down resistance', as at this stage people were and still are all too prone to believe what they read in the newspapers and hear over radio broadcasts. He also noted that no one was allowed or dared mention Goebbels's non-Aryan deformed body with his habitual limp. Roberts wrote that 'it is impossible not to associate Goebbels with malignity. He appears to have an absolutely first-class mind, but one warped and embittered, and now, from his position of power, concerned with hate and revenge, against the Jews and the Communists' (p.28). It was Goebbels who continued to help make Hitler so popular, almost portraying him as a demi-god, and cleverly organising cheering crowds which, when seen on film, astonished foreign viewers at such adoration of a political leader. Goebbels appeared to worship Hitler to the very end, and he had fastened onto Hitler's views and policies and expounded them with fervour, making them even more dangerous, because of his unquestionable misguided intellectual ability. Roberts concluded by adding that 'I should call Goebbels the most dangerous man in Europe, precisely because he is so diabolically clever and so frankly Machiavellian in his views of mankind and the methods he would employ' (p.29). It was an astute summary of Goebbels which would have been revealed at the Nuremberg Trials had he not avoided them by a well-judged suicide, indicating his degeneracy by taking his wife and children with him.

Roberts did not include Himmler at this time, whom he personally met on his investigative tour adding his observations later in the text. Roberts skirted over Rudolf Hess who served as Hitler's secretary in Landsberg prison in writing *Mein Kampf* and who was his deputy. Roberts wrote that 'Hess is not very impressive personally', he simply repeats Hitler's statements and 'he appears washed out and lifeless' which is why no one thinks he would ever succeed Hitler (p.30). Roberts' judgement on Hess by all that is known about him postwar was accurate and raises the curious question as to why Hitler selected him as his deputy. It may be speculated that Hitler did not need having a deputy except for harmless formal occasions, and he would not have welcomed a stronger personality as he hated any form of personal challenge.

He finally turned to the least known of all the Nazi leaders, namely Wilhelm Frick, who served as Minister of the Interior from 1933–1943, whom Roberts described as 'one of the clean-living members of the Nazi inner circle', noting that Frick was an unreasoning zealot for the cause, having the mind of a legal Civil Servant with a 'strictly Nonconformist morality' (p.31). By using this expression, it appears that Frick like Hitler was a non-smoking teetotaller, however, Roberts observed that 'Frick makes one feel that human beings are so many insects to be driven along directed paths' (p.32) and at the Nuremberg trials he was hanged as a criminal.

These views of the various Nazi leaders Roberts came across, provide a valuable insight into some of the men who stood behind Hitler, all later condemned as criminals and all part of the dangerous apparatus of the Nazi movement, which needed to be known by international leaders because of their sheer corruption of thought.

The Nature of the Early Nazi Movement

Roberts came into touch with a variety of Nazis from whom he was able to glean not just information but insights into the Nazi movement, and people who had been part of Hitler's battle-plan towards total power over a nation. Roberts wrote of Alfred Rosenberg that he was obsessed with racial purity (p.33). In using the word 'obsession' Roberts underlined the sheer fanaticism and extreme racism that permeated Nazism. Rosenberg, a Baltic German, was the Party's ideologue, and authored a book called *The Myth of the Twentieth Century* in 1930 which outlined the Nazi theory on race and the pure blood of Germans. He had taken up Hitler's hatred of Jews and his claim for *Lebensraum*, putting it into print as if that justified Nazi views. He even wrote that Jesus Christ was not the Messiah and denied the Old Testament any validity. The very fact that this appeared to pass almost unnoticed in Germany should have caused international observers to ask themselves about the iron grip the Nazi Party was gaining over the German population.

In his early days as Hitler struggled to gain the leadership of Germany, he had not been overly popular, but his zeal for change was more than noticeable, and soon Hitler 'could twist the nominal leader, the simple-minded Drexler, round his finger' taking forward steps towards his personal victory (p.34). He also used Ernst Röhm, Chief of the SA, whom Roberts described as 'a murdering soldier of fortune' who had once said, 'be a patriot or be a corpse' (p.34). Once used when he was needed, but for fear of the future, Röhm was murdered under Hitler's instructions in the Night of the Long Knives, although he was supposed to be a close friend of Hitler. These passing observations by Roberts highlighted the shady background of what amounted to a criminal takeover of Germany. Many of these observations should have emphasised that international leaders should have been more prepared to understand they were dealing with a criminal gang which set its own parameters of conduct and were ruthless.

Roberts noted that Hitler had early on produced weapons for himself by taking over the Party, and with the SA as a private army, and so by 1921 the NSDAP was a party of 3,000 numbers. He was able to do this based on Germany's sense of disillusionment, the war, the inflation, and collapse of national morale (p.35). The demands of the Treaty of Versailles had taken German land, the vast financial reparations with the humiliating Guilt Clause, plus of course the financial collapse of the global market had left Germany packed with a discontented population as easy pickings for a man of Hitler's passion for power. Roberts wrote that the dictate of the Versailles Treaty was always a powerful weapon, and his Party machine was more efficient than others, especially with their fist-fighting against fighting communists (p.40).

The Weimar Republic had started well with great hopes, with Roberts noting that even 'its undoubted virtues were submerged with its faults', and it grew weaker, giving Hitler the time and material to appeal to the masses because their psychology was often the same as his (p.36). Hitler's triumph was based on his emotions and his instinct to 'beat reason', and it used the listless despair of the sufferers, and according to Roberts the very liberty of the Weimar Republic offered no hope (p.37). Hitler played on their sufferings as the keynote, and he 'preached to them diverting his message

The Early Days   125

into political channels', offering hell fire if they drifted on, and heaven if they followed him (p.38).

He had from the beginning demanded a new reborn Germany, and he was also 'lucky', as time and place fell in the right order for him when he was raised to Chancellor at a time when his party was weakening (p.39). Roberts did not note at this stage that many right-wing traditional conservatives had thought they could control Hitler, failing like many other international leaders to understand his warped psychology and passion for ultimate power, but he soon spotted the fact that Hitler had gained the upper hand. He later referred to those who thought they could control Hitler as sorely mistaken.

From the earliest times Hitler had started to grow myths about the German people, calling them 'a politically retarded race' (p.41). Hitler, as Roberts observed, inculcated his myths, offering people power, because 'the Germans never wanted democracy, they crave for authority, and respect the strong arm' (p.42). As Roberts observed, the bourgeoise and returned soldiers were just as malleable as the workers, and here was the key, 'Hitler fitted in the accidental facts of the troubled post-war years' (p.43).

So-called Philosophy of National Socialism

Rosenberg, mentioned above, developed a philosophy called *Weltanschauung* (world view or outlook) which was sponsored by Hitler in 1935 at a Party Congress, demanding that everyone must be educated in this matter. It was, as Roberts noted, that 'the truth is that it can be understood only as a kind of retrospective philosophical justification of Nazidom' (p.45). Rosenberg's outpouring was often regarded as the real interpreter of Nazi ideology, of whom Roberts warned that this man was a mere journalist but who saw himself in the role of cultural and intellectual leadership (p.48). Roberts had been told that Rosenberg was not liked and only Hitler's loyalty kept him safe, and he once heard Rosenberg give a tirade against Jews stating that 'it was not impressive' (p.49). The *Weltanschauung* was no more than the Nazi racial basis, in which 'no Jew or coloured person could ever be assimilated into a Nordic society' (p.51). It encouraged the conception of a *Völkisch* (Folkist) state which dispensed with the need for a political science, which the Nazis replaced with their own pseudo-science, with Roberts cynically noting that none of the Nazi cabal could claim the Nordic features they kept postulating (p.52). It was all part and parcel of the vague concept loved by the party of Blood and Soil (*Blut und Erde*) put forward by Walter Darré, the Minister of Agriculture who took this step to extremes (p.53). He argued the German is the product of the soil, with Hitler claiming they were the products of the first migrant tribes, and they had been a solid edifice ever since, but then adding that the Jewish element was just the rubble (p.54). This was all, as rightly suggested by Roberts, the start of the revival of pagan myth coupled with the idea of starting a race of supermen (p56). Roberts further observed that the so-called Folkic State made the individual totally meaningless (p.57). He concluded by writing that 'the Nazis in Germany have probed back into the subconscious and removed the accumulated obscurities – some people outside Germany call them advances – of centuries. They have resurrected tribal instincts and the mystical sanctions of a savage society' (p.58). This constituted a stark warning to his readers of the atavistic attitude of Nazism, warning readers and observers that the Nazi regime was not only a criminal organisation but saw itself as returning to the brutal days of tribalism.

Chapter Two

Four Years of Power

Technique of Revolution

Roberts, long before historical analysis had taken root, noted that the German *Junker* (noblemen, aristocrats) class thought they had 'Hitler in chains', mainly tending to be traditional right-wing conservatives who thought they could control Hitler, but Roberts had noted that 'Hitler swept off his chains and became in truth the People's Chancellor' (p.61) with immense ramifications. These right-wing traditional Germans thought they had caught the 'simpleton corporal', but according to Roberts 'the joke was entirely on the other side. It was the *Junkers* who were caught' with Hitler announcing his three aims of national unity, prosperity, and equality with other countries, which was the first of the so-called four-year plans. Roberts then wrote that 'then began the purge. The weeks after 30 January saw the most thorough clean-up in modern political history', even those who had mildly criticised the Nazis were in trouble (p.62).

Göring had set the pace as ruler of Prussia using police and demanding violence (p.63), taking in 'his usual fashion the bull by the horns'. It was the time that all opposing parties went to the wall, the communists were attacked at once, and as Roberts wrote the Social Democrats 'actually bared their own throats for the killer's knife', even voting for the Bill which gave Hitler dictatorial powers (p.64). The final blow came on 14 July 1933 when it was made clear that the NSDAP was the only legal party, with the Storm Troopers (SA) enforcing this by working as a private army with the remaining opposition. Goebbels produced the *Law for the Protection of the German People*, which was passed, and gave total governmental control over every written and spoken word (p.65). This was followed by the Reichstag fire 'and the people swallowed the story of Communist arson'. Hitler had only gained 43.9 per cent of the votes, with Roberts noting 'it would be stupid to call this a free election' as 'Hitlerism was a minority movement' (p.66), and many outside observers were mainly unaware of the potential ramifications of a German dictatorship in the hands of a man like Hitler.

One of Germany's major features was that its origins were in the many varied provinces, with every individual area often revelling in its not-so-distant past. Hitler promised to respect the provinces on which Germany was built, but Roberts observed that 'within months [Hitler] was cutting away their roots', with 'Göring taking the lead in the race for centralisation' in Prussia (p.67). Göring, Roberts explained, worked 'with his usual abruptness' ensuring the police were all Nazis, knowing that he was being illegal, claiming he would sort out the legalities later and other provinces such as Hesse fell (p.68). Bavaria proved the most reluctant, but the provincial states were doomed and 'Federalism disappeared' (p.69).

The Nazis were demanding a new unitary system of government, and Bismarck's Germany had disappeared to a centralised autocracy which had always been in the mind of Hitler as he exposed in *Mein Kampf*. Democracy and regionalism had gone, and Roberts explained that the rest of the story were the plebiscites started first when Germany left the League of Nations (14 October 1933), as Hitler told the people if they agreed it would 'restore Germany to her freedom in foreign affairs' (p.70). Roberts also added the ominous note on plebiscites that 'he would have been a strange German who voted against Hitler' (p.71), and perhaps as the years rolled by, he would speculatively have changed this to a 'brave person'.

The Growth of Party Organisation

Roberts then turned his attention to the immediate past showing how the Nazi Party organisation had constructed itself. He wrote that 'it would require a lifelong study of administration to understand the complicated political structure of the National Socialist Party, and even an expert would be driven mad, mainly because 'it grew out of nothing and developed as it grew', adding that today it 'is one of the most complicated, disorderly, overlapping, amorphous organisations in the world'. He was writing this in 1936, and he thought that 'Hitler knows what a mess it all is, but presently does nothing' (p.72). The new Nazi organisation, he noted somewhat cynically, was a happy hunting ground for jobseekers, and 'I was staggered when I was shown how the system works at Party Headquarters in Munich, until I realised that everything depended on finding something to do'. He noted many departments spent their time on clipping newspaper cuttings, creating an elaborate filing system, with trained historians researching pictures of ancient bakers, mainly to prove the worthiness of labour during the centuries. They were also busy collecting plenty of anti-Nazi literature prompting the writer to reflect on the fact the Nazis were still being opposed (p.73), a feature which was and still is overlooked.

Roberts then turned his attention to the evolution of the Nazi structure which had started from 1925 when the Party was reconstituted after the Munich revolt, starting off in a dingy apartment (p.74). It was not long before key figures emerged such as Goebbels in propaganda, and lesser known at the time of writing (1936) was Walter Buch (his son-in-law was Martin Bormann) who headed a disciplinary committee known as *Uschla* to crush dissidents mentioned later in this section. There were large departments for Nazi pensions and insurance, and even Roberts was recompensed from this fund after his raincoat was torn at a Nuremberg rally. However, Roberts cynically noted that Hitler was more interested in rooting out the heretics such as the Strasser brothers than be consumed by office work. By middle of the 1930s there were over 200,000 names on Party Rolls, so he bought the former Barlow Palace, which became known as the Brown House (p.75).

Roberts noted that Hitler was fortunate in his subordinates, because 'they provided the administrative capacities he lacked', adding that the offices 'provide a definite shadow state', giving the impression 'as if they were managing a nation' (p.77).

He studied the Party Organisation when it came to power, noting that some of the more powerful figures within the organisation had more control leaders (apart from Hitler and Göring) than any form of civil service in any other country. The Central Directorate of the Party (*Oberste Reichsleitung* known as OR) was the key to the massive organisation having nineteen members, Roberts noting that most people outside of Germany would never have heard of them (p.78). Roberts recorded that in the OR 'we are getting very near the realities of power' and today it is even 'more cumbrous and complicated' (p.79), especially noting that there were special departments on Race Politics and another for Investigation of Kinship (p.80), both of which should have sent out warnings about the future. He wrote that 'At first sight, this range of departments would seem to run the whole gamut of administration, especially since the Party is only a shadow of the State, and theoretically has not taken over any of the permanent Civil Service' (p.81), though it soon would in places and dominate in the rest.

He met Robert Ley, a powerful figure in the Labour Office department, who was one of Hitler's oldest personal friends and 'a well-known Jew baiter'. There was an office for training young men for Party leadership, stressing the importance of *Führerprinzip* training the mini-dictators of the future (pp.84–5). They all had branches in every *Gaue* (region), with Roberts noting that 'the Party organisation becomes so overpowering an incubus' (that some do not like) and 'fresh parts always added' so 'Germany is weighed down by a vast machine to which fresh parts are always being added, and which has long passed its utmost efficiency'. 'Whether Nazis or not, they [Germans] are becoming the slaves of a machine'(p.86).

He mentioned among the key figures the much-feared Major Walter Buch of the *Uschla* department, mentioned above, noting that 'its records are probably unparalleled anywhere in the world' (p.82), which, given the nature of Buch's work, was ominous. Hitler believed in a check and countercheck within the Party, demanding 'a regime of periodic purges to keep up the morale of the survivors (p.86) which was Walter Buch's post. It was vastly different to the Whip system in the British House of Commons, because with Buch the victims knew that they were in a life and death situation. He was in total command of the *Untersucgungs-und-Schlichtungsausshuss* known as *Uschla*. He checked all Party Members, working as a 'dread punitive organisation', the Nazis called it the Cell or Cell G, and it was given much publicity [probably to instil fear] with no sympathy for any waverers. The Black Guards (SS) told Roberts 'That is the type of system we understand, as if daily scrutiny was absolutely normal (p.87). Buch worked in secret behind the scenes and no records were kept of the summary court martials as the Cell worked for the Party.

Göring had followed the same policies with the Gestapo. It was widely known even at this time that 'once in the hands of the Gestapo a man has no possible means of defence', and 'no body of political police in the past has had greater power than theirs', though Roberts may well have mentioned the Russian Cheka and Soviet NKVD of which he would have been aware.

Interestingly, Roberts then turned to Himmler, who hoodwinked him as Roberts described him as 'modest in manner', 'his glasses make him look insignificant' and he had a 'beaver like capacity for work' which Hitler had noticed, (p.88). Himmler had built up bodies of secret police, and in 1934 was in charge of all Germany's secret police. At that time Himmler was 37 years of age, and as Roberts noted, he 'was rightly considered one of the key men of the regime' noting that the Foreign Office saw him as an ogre, but with Roberts adding 'Actually, he sets an example of quiet dignity and simplicity of life that is often lacking in Nazi Germany, and remains entirely unspoilt, living like a clerk in a simple Berlin flat'. 'Personally, I found him much kindlier and much more thoughtful for his guests than any other Nazi leaders, a man of exquisite courtesy and still interested in the simple things of life' (p.89). Roberts found Himmler totally normal, noting that many think he would succeed Hitler, whereas Hess lacked character with Goebbels too unpopular, and Göring too blunt. Roberts added that Himmler 'seems to have the simplicity of true greatness and yet balances this by an astute mentality' and 'the superficial see in him only a brutal opportunist'. Roberts qualified this by adding the thought that 'while not approving of his methods, I see in him capacities for leadership what may change the future of Europe' (p.90). Roberts noted that 'The Party could not survive without the constant vigilance of Buch and Himmler', however, he further wrote that 'in short, they are as untrammelled a race of young autocrats as the world has ever seen, and the very necessity for them, and the extraordinary range of their powers, throws much light on the real nature of Hitlerism' (p.91), which was a built-in criticism. His judgement of Himmler was the only bloomer Roberts made in all his appraisals. Nor was Roberts the only foreigner to misread Himmler. The astute American journalist William Shirer met him and wrote that 'Heinrich Himmler, who with his pince-nez looked like a harmless provincial schoolmaster', and later observed again that 'he struck me as too insignificant, too mediocre, to succeed for long as such a key man in this repressive regime'.[1] There is no doubt that Himmler could turn on the personal feeling of modesty as he probably did with all foreigners. He had simply hoodwinked Roberts who, like many others, would have to wait a few years to realise that Himmler was a cold-blooded killer, dangerously ambitious, and the main source and instigator of the Holocaust as well as other appalling cruelties.

Roberts wrote that Germany had been a heterogenous collection of kingdoms and duchies wielded by Bismarck into a confederation (p.91), but in 1925 Hitler had divided Germany into tribal districts or an administrative Gaue, all under a Gauleiter, thereby becoming shadow governments which soon grew in number. Roberts wrote that 'It was of course, the Russian system of Soviets transplanted wholesale into Germany, but Hitler chose to overlook this fact and viewed his territorial organisation as the most novel of ideas' (pp.92–3). It was a question of administrative organisation, and 'Hitler chanced upon the device of *Statthalters* for each state', which gave them total power in their area (p.93). Roberts wrote that 'Hitler does not intend to leave the matter at this stage, however. He insists on recasting the entire face of Germany, and he had made many speeches insisting on a uniform administrative structure' (p.95). Nevertheless, some areas like Bavaria did not like the divisions and even Göring was unhappy for a time in Prussia as he probably liked being the lord and master (p.96). As Roberts noticed that 'you cannot take from people their local affiliations', 'and healthy regionalism is stronger in Germany today than ever,' 'their traditions and distinctions are a question of their very soul'(p.97).

In terms of the Party and the Civil Service, Roberts found the relationship between Party and State 'as almost impossible to define'. The Party had not taken over all State activities, but 'Hitler has defined the relationship by saying the Party is the mainspring of all public activity' (p.97). It takes little imagination to read between the lines here and see the threat that Germany was going to be controlled by a single political party which was headed by Hitler who would not accept any challenge. Hitler 'violently repressed those extremists who followed Röhm' and anyone else who was perceived to be a danger to his rule (p.98). It should also be recalled that Dachau concentration camp was opened on 22 March 1933 to imprison even the mildest critics.

A law of April 1933 allowed Civil Servants to be discharged for the simplification of the administration, and adding other undesirables, Jews, Communists and Liberals, some of whom received pensions, but not the Jews and Communists (p.98). Various purges continued which mainly applied to non-Aryans, or those considered undesirable, Roberts observing that the ranks of the police were most heavily purged, that the postal service demanded only Party members, and in technical areas most stayed except those under race laws or who had previously held anti-Nazis views (p.99). A Foreign Office spokesman explained these purges were not necessary with them because they had already done that, and they tended to emerge unscathed, though 'naturally this is far from meaning that the Party has no influence' (p.100). Roberts wrote that 'Hitler obviously leans towards increasing the duplication of functions rather than merging the two sets of bodies' (p.101), but it was already clear that the Nazi office dominated everything, especially the Foreign Office.

In terms of the problems at the administration level, Roberts observed that the weeding out of undesirables was on a greater scale. Hitler always wanted to reward his supporters and the Gauleiters and Statthalters always followed the same policy. There was still some confusion when a new Municipal Law was announced in January 1935, as it created a single uniform law for the whole country (p.102). Roberts shrewdly observed that 'Germany is becoming one great administrative machine…all controlled from the master-switch at Berlin. The theory of a totalitarian State is there; enabling laws having been passed; and henceforth the administrative practice of totalitarianism will grow up as well' (p.103). Roberts with these observations was ably informing his readers that Hitler's dictatorial system would continue into the near future, with all his insane, immoral, and criminal thinking.

The Eclipse of the Brownshirts

Roberts wrote that Germany was a land of uniforms with 'no less than 315 distinct types of uniform, each of which a zealous Nazi is doubtless expected to identify at sight'. He observed that Brownshirts varied in the way they presented themselves, some reflecting the relics of the past or their areas. Which, Roberts noted, is all quite different from the straightforward black of the black guards, namely the SS (p.104). He noted that the SS had a more Spartan simplicity and 'they contrive to be the most impressive body of men in Germany', contrasting with the 'the pell-mell mixture of Brownshirt uniforms'. He recalled sitting opposite two Brownshirts who complained they were tired by long duties and pointed out the SS who were younger, whereas they were nearly old veterans with Roberts noting it was a conflict of generations (p.105). Roberts observed that Hitler 'now wanted a disciplined Praetorian Guard to maintain his own government', thereby hinting that Hitler saw himself as the emperor.

Roberts was aware he was in Germany at the time of the twilight of the Brownshirts. He noted the Brownshirts had anticipated rewards and better posts, especially as the old fighters. They had hoped for jobs, but they were aware the army was not interested in them, but there were some Brownshirts who thought they should run the army. Criticisms of how they were now being treated was spreading through the ranks, but their troubles were becoming superfluous. It was known that Göring did not appreciate them, and there were rife rumours that Hitler did not want some form of revolt (p.106). Roberts observed that some of the SA still believed in the old Socialistic side of the Party, but they were now aware that nothing was happening. He observed they were mainly working class, whereas the SS were more bourgeois and disciplined, recalling however that the Brownshirts never forgot they were civilians with an interest in politics, seeing themselves as representing the nation (p.107). There was evident discontent, despite the propaganda image that Germany was one large happy 'folkish' family. Hitler had already issued a warning (July 1933) promising to supress any disorder ruthlessly, and in 1934 special campaigns had been launched against grumblers, not helped by some conflict between the Brownshirts and the Stalhelms, (League of ex-front-line soldiers) so a month's holiday was granted to quieten them down (p.108).

Roberts commented on the Night of the Long Knives, offering the official story that it occurred because the government was putting down a conspiracy (p.109). Roberts decided that the real explanation was to do with the Brownshirts, political freebooters, soldiers of fortune and gangsters who had helped Hitler but now felt that Hitler had stopped half-way and forgotten his socialist promises, and it was not helped by Ernst Röhm and Göring being at perpetual loggerheads. It was highly unlikely Hitler was in personal danger, but Roberts had noted the discontent between the Army and Brownshirts which had triggered some alarms (p.110).

Roberts wrote that 'it remains uncertain, I repeat, whether or not an actual revolt was planned', and those who were involved were doing their own things, as Karl Ernst (SA Commander in Berlin) was about to go on holiday with his wife, making a plot doubtful, and the tale of von Schleicher's plot was equally unlikely. He further added that there was no evidence that he and Röhm planned anything together, and the killing involved a wide range of people (p.111). He added that 'however murky all these matters may be, there is no doubt about Hitler's actions', who was claiming he knew the night before something had to be done, but later Göring told the press it had been planned (p.112), leading to an inconsistency of official accounts. Roberts noted that Gregor Strasser had been taken from his home and killed as well as General von Schleicher and his wife (p.113). Hitler claimed he had been confronted by a mutiny aided by a foreign power (p.114), and in a 'speech in the Reichstag of 13 July left nothing more to be said as to the moral standards of the German government', stating that 76 conspirators were killed, but as Roberts noted, there were many more (p. 115).

Roberts further noted that 'the attacks on Gregor Strasser were equally unworthy. The suggestion of his complicity in a plot against Hitler was 'merely silly' (p.117), as 'Hitler wanted to break the hold of the unwieldy Brownshirts and free himself from the incubus of the lower middle classes, and the 'next step was the reintroduction of military conscription (p.119). Roberts had grasped the essential themes of the crisis amidst its myriad official explanations, that now in power Hitler was intent on ridding himself of any possible opposition, even though it included his purportedly best friend Ernst Röhm who had controlled the extensive SA. Hitler was clearing his way of any potential rubble as he extended his grip on Germany, and Roberts, by spending time on his analysis clearly sent out again the warning that Germany was being led by a dangerous criminal where no holds were barred.

The Army and Hitlerism

Roberts turned his attention to Hitler and his perceived relationships with the German Army. During this year of 1936, for Hitler the army was already more about what he described as 'militant patriotism', an expression which needs some unpacking. For Hitler this was more like what is best described today as an 'aggressive nationalist', because he had made it clear in both *Mein Kampf* and from Roberts' observations, namely he had every intention of reclaiming territory lost in the Versailles Treaty, expanding east for *Lebensraum*, and he had often stated it would need force of arms. At this stage of his writing Roberts makes the curious observation that as he was an Australian, many German people he met expressed their sympathy for him, because he belonged to the decadent British, and pointed out to him that the Party claimed the war was forced on them because of the Jewish stab-in-the back, and that the Treaty of Versailles had been a deliberate attempt at humiliating the German nation (p.120). There was no question that the infamous Treaty had given Hitler's vitriolic attacks a sense of justification for many Germans, and the ridiculous stab-in-the-back theory (*Dolchstoßlegende*) had been widely and unbelievably accepted.

Roberts had noted that Hitler had loved the army life, and he had rushed to war in 1914, loved the military displays and had started his own brown army (SA) with a black army (SS) to follow, and he clearly enjoyed uniforms. Roberts asserted that 'Hitler wanted the strongest army in the world for many reasons, and he was at his best when talking of the comradeship of war, but he added the warning he had heard so many times that if they wanted to recover lost provinces, it could only be done by violence (p.121). Today, given that *Mein Kampf* and men like Roberts had made this more than clear, it seems extraordinary that many international leaders, especially in France, Britain, and even America still hoped that Hitler could be reasoned with and controlled.

Roberts observed that Goebbels supported this viewpoint and was the brains behind Hitler, and that Göring was a born military man playing with his 'gigantic toy' the proposed Luftwaffe. How far Goebbels was that influential at the time may be questionable, but there is no doubt he was clever, and always gave Hitler total support. It was enough for Roberts to warn that 'dangerous men, these, to be in charge of Germany at a time when the nation was reawakened and was in a mood to accept any sacrifice for the sake of rearmament', adding that Hitler was plunging the world into a new arms race, and even risking economic disaster in so doing (p.122).

Roberts referred to what he called the rebirth of the Army, noting that the Versailles Treaty had been broken by the Germans, even though there had been rumours the rest of the world would disarm (p.122). Nevertheless, Roberts makes little mention that in Germany during the 1920s under the Weimar Republic, they had continued to restructure their forces, sometimes working in tandem with Russia as the two pariah states. This had been led by General von Seeckt who is often accredited with what would later be dubbed the blitzkrieg war, but also a man who disliked Hitler and Nazism. Roberts observed that General Blomberg had said no nation could be denied the right of defence, because it is 'man's primitive birthright' of defence, even though in his early days, Hitler not wanting to provoke the old enemies, had preached 'equality'. However, as Hitler grew in power this changed and on 16 March 1935, he announced conscription, and the picture changed with the armament factories becoming noticeably busy (p.123). The Army command had to learn how to change a massive force of conscripts into a 100,000-strong army, causing concern abroad, but General Beck, Roberts noted, fought valiantly to achieve this, and progress was made (p.125). General Beck would soon turn against Hitler and resigned when his intentions started to become a reality, later becoming a key figure in the attempt to assassinate Hitler in the 20 July Plot. In 1935–6 traditional military men like Beck thought it correct to be able to build up the German army.

Roberts managed to watch some army manoeuvres in 1936, and he was surprised by their mobility, which was a product of Seeckt's work in planning a new army. He saw new types of anti-aircraft artillery which British experts told him were new, and a massive increase in mechanisation (p.126). Foreign military guests were often invited to these events, some enjoying the companionship of the old enemy, some seeing the Germans as showing off, and a few expressing concerns. It was Roberts' analysis of the Nazi political leadership which should have taken the most attention. He made a pertinent comment in his book when he observed that factories are busy pouring out guns and aircraft, so rapidly they are short of flying personnel, but 'there is no doubt' he noted that in a few years Hitler 'will have the finest army in Europe' (p.127). Like many others in Europe Roberts claimed the French army and its leadership was the best, which may have been numerically correct, but the 1940 Battle of France proved it to be grossly wrong. Roberts noted, more justifiably, that Hitler cannot be believed over the figures he announces on the world stage, with Roberts estimating that Germany already had up to 42 divisions (p.128). As Chamberlain would eventually realise after the Munich Conference, Hitler could not be trusted and was a liar, a point which Roberts consistently drove home at every opportunity.

Roberts then turned his observation towards Göring who had been planning the future Luftwaffe for many years, claiming that this was the war of the future. This prompted the dangerous thought to Roberts that 'this means an aggressive war…and it would be won in the first few days by bombing planes' (p.128), a fear which was occupying many international leaders. Göring had the support of Hitler and used flying clubs and major advertising thrusts to find recruits. On 24 June 1933, Göring had organised what appeared to be foreign planes to drop leaflets to stir the propaganda about defence planes, it was a ruse to garner support (pp.129–30). This with

138   Why Appeasement Failed

other facts worked, and recruits grew rapidly enabling Göring to pave the way for the Luftwaffe, which Roberts warned was an embryonic air force gathering pace (p.130). Again, Roberts doubted the truth of the figures which he found elusive because of the many misleading statistics, noting that construction is growing apace, with Roberts proposing there were at least 2,500 machines, and they are all new (p.131). Roberts knew there was still a problem finding pilots, but acknowledged the German air-force is viewed as Hitler's greatest achievement (p.132).

He finally turned to the German Navy (Kriegsmarine) which was not Hitler's strongest point and was not within his personal favour (p.132). In June 1935 there had been the Anglo-German Naval agreement with England, which limited the German navy to 36 per cent of the British fleet, but significantly, there was no mention of submarines. France had objected, but many had thought Hitler had been moderate, finding it reassuring on the grounds that it suggested Hitler was not planning an aggressive war (p.135). Few reflected on the fact that Hitler had long outlined his wish to re-occupy German territories and expand east, which for Hitler was a land and air war. It equally demonstrated Hitler's limited military thinking in regard to the significance of a powerful navy.

A Nuremberg Rally

In any day modern democratic society any opposition party would want to have advanced notice of another Party's manifesto, as well as an insight into the sort of voters it was attracting. It would also be useful to hear about that Party's overall views and attitudes, and above all its intentions. This had played a significant role in the 1920s with the constant physical conflicts between the Communists and National Socialists, but after Hitler grasped power there were still major Party functions to hear the rallying call. Roberts attended one of these major functions, called rallies (*Partei-Tag*) which had become an integral part of Nazism. He watched the shot-filled blood banner once carried by Andreas Bauriedl at the Munich revolt being given almost religious overtones, setting the mystical atmosphere for these rallies once Hitler had achieved power. Roberts noted that 'Hitler acted as the pontiff of a Nazi Rome' during the grandiose parades which after 1933 became a fixture (p.136). He noted that people saw it as a 'circus and revue' making it an institution. He had heard that there had been an atmosphere of depression in 1934 as 'the cleaning up of 30 June [Night of the Long Knives] had left gaps', but the 1935 Rally was called the Party Day of Freedom with the reintroduction of conscription (p.137).

Roberts attended the 1936 Rally which was a culmination of a long series of speeches, in which Hitler gave his address to the Germans and the entire world. He announced the four-year plan for economic self-sufficiency and a campaign against disorder, which he identified as Russia. Roberts noted that citizens from many countries were there, including American and English peers, one of the latter telling Roberts how impressed he was (p.138), hopefully, Roberts noted, more impressed by the arranged massive grandeur than the speeches.

At this 1936 Rally, Roberts heard a Victor Lutz slowly read over 400 names of Nazis who had died for the cause, heard speeches dwelling on whether Germany might intervene in Spain on Franco's behalf. Roberts noted the upsurge of emotionalism, and a strange cry which eventuated into *Heil Hitler*, with him noting that the 'German excels in mass meetings' (p.139). There followed the consecration of new banners, with Hitler taking the salute for five hours, while Göring had to rest against his car. He watched planes fly by overhead, and there were mock aerial fights, which he described as 'a triumph of organisation and showmanship' with 'a million and a quarter visitors crammed into a town of 400,000 people' (p.141).

Roberts concluded with the critical insights that 'the Party rally was a miniature mobilisation, and 'Hitler's speech against the Bolsheviks was still ringing in one's ears', it was full of pseudo religious ceremonies creating an impassable mental gulf between Germany and the democracies (p.142). The contrast with the democracies was itself a warning, as these events were built on pseudo-religious feelings and based on crowd emotionalism to a degree unlikely to occur in any democracy. It was the way that Hitler gained so much support from so many classes of society. The English peer who commented on its magnificence probably reflected some of the Junker class, normally the last social class to be affected. Attendance at these rallies clearly indicated the amount of emotional support Hitler had manipulated in his favour, so even some of his most bizarre and immoral shrieks were taken on as if announced from Mount Olympus. This, as seen by Roberts, did not bode well for the future, as Hitler was enlarging his fanatical support.

Chapter Three

The Economics of Hitlerism

Several times Marx and Engels made references that money often drove history, and many books have been written on the driving forces of economics. After the First World War Germany was in an impoverished state more so than other major European countries. It had not been helped by the infamous global monetary crisis, and Hitler had used the feeling of public depression to bolster his way to the top by making promises of a better future. To do this he increased, as is known, employment in public works, increased production for gathering military resources, not least expensive aircraft manufacture, and even the money spent on the Nuremberg Rallies, parades, and Nazi paraphernalia was immense. This needed paying for which the German government could not be unaware. International observers had noted this expenditure, with some predicting that it would collapse Germany, and others suggesting that it might lead to war. Roberts as a gifted and intelligent academic spent time in his book to outline the Nazi response with its hopes and fears.

The Doctrine of Self-sufficiency

Roberts knew that Hitlerism had to win on the economic front, noting that the German government had claimed they were facing an economic blockade, just as they had in the First World War. Many Germans saw National Socialism 'as one of the greatest phenomena in all history' but recognised these problems, as the Nazi Party looked to economic self-sufficiency, known as autarky, claiming they wanted to make Germany a self-sufficient citadel' (p.145). Roberts wrote that 'Germany is a country suffering from a marked neurosis' because it is always dependent on outside resources, noting the paradox that Germany was on the gold standard with practically no gold reserves (p.146). In June 1933, the authorities had imposed severe penalties on people concealing foreign assets, and no one was allowed to send more than 10 Marks out of the country per month, even to their relatives (p.147).

The critical problem often centred on foreign trade, and the only way was to cut down imports or by increasing exports, otherwise Roberts wrote 'the only alternatives are either a recourse to war or the complete success of the Four-Year Plan', but either way foreign markets were essential (p.148). In September 1934, Schacht had introduced his famous 'New Plan', wanting to restrict imports to the level of exports, so there should be no drain on resources (p.149). This meant that Germany had to stick to the plan of only buying what she could afford, nevertheless, the volume of exports was declining (p.150). Roberts noted that despite Schacht's plans Germany felt like a man who lacked any money (p.151). It was, as Roberts pointed out, the Quest for Markets which was Schacht's offensive which Roberts rightly referred to as producing a 'Stone Age bartering' of goods for goods (p.151). As such imports from Britain and USA were declined; the system worked with Italy, but the Balkans pressed for money for their corn, with Germany only offering armaments instead. In this scenario the Balkan negotiators knew they would become dependent on Germany for their replacements, with Roberts noting that 'such retrospective Machiavellism is rather forced' (pp.152–153). Roberts observed that Germany by increasing its armaments had created an internal boom but knew 'it can't go on forever' (p.154).

Financial Jugglery

Roberts wrote the Nazi government was operating a 'multiple geared currency' (p.155), observing that 'international trade is as much of a battleground as any war could be', with Germany 'evolving a currency system with an infinite degree of flexibility', and 'on the surface Germany has grossly over-valued currency, and is tied to gold when in reality she has no gold backing' (p.158).

This situation enabled Germany to buy materials from abroad with advantageous rates, and Roberts was told that no dictator would want to see devaluation, recalling that when France devalued its currency in September 1936, the German press announced this as a sign of weakness (p.159). Based on his astute observations Roberts asked 'how is Germany able to keep going from month to month?' He observed the evident truth that Germany was surviving because the administration was offering no reckoning or accounts.

The 1934–5 budget indicated a massive deficit, which he noted, 'in German eyes, she must have equal trade with each country...or she will breakdown and lose everything' (p.160). The financial situation was so appalling it is easy to understand why Roberts and others saw war as highly possible as the one way the problem could be resolved. Roberts raised this question in his direct way by asking how they could pay their bills and how does Germany keep going month to month? He believed they were postponing the evil day as long as possible, and it seemed the Nazi state had to increase taxes, but this would be unpopular and was such a sore point that editors who mentioned it in their papers were swiftly punished (p.161).

Roberts wrote that the 'fundamental weakness is that over 98 per cent of the Reichsbank's note-cover is represented by short-term State bonds which may easily become worthless', and that official figures about expenditure are obviously incomplete and sometimes contradictory (p.162). He raised the question as to whether Germany could prevent a breakdown in the next few years, noting that town residents had more hope than those in the rural areas who were less willing to take risks (pp.163–4).

The Internal Boom

Roberts wrote about the deliberate creation of an internal boom if only because of foreign loans (1926–9), noting that 'Germany had probably the most up-to-date factory system in Europe... when Hitler came to power six million were unemployed', and the government's plans amounted to simple and direct ways to finance their ambitious programmes of public works [which tended to be the motor-roads and arms industry] and credit was created (p.165). The centralisation of the banking system helped mainly because it was public investment rather than private enterprise, but 'it led to a tremendous growth in industrial activity' (p.166). The main basis was 'not for consumer goods but for armaments, machines and cement', not for textiles and food. He wrote that 'it has been rather wildly asserted by some British politicians that Germany spent £800,000,000 sterling on armaments in 1935 alone, but this was untenable', adding that to explain the money and credit problems 'would require a magician to be more explicit' (p.167). The truth was, Roberts observed, that Hitler received subsidies from various industrialists, and by 1935 the armaments industry boom had revived, adding that 'to say Hitler is a puppet pulled hither and thither by the Thyssen family [major industrialists] seems inaccurate' (p.168), which was all too true.

Roberts turned to the position of labour, pointing out that the government had claimed it would reduce unemployment and was proved successful. He observed that Marxists, Socialists, Jews, and pacifists were never part of the figures, and that a million men had been absorbed into the army, the Labour service camps, and the vast Nazi organisations. Over half a million had been taken off the labour market with a marriage allowance to entice them away, [which was probably based on the Nazi theory that women should be at home producing children] and there were a series of emergency steps to achieve this, backed by ceaseless propaganda (p.169). Also assisting in this game of statistics were the Hitler Youth and compulsory labour camps as they all belonged to the newly created Labour Front, and received allowances, holidays, and other benefits (p.170), a deliberate effort to make the Nazi government popular.

Roberts wrote that 'Hitlerite Germany is reviving the Bismarckian expedient of social oil, the free use of palliatives to keep the workers in a satisfied frame of mind', noting that was more successful in Berlin and much less elsewhere. He noted the curious rumour that Hitler preferred individual home-plots for workers and not flats thinking this policy would clear communism from the land (p.171). However, Roberts noted that agitators were always visited with penalties for sabotaging the work of the Third Reich, [which would become worse] the official attitude was 'that no complaints exist anywhere…to talk like this is to insult one's intelligence… and the whispering campaigns would refute this', with Roberts adding the pertinent insight 'that the truth is none of them are free' (p.172).

The Fight for Raw Materials and Substitutes

Roberts wrote with much justification that 'modern international history can be written in terms of deficiencies in such raw materials', and regarding such critical and vital materials, Germany was worse off than any other major state in Europe. Nevertheless, Germany desperately wanted to reach self-sufficiency, which was highly unlikely. Roberts noted that the population tended to believe Hitler's claims, especially with the news that they were trying to produce rubber from scientific experiments (p.174). Roberts devoted pages to his personal observations and conversations on the German inability to make woollen clothes, as their substitutes either caused itchiness or let the rain through to the skin (p.174). He noted their efforts in trying to produce oil from coal (p.176), and that currently their cars were fuelled by 40 per cent local benzol [organic chemical compound] which consisted of 10 per cent alcohol, 50 per cent foreign gasoline. They even tried wood fuel, because frantic efforts were being made to avoid foreign imports (p.178), and the same was being experimented with vegetable oil, but observing that with all these efforts they still had to import special coal (p.179).

Roberts wrote that 'self-sufficiency for Germany in her present territories is a chimera, a dream impossible of realisation' and 'the only sensible policy would be co-operation with other countries' (p.180). Roberts did not state it explicitly at this point, but between the lines the lack of self-sufficiency was a possible ingredient of war already seen in Hitler's desire for so-called *Lebensraum*, and the idea of co-operating with other countries would be rare for Hitler.

Schacht Versus the Extremists

Hjalmar Schacht, President of the Reichsbank and Minister of Economics was, according to Roberts, unwanted amongst most of the Nazi economists, because although he had a top reputation in this field, he never held back at what he thought about the Nazi leaders. It was him, however, who managed to get Germany out of the inflation years and had negotiated the Dawes loan. Roberts described him 'as the most amazing person. Amongst all the German leaders I met he stands out as the most distinct personality' (p.181). Roberts noted that 'nothing is sacred to him, except his belief in himself', and he hated any interference from some of the 'ignorant Nazi leaders' (p.182).

When Roberts was in Germany, Schacht had only just become a Party Member, but he remained unpopular (p.183). He had clashed with the Nazi economists, and he had not helped himself by suggesting financial cuts in Nazi administration spending, and the military and secret police he described 'as heresy to the Nazi Party'. Soon complaints became serious as he was accused of sabotaging the State (p.186), so Hitler put Göring in charge the moment Schacht advised that Germany should stay in harmony with other countries (p.187). Roberts' estimation of him was correct, he was somewhat self-confident but critical of the Nazis and good at economics. Later he would stand trial at Nuremberg, but the British prosecution demanded he should be acquitted despite the Russians demanding his execution. He was imprisoned after a denazification trial but soon released and postwar continued working in finances.

The Agricultural Fiasco

Finally, in his analysis of the economic picture of Nazi Germany, Roberts turned to the agricultural scene and the rise of Walter Darré, Nazi Minister for agriculture. German experiments had depended on agriculture as much as industry because food was essential even if, as Roberts commented, Goebbels thought bullets were more important than bread. Roberts noted that Germany had poverty in its soil, and there had always been a conflict between the Junkers in the rural east, compared to the west German industry (p.189). Roberts reflected that 'one of the reasons for Brüning's fall was his attempt to make the Junkers more efficient in their farming…but they were also corrupt'. This was when Walter Darré entered the scene, who wanted the return of the Nordic peasant, older he said than the Junker's class (p.190). He saw his task as rallying the peasants, an archaic term for agricultural workers (p.191).

In 1933 Darré became the agricultural dictator and was a fermenting racist and a strong believer in Autarky (p.192). In that same year the 'Food Estate' was set up, and it was controlled from Berlin. It was no longer a profit and loss job, as all food, after the feeding of the farmer's family, went to the state with penalties used to enforce their decisions. It was Darré's 'Blood and Soil' theme which captured Hitler's imagination to enhance his despicable race and biological ideas (p.193). It was ruled that the farm could not be sold but had to be passed onto the eldest son, and no Jews were allowed access. There was a drive for agriculture, but all this cost money, and city consumers complained about the price of food, nor were the farmers pleased by being under rigid control and being obliged to deliver 'x' amount of food at given times. On top of all these problems, Roberts pointed out that the administrative system was bewilderingly complex (p.195).

Roberts was aware that Germany simply could not produce enough food, and had insufficient foreign exchange to buy it in, with the herds suffering from lack of food and these herds dwindled by almost a quarter (p.196). This was another reason for Hitler's determination to activate his proposed policy of *Lebensraum*. Roberts observed that Germany simply could not feed itself, and consumers had to pay more for what they could purchase. It was noted that since Hitler came to power wheat had gone up by 16 per cent, eggs by 50 per cent, butter by 40 per cent, potatoes by 75.5 per cent and most meats by 50 per cent, clearly indicating serious economic issues (p.197).

Hitler had not managed to resolve the long-term problems of German agriculture, and as always, the measures benefitted the Junkers classes, while agricultural workers were not allowed in factories or to migrate to cities. Roberts noted that 'Blood and Soil' was 'a poor exchange for an economically sound system of agriculture' (p.198).

Chapter Four

The Balance Sheet of Hitlerism

In Part Four of this major work, Roberts presented a major overview of the way the Nazi regime shaped Germany to meet the Party's ideals and aims in nearly every aspect of the national life. He demonstrated in a variety of ways how the regime swiftly changed traditional German life, so it was prepared to fulfil Hitler's future intentions, thereby presenting to international observers what was happening in Germany, and the dangers it reflected for global peace.

The Youth Movement: the fight for the first 18 years

Roberts turned his attention to the Hitler Youth movement [*Hitlerjugend*] which was described as 'primarily a spiritual movement, a development through constantly renewed ecstasy to endless achievement', but he recorded that as soon as he approached their banners to see them, he was stopped by a sentry telling him that 'this is holy ground, untouchable'. This was a giant hint to him that this Nazi movement was far removed from the international Boy Scouts movement, and he noted that nationwide it included 6,000,000 young people (p.201). Roberts explained that Kurt Grüber started the organisation and the whole country was mapped out in youth maps. Grüber had been quickly overshadowed by Baldur von Schirach his 23-year-old protégé who was a dedicated Nazi (p.202).

It was an entirely sponsored Nazi movement and one by one all other children's organisations of traditional Germany, including most of the religious groups, were obliged to become members of the Hitler Youth (p.203). Schirach grew in power and was 'pampered with posts of great responsibility', and Roberts noted he was entirely dependent on his friendship with Hitler, which meant that 'apparently nobody can check him' as he demanded the unification of all children (p.204). He created the image of Hitler as a demi-god, namely 'the Führer is the man sent from heaven'. At the same time as the boys were being organised into the Nazi ideology there was the Band of German Maidens [*Bund Deutscher Mädel*, the BDM) as well. Roberts noted that the 'little boy and girl alike are pledged to sacrifice everything for the Führer and are taught that he is everything and themselves nothing' (p.205). Roberts observed that 'the Party attributes great importance to the training of future leaders' because 'Hitler wants faith, obedience, zeal, and the unceasing hatred of certain doctrines', and 'it would be foolish to underestimate the enthusiasm of young Germany for their Führer' (p.207). Roberts wrote that 'it is a queer form of fanaticism' (p.208), and 'they must submit to a mental uniformity which by its nature is downgrading', and 'it represents a giant with glandular trouble. The outward husk is imposing, but beneath is only mental aridness' (p.209). He added that if only one of the boys he saw in the camps while listening to propaganda 'had asked a penetrating question, I would have felt more hope for the future of Germany'(p.210).

There is no question that although Roberts was only touching on children and teenagers, he had foreseen the danger of the politicisation of the country's youth. They were being groomed to become ardent Nazi members treating Hitler as their adored God. They were being disciplined to become robots, obeying all commands even though their families may have had serious doubts, because Nazism put their family or religious affiliations on the bottom shelf. It was a major military conscription exercise which would soon produce resolute soldiers for the Nazi regime, as is now well-known with the benefit of hindsight.

The Labour Service: the fight for young men

Following on from his observations of how the Nazi regime indoctrinated children and teenagers, Roberts immediately turned to the labour service, almost with a seeming appreciation of this organisation. He wrote that 'the Labour Service seems to me one of the most desirable of the Nazi experiments', qualifying this by adding 'at least under German conditions'. He noted it was started by Konstantin Hierl, who in Heinrich Brüning's time had organised Nazi camps (p.211). Hierl, Roberts noted, had announced this work was an honour, stating it was a proud privilege of German youth to serve the *Volk*. On 26 June 1935, the Reich Labour Service Law was promulgated, announcing that six month's service was law for everyone between their 18th and 26th birthdays (p.212).

Roberts was told that at that time (1936) some 200,000 were serving, and the camps were organised on military lines, but with a spade instead of a rifle. He described the camps as being more like barracks, with uniforms and intensive drill, he noted that 'individualism has no part in the scheme' with Roberts watching a reveille at 5 am with the raising of the flag, followed by eight hours work each day (p.213). He was giving the impression that his initial views of this movement were changing as he noted the inbuilt aspect of their lives. They had lectures on the New Germany and on international affairs, with Roberts noting that 'the whole time, there is deliberate leading of his mind in certain directions', with the Nazi creed of putting the *Volk* (German people) before self, and each camp is a duplicate of another (p.214). Roberts noted that each camp had precisely 152 men, and at the time of writing they could put '200,000 drilled and well-organised infantrymen into the field' (p.215) cynically noting it was yet another form of military training.

Roberts was informed that their key role was mainly reclaiming marsh lands, which Hitler called the fight against water (p.216). Roberts saw the red flag and black spade in the remotest of places, remarking that in Germany 'somehow, it does not seem absurd to be saluted with a spade' (p.217).

The Labour Front: the fight for workers

Roberts turned towards another Nazi development which was amongst the first to be set up, namely the Labour Front (*Arbeits-front*). As Hitler had forecast in *Mein Kampf*, trade unions would change. It was because the Trade Unions had opposed Nazism that they were banned (2 May 1933) and within four days Robert Ley had taken over at least 169 workers' organisations. Hitler had stated that it was because Nazism had banned class-warfare. Roberts noted that Ley had been more honest when he stated that 'the unions were so many anti-fascist nests', with Roberts adding that the Labour Front was a national takeover of Unions (p.218).

It was claimed, Roberts observed, that Nazi theory was that all workers from the physical labourers to managerial level were the same insofar as they were working for the State. Roberts was told that at that time the Labour Front had some 26,000,000 members, though he warned that these figures were supplied by the Nazis, who claimed it was a separate organisation and not a government department, but Roberts pointed out, almost cynically, that there is close collaboration (p.219). He noted that the leader is Hitler and Robert Ley the executive director, and there was an office to investigate complaints, with Roberts noting it was similar to what the Russians did, though he noted that the Nazis would not like this comparison (p.220). He was told that when complaints were received they were reviewed by committees and there is one token 'official' in every district who gives the final verdict…'there is much talk of the social honour of workmen…the workman may apply to the Court of Honour…but strikes are out of the question because they are viewed as State Sabotage' (p.221). Hitler was achieving all he had projected in his *Mein Kampf*.

In regard to employers, the State classified them as Leaders, but they 'have responsibilities which go with the privilege'. When Roberts raised questions about distressed regions such as Silesia and Westphal his questions were 'not kindly received' (p.222). It was no surprise that Jews were legally forbidden, and 'beyond everything in the German world is the dictatorship of the State, so that even measures which are nominally voluntary (such as Labour Front) have ultimate coercion behind it and everybody knows this' (p.223). It amounted to a rigid form of state control in every aspect of German life, every individual obligated to follow Nazi demands.

Roberts mentioned the 'Strength through Joy' (*Kraft durch Freude* the K.d.F) movement which supplemented wages by offering cheap travel and holidays. The idea was to get workmen away from their everyday surroundings, and Roberts was informed that this year (1936) some 6,000,000 had enjoyed this offer, travelling on vessels to Madeira or Norway with 80 recreation homes built, and he saw many huge holiday buses with the K.d.F. everywhere (p.224). Roberts found it amazing that the effort was supposed to be self-supporting, with the authorities claiming they were even building their own huge liners paid for by the workers (p.225). They were given special seats in the operas and theatres, but more limited in films with only moralised historical presentations being acceptable. Roberts noted that 'if one puts aside the propagandist element, one must admit that this movement is definitely providing facilities that would otherwise not exist' (p.226). The K.d.F organisation also provided cheap sport which bemused the writer as that was different from British life where no such aid was needed. When

Roberts commented on this, he was met with 'kindly sympathy' and told the British were losing the race (p.227). He added that 'I realised that it is one of the most striking forms of social service I had yet seen and, at the same time, a most efficient method of propaganda' (p.228). He was evidently correct that few could criticise such an effort for making a better life for the worker, but also noting its propaganda value. It was excellent propaganda for overseas, and at home it gave the Nazi Party a major boost and for many (but not all) would seem to compensate for the loss of trade unions. Hitler had promised a better life for all, but he had not explained to everyone the future was war.

Women and Population: the fight for the race

Roberts noted that the Nazis never made any bones that a woman's duty is primarily domestic, and that her only interests and activities should revolve around the cult of the *Kinder, Kirche, Küche* (children, church, kitchen). Hitler was recorded in a speech instructing women 'That in my new army I have provided you with the finest fathers of children in the whole world' (p.229) as if that was all they ever needed in life. To his female audience he denied the benefits of higher education, expecting them to make good cooks and prolific mothers, and yet, Roberts observed, 'they cheered him'. Roberts noted that the Nazi organisation had experimented with a Women's Labour Service, but it amounted to a vigorous routine plus exercises and singing. He was taken to one of their hostels outside Berlin where the person in charge told him he was sceptical about the whole project (p.230).

Roberts wrote that in his opinion it was a patronising attitude typical of German men, and he reported that a Scandinavian observer had noted the Nazis were ignoring the potentialities of half their nation, which was an astute observation. For his part, Rudolf Hess had stated that no outside criticism should be raised, because Germany did not comment on other nations' attitudes, and Hitler only wanted to increase the size of the German population. Roberts observed that the plan was failing, and not helped by the demand that this human growth had to be racially acceptable. The Nazi demands had been 'no race pollution' and 'only biologically desirable physical specimens' should bear children. As a consequence of these rulings,

Hereditary Health Courts were set up (p.231), and abortion made an offence, but rewards were given when babies were born (p.232).

Hitler organised a form of national health service but only for the healthy side of society which meant being based on a 'racial and hereditary culture' which remained a priority. In a slightly cynical note Roberts observed that 'the Nazis are raising a generation of blond physical beauties' (p.233), writing that provisions are made for sport and physical training from the kindergarten onwards, and it is little wonder the Germans won much of their Olympics (p.234). Hitler would have been astonished if he had witnessed the rising role of women in the postwar years after 1945, eventuating in a female Chancellor, Angela Merkel.

Public Works and Great Roads: the fight for employment

Public works had been part of the Weimar Republic's policy, but Hitler took a personal interest in this area of the nation's life. He had always considered himself a good artist and saw himself as a potential architect. He was now seeking a great building revival, as well as new roads (p.235). In September 1933 Hitler ceremonially turned the first sod of earth for the new motor roads, which was the beginning of a massive enterprise, demanding a relieved and massive workforce because almost a third of the working population had been unemployed. Roberts noted that those without work or income were always a possible menace to the government with their political activities of resentment, but this work brought them back into the market and reduced their psychology of despair. Roberts believed that Hitler's intention was to use the road system to join north and south and unite Germany. Later others, including a man who quietly spoke to Roberts, would voice the opinion he was seeking the best communication routes for his military forces, telling Roberts to note where the roads led, claiming it could predict Nazi foreign policy (p.239).

Roberts noted this work was done under the well-known Fritz Todt who had drawn up plans for 5,000 miles of new roads, the first of what today are called motorways (p.236). It was a costly enterprise, but Hitler was using cheap labour, and when Roberts was given the financial statistics, it struck him as somewhat 'optimistic' (p.237). He noted that their analysis was far from convincing, and that their Labour Service, which he had observed earlier, was obliged to work on the roads in their semi-military life in barrack-like buildings. He wrote that 'I would say life is hard for a road worker in Germany' adding that 'generally the standard of life is low in their industrial cities' (p.238).

Roberts later found it strange driving on the new roads, especially with the high speeds needing super-charged cars, and Roberts decided that car companies would make money. He wrote that they are efficient but somehow 'needlessly grandiose but most impressive...and somehow seem to reduce the individual to insignificance' and 'rather inhuman'. In 1936 he noted that 600 miles had been finished with another 2,800 miles to go (p.240).

Author's note: *At this stage Roberts turns the reader's attention to the highly significant area which he describes as 'What the Onlooker does not See'.*

The Drive for a Common Mentality: how a nation is hypnotised

Roberts starts this part of his book with an overview of German culture, pointing out that there was no aspect of life which could stand outside of the totalitarian State. The government had established bodies which would cover the entire cultural field, and in October 1933 a Reich Chamber of Culture had been established under the ubiquitous Dr Goebbels (p.241). The Nazis were seeking a uniformed and spirited leadership, but Roberts noted that 'the real aim is to develop culture along national Socialist lines' (p.242). He observed that Hitler, Rosenberg, and von Schirach were Germany's best writer sellers, but noted that '*Mein Kampf* does not sell for its literary merits, that Rosenberg's efforts amount to turgid outpourings, and that Schirach was nothing but the jingles of an undeveloped teenager'. All these efforts, he noted, marked the paucity of literary output in Nazi Germany, which explained the vogue for translating foreign novels, which indicated the German lack of creation (p.244). He wrote that 'Hitlerism was associated with intellectual intolerance from the outset', and 'although they called the elimination of decadent thought as essential', Roberts noted that 'one of the most disgusting episodes of the regime was Goebbels's famous bonfire of undesirable literature' (p.245), though perhaps 'infamous' may have been a more precise description. Roberts had recognised the iron grip that Hitler and his regime had forced upon the German people, writing that the 'rigid control of the mind is so much an engrained principle of National Socialism that it was almost a heresy to question it' (p.246).

Roberts turned to the Press, which in his and other democratic countries was not controlled by the State. A free Press, as in all democratic societies can be both the burden and bulwark of democracy, and only comes under prohibition in times of war, such as the 'D-Notices' in Britain. The President of the German Press Chamber was Max Amann, one of Hitler's old fighters, and only the so-called Aryans could be journalists. When there were protests over this, Goebbels obliged newspapers to give him lists of their shareholders to ensure they were Aryan since the year 1800 (p.247). Summary powers were granted to Amann to sack anyone he doubted, and all newspapers were subordinated to Goebbels's office, which meant even by 1934 a thousand newspapers had been suppressed (p.248).

Many newspapers were forced to unite, even the Nazi ones, Ley's profitable *Der Deutsch* had to give way to Goebbels's *Angriff*. Roberts noted that the face of German journalism had changed, creating 'a deadly uniformity of the press' as they sold 'the same line'. Goebbels claimed it had nothing to do with liberty of opinion, but there were still protests, so it was slightly changed, but everyone had to follow orders, and serious criticism was out of the question, with Roberts noting that 'one misjudgement will lead to a person's downfall' (p.249), which in Nazi terms could range from loss of post, to interrogation by the Gestapo, to Dachau, and even to death.

The editors were therefore obliged to blindly follow Hitler's paper *Völkischer Beobachter*, and events in Russia and Spain could only be written from the Nazi point of view. The natural consequence meant that most Germans thought Russia was a military menace, and Czechoslovakia had permitted the Russians to build airfields along their borders (p.250). Roberts wrote that 'I view this control of the Press, together with the control of the minds of the young, as the most important factor in German life', while Goebbels was busy claiming the liberty of the press as one of the abuses of democracy, because their job is to strengthen the nation, claiming there had to be a process of adaptation (p.251). It had already been argued in *Mein Kampf* that the press was meant to strengthen the nation. Roberts observed that a German journalist had been imprisoned for sharing these views with foreign journalists. Goebbels was stringent in his views, and he was also in charge of broadcasting (p.252).

Germany had over six million radio listeners due to a cheap set authorised by Hitler, but many liked to hear the foreign broadcasts which became illegal. The German public were also subject to another form of radio domination when broadcast systems blasted out propaganda and Nazi speeches in public places. Over this Goebbels had a monopoly for National Socialist ends (p.253).

Roberts noted that most Germans fell victim to all this, because Goebbels had seen the power of propaganda being conveyed through these channels, with Roberts writing that 'we may call it the subordination of the truth to propaganda; he describes it as employing a mighty weapon in the interest of the nations' (p.254). It was once again a signal of the grip the Nazi Party held over the thinking process and views of the bulk of the population.

Roberts wrote that 'the Nazis laid a heavy hand on education', even using military scenarios such as 'bomber planes' to test time and distance equations in mathematics. He found that at the age of six years the Nazis were portrayed in such way that Hitler was idolised, and they were taught to think of Hitler 'in the way we regard Christ and His disciples' (p.254). Roberts could clearly see that 'the whole of their education is tendentious', and he was asked by one historian 'what is the difference between 'propaganda in peacetime and wartime?' (p.255), as if that explained everything. Roberts found that most scholarships were reserved for Party members, that non-Aryans were excluded with many German teachers adopting a defeatist attitude (p.256). He then added the line that 'I have seen curricula from working-class schools of Berlin and Hamburg that are grotesque travesties on education' (p.257), and in this comment it must not be forgotten that Roberts was a highly professional educationalist.

In this chapter Roberts clearly demonstrated the dangers of what might be called the governmental grip on the German mind, heart, and soul. Goebbels was the leading figure in much of this process, dictating which books should be read while burning others, and which films were acceptable. Individuals were no longer to make their own choices or form their own opinions. He controlled the press and broadcasting, and German education was obligated to follow Nazi propaganda from the infant school upwards. Roberts understood and successfully conveyed the image of total Nazi control, and the danger of producing Nazi robots and worshippers instead of a free society. This was a stark warning to the international community that the Nazi movement was not going to fall at an election or be crushed by a revolution, and in any war the young would be fervent in serving their leader.

The Present Place of Jews

And Roberts wrote that the treatment of the Jews and the 'degrading anti-Semitic measures of the Hitlerite government have made the name of National Socialism despised throughout the world'. He examined Hitler's case, noting that there may be only one Jew in every 100 German people, but they held a peculiar position. One of the problems Roberts noted was Germany's place on the geographical European map, as it meant eastern European eastern Jews fled to Germany [from the Russian and Polish pogroms] and had mainly congregated in Berlin. It was believed they had no disposition to work the land or labour, and they had taken all the professional positions (p.258). It was not regarded as an asset as it was argued they had taken the principal posts in all professions by personal influence, and Nazism associated them with Russian communism, as they had purportedly taken over the theatres, newspapers, education, and the law (p.259). They were also accused of being involved in political activities with constant reference to a Jewish communist revolution (p.260).

Roberts wrote that 'on analysis it waters down to very little except racial prejudice' pointing out that Hitler from the start screamed there could be no good Jews, thereby condemning 600,000 human beings irrespective of their abilities and individuality. He constantly stated that Jewish blood contaminates and pursued the atavistic doctrine of blood and soil (p.261).

Roberts using the language of the day referred to the 'Jew baiting', which was growing with Hitlerism, reaching its nadir with Julius Streicher's anti-Semitic paper *Der Stürmer*. Roberts described the obscene cartoon type caricatures of Jewish people as 'monstrous cartoons', noting that the Nuremberg Race Laws reduced the Jewish element to serfdom, and forbade interbreeding, amounting to an obnoxious law (p.262). He pointed out that in Nazi Germany no Jew had any civil rights or could hold any position. Those who were starving were refused any aid, and he suggested 'it is a campaign of annihilation – a pogrom of the crudest form, supported by every State instrument'. This was a prescient view in 1936 because as is now well-known the annihilation of the Jewish race was Hitler's obsession resulting in the Holocaust. He saw that many local areas boasted they were Jew free, yet he estimated there were more than half a million Jews still living in Germany (p.263). He wrote that 'I met nobody in Germany who adopted an apologetic attitude – nobody who saw anything wrong in the attack' and everywhere there were notices forbidding Jews, such as 'no Jews or wandering animals allowed in these precincts', cynically wondering if this grouping were intentional (p.264). Roberts rightly pulled no punches on this irrational and immoral crusade, stating that 'the most tragic thought of all is that Germany is behind Hitler in his campaign' (p.266), and it 'is the measure of the New Germany's degradation' (p.267).

The Nazi degradation of Jewish people which Roberts focused on was generally known about at the international level, and during the 1936 Berlin Olympics it was observed that it was temporarily suspended for the sake of German reputation. This action tended to reveal the fundamental fact that even the Nazi adherents knew it was unacceptable, and other national governments should have been more aware that the new German regime was criminal and immoral, a government which in terms of negotiations and trust could only be viewed as worthless. This insight by Roberts turned him to the next section of his analysis.

Swastika Versus Cross

Roberts wrote that in Nazi Germany 'it is the age-old struggles between laws temporal and laws spiritual, a struggle in which neither side can surrender without sacrificing its principles'. He noted that ironically Article 24 of the Party Programme stated, 'the Party is built on the base of a positive Christianity' (p.268), which, with the benefit of hindsight, is virtually outrageous.

Roberts argued that it was impossible for a man to be a good Nazi and a good Catholic, and 'Hitler felt that he had evolved a force greater than that of any religion' with von Schirach and Himmler developing their puerile neo-paganism themes (p.269). Hitler had claimed that 'we wish for no other God than Germany', while Schirach was busy telling the Hitler youth 'I am neither a Catholic nor a Protestant; I am a National Socialist' (p.270).

Hitler had several times claimed he wanted nothing to do with Church matters, but he appointed Pastor Ludwig Müller (a 50-year-old army chaplain whom Hitler liked) of the Lutherans as the Bishop of the Reich, who announced his changes from Luther's pulpit (p.271). Hitler was wanting a National Socialist Church, but his efforts failed because the evangelical wing knew their religious liberties were threatened. They took a stand led by Martin Niemöller, who had been a tough ex-naval submariner from the First World War (p.272). Hitler gave Müller the right to sack anyone, but the Lutheran Church split and survived (p.273). Roberts somehow estimated that 'less than one Bavarian pastor in twenty favoured the Reich Church' (p.274). Pastor Niemöller was powerful in his objections and the new Confessional Church continued to challenge Hitler when he interfered in their faith.

In the meantime, Roberts noted 'the organisation of the pagans was called the German Faith Movement'. Its prophet was Wilhelm Hauer, described by Roberts as a theological professor, but who, in fact, was a mere writer on religious matters, and who preached the idea of an Aryan faith, claiming that 'the real Deity was the spirit of the race'. In such proclamations he almost rivalled Rosenberg. However, Roberts observed that 'on the whole it may be said that the neo-pagan movement has no real strength in Germany', but added the urgent warning that the youth were susceptible to its influence (p.276).

Various pastors published their views in a public statement, calling on all protestants to 'defend their Christianity against the folkic and totalitarian claims of the Nazi Party', which given the power of Nazism was a brave stand (p.277). This led Hitler to reconsider his position, because having to stand against such theologians as Karl Barth and Martin Dibelius would be challenging and might undermine his popularity. To meet him part way they assured Hitler that they would support him in his stand against communism (p.278).

The Lutheran Church was very German, but the Roman Catholic Church was international, they could never submit to state control, and there was no question over their leadership, and in 1936 Roberts noted that Hitler had made no attempt to dragoon them (p.279). He did, however, send von Papen to arrange a concordat, maintaining that Hitler would not interfere in their church so long as their priests did not meddle in politics, which Rome found acceptable. Nevertheless, the fight against Nazi behaviour continued, led by some brave Catholic Bishops, but the Nazis insisted their youth organisations become part of the Hitler Youth (p.280).

Roberts noted that the current dictum was 'To serve Hitler is to serve Germany; to serve German is to serve God', adding that 'no Church can accept such impious reasoning' (p.281). Often in history the church and a nation's political body has clashed, the Church has sometimes become a servant of the State, but the Nazi obsession with its leaning towards the old tribal paganism was a warning to international observers that this regime was intellectually primitive. It was also another aspect of the Nazi grip on the public mind, and even this religious aspect should have been sending warning signals that this infestation was potentially dangerous, as even children suffering from mental instability in their communities could be in danger.

Law as a Political Instrument

Roberts wrote that 'the Nazi theory is that law is merely a weapon in the political struggle', which Hitler endorsed in a speech in March 1933. It meant, Roberts argued, that 'in other words, that the same crime would be a different offence if committed by a well-meaning Nazi', and also the law could be retrospective, so a man could be hanged for an offence, which when it was committed, carried only a light sentence. Naturally, Roberts observed that a general amnesty would be given to those Nazis who committed offences during the struggle for power (p.282). Roberts pointed out that 'Hitler's conception of law, as primarily a political weapon, has set the clock of the jurists back to the eighteenth century, back to the days of irresponsible despots', and a People's Court was set up in April 1934 to deal with treason cases (p.283); from his opening lines Roberts was clearly outlining the Nazi corruption of the Rule of Law.

Roberts explained that propaganda displayed these views as a part of 'national Ethics as a source of Law and the distinction between law and morality is done away with', with Hitler claiming it must be based on common sense, 'so that depends on the judge', who, Roberts pertinently argued, will presumably base it on whether it is in the interests of the Nazi regime (p.284). When the 'law is personal, emotional, political' Roberts argued this belief represented 'the law of the cave man', noting that 'the German legal system today is but the servant of the administration'. A servant of the Party can escape the penalties, making it so absurd it is hardly believable.

Roberts noted that 'we have the evidence of the new penal code' with the Nazi claiming that 'the Penal Code is an expression of the moral standard of the nation' (p.285). He pointed out that the new Code is based on the spirit of the law rather than the letter, so they also reject that a petty criminal's poverty background is an excuse, and surroundings do not count, claiming he is just a degenerate (p.286).

Apparently, according to Roberts, there was no need for uniform punishments for the same crimes, and one must always be conscious that one is breaking the law. The code embodied novel punishments, 'the most severe is decapitation, and the hard labour must be genuinely hard' (p.287). It was a matter of the protection of Honour, so serious 'punishments are given to those who insult the German nation or Hitler', because the keynote for the Nazis was loyalty to the nation, its leader, and the Aryan race (p.288).

Roberts added that 'it is no wonder that an eminent British authority recently stated that the Rule of Law, as we know it, has disappeared from Germany', Roberts adding that 'for National Socialism the law is but its maidservant', with Göring stating 'the law and the will of Hitler are one'(p.290).

This question of the new German law was another aspect of the Nazi grip on power, which after Roberts had left Germany, would increase exponentially with the subjugation of the populace with the fear of the rising powers of the Gestapo and SD, who would be able to interpret the law whichever way suited their purposes.

Chapter Five

Hitlerism and the World

General Foreign Policy

Roberts observed there was a conflict of policies in the Wilhelmstrasse explaining that Hitler's foreign policy had first been based on undoing point by point the Versailles Treaty, to later wanting to expand from the German cramped frontiers. The Germans, Hitler had argued, are a people of destiny in a decadent world, and this conviction was based on the belief that everything goes to the man with the greatest force. This naturally presupposed that the validity of treaties cannot be taken for granted, and the old diplomacy systems would go by the board, with Roberts noting that the dictator will blunder through complex problems with a resounding blow (p.293).

Roberts wrote that there were others who supported this reasoning, believing a strong leadership can bring profits, and international 'powers will be content to offer bribes to keep out' of the possible mess. He added that Germany can bluff by bringing about a *fait accompli*, sometimes relying on divisions amongst her opponents, or offering an ultimatum, the biggest card in the opportunist's pack. He added that there are the imperialists and pan-Germanists who all want expansion, some like Rosenberg wanting to head east, some south to the Balkans, and some like Ribbentrop seeking Anglo-German co-operation. Roberts claimed Hitler listened to all of them, presenting himself with a vast reserve of opportunities. He further added that Hitler relied on instinct and political gains, and as a demigod he had neither the mentality nor the facilities to analyse a grave international issue, and to date, Roberts noted, he has gone no further than repudiate the Versailles Treaty (p.295).

Roberts described Hitler's methods of using what he called thunderbolts, describing this policy with five examples. The first was on 14 Oct 1933, when Germany left the League of Nations and Disarmament Conference. Secondly, on 16 March 1935, he had announced universal conscription looking to an army of 36 Divisions, thereby repudiating Part V of the Versailles Treaty. Thirdly, on 7 March 1936, he reoccupied the Rhineland (articles 42–3 of Treaty). Fourthly, on 30 November 1936, he seized control of the rivers, and finally, as Roberts was finishing his book, on 30 January 1937, Hitler withdrew the signatures from Versailles and declared the Treaty as finished. It was all based on the Nazi belief that they had been betrayed as the Allies had purportedly broken their promise to disarm and were, to use the age-old excuse, encircling Germany (p.296).

In January 1934 Hitler had signed a non-aggression pact with Poland guaranteeing peace for 10 years. It was believed that France had been busy hemming in Germany with treaties, and Roberts knew that Hitler was turning to 'the dangerous waters of Austria, which had failed first time after the assassination of Dollfuss' in July 1934. Roberts rightly admitted that 'Germany had much cause for complaint…no proud nation could endure the yoke of the treaties' and his hint that the French had not helped carried much weight (p.297).

The Macdonald Peace Plan of March 1933 had not helped the situation, with Germany technically deprived of all military planes which had been demanded for defensive means, and France countered these plans and would only accept 200,000 German soldiers. Roberts pointed out that Hitler wanted equal rights, adding that 'one must admit that the thinly veiled hypocrisy of the French arguments at this period did much to produce the German exasperation, as the German military needed real tanks not dummies (p.298). It had been the breakdown of these interchanges, Roberts argued, which meant that Germany accelerated the pace of her surreptitious rearmament. Contrary to Roberts' view it could be argued, but only with the benefit of hindsight, that Hitler did not need any excuses to build up the German military and its resources. There were international protests about Germany's conscription, but they were ignored causing concern, and all these efforts by the Nazis hastened negotiations between the other nations, which Roberts wrote, 'meant that Germany really was encircled' (p.299).

International activity and friction were now redeveloping. Hitler had accepted the Naval Agreement with Britain on 18 June 1935 [to French annoyance with the British] but meanwhile all eyes were on Mussolini busy invading Abyssinia. The Stresa Front (between Britain, France, Italy aimed at

Nazi Germany) was seen by some historical commentators as the last means to close down the Nazi threat. Following the Rhineland Occupation Hitler had told the public he was tearing up the Versailles and Locarno Treaties, and he called an election with 98.81 per cent voting for him, Roberts noting that 'it would have been miraculous if they had not done so on such an issue'. There were notes of protests at the League of Nations, but it was noticed that Britain did not feel strongly on the matter (p.301). Roberts noted that in terms of the Rhineland Hitler had taken the chance 'that the nations would not go to war to keep Germany out of her own territory, and events proved him right' (p.302).

On 21 May 1935, Hitler made a security pact with Lithuania but not Russia, and Roberts commented 'there was much to justify the French contention that they gave a temporary peace in the west while allowing Hitler a free hand to shape his destiny in the east'. The Soviets soon noted this possible policy, while the French suggested some mutual assistance pacts within the league amounting to agreements there should be no territorial changes for 25 years. However, they then pursued 'an untenable idea of a commission of control', and Britain sent Hitler a questionnaire about peace plans, but Hitler never replied (p.303). Roberts thought that Hitler was more concerned with the erection of a Front against Bolshevism (p.304).

In Spain there was more chaos with growing Civil War, and Roberts believed Germany 'sees herself as the guardian of European civilisation against the oncoming wave of destructive Bolshevism' as Hitler announced the time had come to overturn the Versailles Treaty. However, he added the pertinent conclusion that 'it is inconceivable that any other Power should take her word as binding when she has treated her past engagements so lightly' (p.305).

Roberts had ably demonstrated that 'the milestones of Hitler's four years of power are broken treaties; and on each occasion Europe was deliberately threatened with the spectre of war', and today Germany is now 'encircled not because of the malice of her enemies but solely because of the fears aroused by the so-called surprises' adding that 'if ever there is a country without friends, that country is Germany today' (p.306). At the time of writing the Munich crisis was still distant, and had Chamberlain read Roberts' analysis he may well have emerged from his shell earlier and seen the danger of Hitler, and he would have known that the much-hoped Munich Conference would be a matter of paradise lost.

The Soviet Bogey in Theory and Fact

Roberts wrote that Germany thought that she alone was awake to the menace of Moscow Comintern, seeing it as a disruptive force. He decided the trouble was that the Germans look back to their own civil war with their communists, and they take in all Goebbels's propaganda which 'tickles their feeling of racial superiority to think they are the first, the only people in Europe to realise the menace' (p.307). Roberts wrote that 'a cardinal feature of the bitterness between Germany and Russia is that it is most convenient for both sets of dictators', as they find it difficult to find emotional propaganda. He noted that this 'friction between Germany and Russia is the most demanding element in European affairs', and is the third of Hitler's hates, the first two being Jews and the Treaty of Versailles (p.308).

Roberts expressed his view that it was difficult to see why this tension between the two powers continued. He noted that the so-called proofs put forward by Goebbels and Rosenberg at Rallies 'are nothing more than a collection of unproven assertions', which started in Germany, and were mainly based on Marx being Jewish. There was no doubt for Roberts that Germany was looking east, even to lands beyond the Ukraine. Following the Treaty of Brest-Litovsk, Roberts believed Germany had anticipated a German gateway to the vast plains. However, a neutrality treaty was signed in April 1926 and extended in 1931 by Hitler himself (p.309). Trade between Germany and Russia continued between the two, but Russian concern started Stalin to reach out towards Paris and Prague (p.310). It was curious given the ideological class and all-round bigotry that trade between the two countries was expanding. Roberts noted that the German army thought the Russian one good, and even wondered whether a German-Russian bloc could dominate the world (p.311). However, Roberts noted that despite the trade deals 'the anti-Bolshevik tirades in Germany have lost none of their force' (p.312), and never would as later Operation Barbarossa would prove.

The Lost Germans

Roberts had visited the Feldherrnhalle (Hall of Field Marshals) in Munich which the Nazis had taken over for a shrine, for those who had given their lives in the Nazi cause. He noticed that there were lists of territories which were no longer part of Germany (1936), including ten areas which were supposed to have been torn from the body of Germany, and although they were all grouped together, not all arose because of Versailles, so it amounted to a list of so-called territorial grievances (p.313).

He noted that the first article in the Party programme read, 'We demand the union of all Germans to form a Great Germany on the basis of the right of self-determination of nations' which was based on Pan-Germanism (to unify all Germans). Roberts reminded his readers that for Hitler, Race and Nationality were synonymous, and that a State must be racially homogeneous, and for Germany it therefore had no minorities and Jews were not counted. Roberts added the warning that 'National Socialism without a racial basis is unthinkable', and while the Versailles Treaty had taken some lands, 'others were Germanic by race' (p.314). Pan-Germanism was claiming all these areas, with Roberts reminding the reader that in Austria there were 6,500,000 German speakers, and there were many others spread right across central Europe from France to Russia (p.315).

There were 15,000,000 so-called Germans outside Hitler's borders which were regarded as the 'lost Germans'. Hitler, Roberts warned, was not concerned about colonies until Europe had settled its Pan-Germanism as 'an active and immediate political force in Europe' (p.316). Roberts wrote that 'Germany works up campaigns only for the Sudeten Germans in Czechoslovakia who receive (relatively at least) the best treatment of all the lost peoples'. He also noted that much therefore is also raised about those in Danzig and Memel, but 'their actual sufferings do not matter; the cynical truth being that each group of 'lost Germans' are used as pawns on the wider chessboard of diplomatic Realpolitik (p.317).

Roberts was presenting serious warnings, without expressing them too openly, of the element of dangerous irredentist nationalism raising its head. This is a form of nationalism which demands, by force, when necessary, the return of territories which once or were presumed to be part of a nation's natural landscape. For Germany this included Baltic areas, Czechoslovakia, Poland, Austria, and parts of France. It would be this policy of irredentist nationalism which would lead to the catastrophe of the Second World War. There were many in Britain, France, and many European countries who were concerned about the German build-up of arms, but Roberts was carefully outlining the emotional reasons behind the Nazi thinking, which was far more important than counting the number of German tanks. Tanks and planes may win a war, but the thought processes of the potential enemy first need the closest scrutiny, which Roberts was providing either directly or between the lines.

The Southern Danger Zones

Austria was a complex puzzle for the Nazis, and Roberts claimed that Hitler preferred the south, with Bavaria and Austria, and disliked Berlin, preferring southerners to Prussians. Hitler always liked the Austrian Nazis, and he had long wanted an *Anschluss*, which as Roberts noted, so did many Austrians but mainly from an economic point of view (p.318). Following the Dollfuss death it had not augured well for the Nazi Party as many citizens were indignant about the assassination, and Hitler's disavowal of the deed had done little to help. Dr Kurt Schuschnigg had maintained the ban on the Nazi Party, stating the country's three foes were Communism, Nazism, and indifference (p.319). The Austrian government, Roberts noted, had so far maintained a precarious isolationism. However, Schuschnigg had managed on 11 July 1936 to reach an Austrian German Agreement in which Germany recognised Austrian sovereignty. Roberts took a holiday stop in a Tyrolean village above Innsbruck, where he noted the Nazis were not strong (p.320). The place, like many others had its political divisions, with Roberts commenting that it was the young Nazi hotheads who resented Hitler seemingly disavowing their effort to kill Dollfuss. There were many government supporters in the village, who told him that 'our souls are still our own', and he found out that the local postmaster had blocked his letter going to the Nazi HQ in Munich. Roberts discovered that these locals knew they were a buffer between Germany and Italy (p.321).

Generally, Roberts concluded that 'on the whole, I should say that Austria wants Germanism but not Hitlerism, and it will be a long time before an Austrian Nazi Party becomes popular' (p.322). Nevertheless, he noted that the 'well-oiled machinery of Nazi propaganda continues to pour out its material', adding that their dilemma is insoluble, across the Brenner is Fascism and across the Inn is Hitlerism' (p.323). When Hitler later authorised the *Anschluss* in March 1938, Roberts, safely tucked away in Australia, would have been as surprised as the American journalist William Shirer was, at the prompt anti-Semitism of the Austrians, with Shirer writing 'What one now saw in Vienna was almost unbelievable. The Viennese, usually so soft and sentimental, were behaving worse than the Germans, especially towards the Jews'.[1]

Roberts was told by a Czech diplomat that the Austrian and Czech borders formed the central axis of European affairs, and that Hitler saw it as a place which had 'wrenched three and a half million Germans away' from their homeland. The Czechs, Roberts noted, were confident of their new-born nationality, and 'the Germans had reasons for resentment,' and much of 'Konrad Henlein's (Sudeten German politician and Nazi) subsequent misery propaganda is based on fact' (p.324). Painful as this may be to the modern reader the Czech government had not overseen the new area well. German schools were closed, and the Czechs 'foolishly adopted a policy of unification instead of federalism'. The Germans lodged 19 petitions before the League of Nations but with no result, and Henlein rallied them into the SDP (*Sudeten Deutsche Partei*) although he personally lacked, Roberts noted, the fanaticism of the Nazi leader (p.325). The Czechs had believed he wanted separation, and President Beneš refused to listen despite professing some sympathy for the more moderate claims (p.326). The Nazis played on the various grievances, turning a local problem into a disturbing international issue, with endless bombardments in the controlled press. Beneš allayed much of the discontent by abandoning the earlier centralising policy of Tomáš Masaryk, and it was, Roberts observed, 'doubtful if the great mass of Sudeten Germans would have favoured a secessionist movement against the Prague Government (p.327).

The Nazis mounted the pressure claiming that the 'Bolshevik Dagger is at our Throat'. In 1936, during Roberts' visit, the German press became more bitter, claiming the Czechs were pawns of the Jewish-Bolshevists, allowing myths of Russian aerodromes to be built, insinuating the threats that Dresden and Munich could be bombed in minutes, and on top of this, they had new strategic railways forming an axial corridor with Russia (p.328). Roberts observed the German Press was hysterical, while the Czech government denied their claims. The overall effect was to throw the Czechs more into the arms of France and Russia, and their Pact with Russia was seen as an aggressive one when it was only defensive (p.329).

Roberts observed that the Czechs had based their hopes on Russian support. The Russians were receiving armaments credit because Czechoslovakia was wealthy and strong with a good industry (p.330). More to the point Roberts as early as 1936 wrote that 'if Germany persists in wanting to absorb the Sudeten Deutsche it means war' (p.331), and he was proved correct a few years later.

The Baltic Pressure Points

Hitler had constantly protested against the cleavage of East Prussia, but Roberts noted that the corridor had been quiet, apart from economic disputes, and that Danzig was a free city protected by the League of Nations (p.332). There had been free elections which gave the Nazis a clear majority, and the Communist Party had been banned in May 1934. By March 1937, the Nazis only needed two votes for a two-thirds majority which Roberts wondered would lead to a single party state. He noted that it was an international problem as it came under the League of Nations (p.333). The idea of a putsch seemed slight, but Roberts wrote that 'I found an astonishingly widespread impression that Hitler could successfully carry off a coup in Danzig without any real fear of a war' (p.334).

Roberts was aware that the Germans felt bitter about Memel as it was regarded as belonging to East Prussia (since 1252), and the Germans claimed it was only because Lithuania wanted a window on the Baltic, with Germany arguing that most of the residents were German (p.335). Again, Roberts observed that the Lithuanian government were far from sensitive, and acted in dictatorial fashion by removing German schools, refusing to recognise the German language, and they dissolved the Diet. In addition to this they tried some 126 Germans for treason, four were to be executed, but the protests were loud, so they became life-sentences. All this became very bitter in their 1935 elections (p.336). From the German point of view, Roberts pointed out that it was Germany's best 'jumping-off area for an eastern expansion…and could be a place to bottle up the Russian fleet'. Germany had long known that with the Baltic States Germany could hold a dagger at Russia's throat (p.337). Hitler, Roberts warned, had claimed Lithuania was a Russian outpost, with the usual story they had aerodromes there. The final problem, Roberts wrote, was those German elements in

Memel were not united in their desire to come back to Germany, noting with some irony, that part of the German national anthem. *Deutschland über alles*, had the line 'from the Maas to Memel' (p.338).

Roberts explored the enigma of Poland, observing that it was its bastions which kept Russia and Germany apart, and that it had long been a buffer state. He knew that Hitler wanted to drive a wedge between the French and the Poles, but Roberts had picked up that there was a general feeling in Poland that Germany would respect the non-aggression pact which would run until 1944 (p.339). Roberts was well alert to the situation and wrote that 'all that one can say is that, in case of any major upheaval in eastern Europe, Poland's attitude is highly problematical'. Poland had wavered in her policy for years, and at the moment the army was pro-French but there were signs that the Poles were more worried by the Soviets than Hitler (p.340), and a few years later (September 1939) they would be right to have been worried by both.

Germany's second hope in the Baltic was Finland, where Baron Mannerheim had freed Finland from the Russians and their fear of communism which had led to a fascist movement known as Lappo [The Lapua Movement; fascist, anti-communist, pro-German, which was only active between 1929–32] wanting a Greater Fascist Finland (p.340). Roberts also noted that most of the Baltic States had some form of authoritarian government (p.341).

Germany and Western Europe

Roberts turned his attention to what he called the 'Obstacle of France', noting that during his four years in power Hitler had been diplomatically correct towards France, but warning that in *Mein Kampf*, he had clearly indicated he had little time for the French, seeing them as encircling him with pacts even on the eastern borders. Hitler wanted to 'smash these pacts', recalling that in *Mein Kampf* he wrote that 'France is and remains by far the most terrible enemy' and 'they are becoming negrified [sic] with the aims of Jewish world domination' (p.342): his bigotry was simply mind-boggling. Hitler felt that 'the inexorable and deadly enemy of the German people is and remains France' and the Maginot Line must be countered. He added that this demanded force, and he had even 'ranted about it at his trial… the French, he said, were responsible for the Versailles Treaty…they had formed the Russian pact...and felt they were weaker than the Germans' (p.343). Hitler believed that France's commitment was so wide that they would even become involved in eastern Europe, but whichever way Hitler looked to the future it appeared to his thinking that the French were always in the way (p.344).

In the Rome-Berlin Axis, Roberts claimed Italy and Germany were flung together by a general antagonism concerning their foreign policies. Inter-German and Italian diplomatic visits started with distinguished visits by people like Ciano. Roberts would later perhaps read Ciano's diary and discover that Mussolini's son-in-law and foreign minister was soon to hold low opinions about Hitler. The main focus at this time was on the Italian occupation of Abyssinia and Franco's civil war in Spain, and in the latter case with both Hitler and Mussolini offering support at the same time (p.344). However, even at this stage Roberts recorded that the Germans had little faith in Italian fighting power, noting that 'the two countries are only in harmony because of their common enemies'. Roberts wondered if an immediate threat might draw them together, despite Mussolini's critical estimate of Hitler. He further raised the issue that Germany and Italy were partners in dividing Europe on doctrinal differences, with Germany grumbling over Italy's new understanding with Yugoslavia, and noting there were significant differences between the two dictators (p.345), which with hindsight has proved how perceptive he was.

The Colonial Question

Roberts turned again to the post-First World War treatment of Germany, when on 7 May 1919, the Council of Three decided to deprive Germany of her colonies on the grounds of 'colonial unworthiness', which Roberts wrote was 'still an occasion for mourning in Germany', adding that especially when a country like Portugal was allowed to keep her colonies. He noted that Germany had built up a colonial empire of a million square miles, five times larger than the Reich, but most of her possessions were 'undesirable', implying they held little economic benefits. Germany had invested £20,000,000 in them and they cost more than she received, and in 1914 they only provided 1 per cent of Germany's total trade. Roberts also claimed that before the war ended, the Allies had secretly decided to share them out, which he described as hypocritical, and with some justification (p.346).

Roberts pointed out that Schacht had organised nation-wide propaganda long before the 'Hitlerites' had thought about it, which was perhaps no surprise because in his *Mein Kampf* Hitler had showed no interest in the colonies, because pan-Germanism came first. He had allowed Ritter von Epp to organise a colonial department, but in 1934 Hitler was still divided on the matter, whereas Göring, son of a Colonial Governor, supported von Epp (p.347).

On this issue Roberts wrote there was no uniformity in the Party, and Darré said they should only think of the Reich in Europe. Hitler had said we 'are finally done with the pre-war colonial and trade policy', though he returned to it in the 1934 Rally, but in a half-hearted way. Hitler appeared uncertain and he looked at it diplomatically suggesting 'colonial equality', but by 1935 was seeing the issue as part of the national honour, with von Epp adding the 'bread and honour' theme (p.348). Schacht continued to argue that the colonies would provide raw materials, because German excess in population needed this support. Schacht's propaganda intensified during 1936, and consequently some Germans thought it might lead them out from their economic problems. Meanwhile the official German press 'made virulent attacks on the colonial guilt clause' (p.349), and this culminated in Göring's famous speech on 28 October 1936, that they should follow England and France and simply take what they wanted. Goebbels followed by staying 'we will, of course, take up the fight against the world for our colonies', but the British Ambassador responded that they could not accept the implications, and Roberts noted that at least the German viewpoint was now known (p.350), implying a form of world domination.

The main area of concern for Germany was south-west Africa, and many international observers believed this area would revert to Germany, notably in Tanganyika where there were five million natives and fewer than 8,500 Europeans (p.352). Roberts observed that 'Schacht's argument that colonies are essential to the economic recovery of Germany is completely untenable', but also noted that the colonial question had become a one-off issue in terms of national prestige and diplomacy, though it was note-worthy that Hitler had made no formal demands for their return (p.355).

There were, Roberts suggested, three arguments against giving them back to Germany: first, she was unfit to rule, two, she agreed to their loss in the Treaty; and finally, the natives may not want this, not that they were asked in 1919. The British had suggested a plebiscite, but Germany responded that this was hypocritical (p.356).

When Roberts, himself with a German grandfather, and product of the British colonies decided colonial redistribution was one of the world's greatest problems (p.358), he was correct, and it became a major issue in the decades following the Second World War. However, Roberts made it abundantly clear that Hitler, who was the driving force, had his mind turned towards pan-Germanism first, but to be followed by German expansionism in Europe.

Conclusion by Roberts

Roberts wrote that it was impossible to give a final evaluation of the socialist revolution in Germany, but he noted that it was 'inconceivable that Nazidom shall remain in its present inchoate stage'. The only question he raised was whether 'the mind which wrote *Mein Kampf* had changed'. He did not think this was the case, as Hitler was now a popular dictator, developing an Army state which was growing in power and keeping the Führer as the figurehead (p.359). On the assumption that people had read *Mein Kampf*, which few had, this was a clear warning that the outside world was dealing with an abnormal leader, supported by a few henchmen made from his own corrupt mould.

Roberts noted the cumbrousness of the present Party would need pruning, but more to the point he wrote that Hitlerism would become a reversionary process going back before Weimar days. Roberts could have argued that Hitler with his atavistic attitude was almost returning to the pagan tribal era. Roberts found it difficult to explain why the mass of people had accepted the restrictions on their liberties, especially in the matters of religion. He thought the only explanation was the restoration of national pride, believing army rule would lower the emotional tempo of the New Germany. Roberts rightly believed that it was always the uncertain and unpredictable that caused the trouble in international affairs, this had been Hitler's greatest menace in the past. Many felt, Roberts continued, that Hitler was now an army spokesman with Germany becoming an army state unless war enters as a complicating factor (p.361). It was not that Hitler was an army spokesman, but that he was subjugating the military to his wishes, and in a few years, Roberts was correct that Hitler had changed Germany into a military and police State with himself in total control. The masses had initially followed Hitler because of his dreamlike promises and his ability to overturn the humiliating and poverty-inducing Treaty of Versailles. Later, beyond Roberts' time in Germany, when some started to doubt Nazism, they were in turn subjugated to silence by the fear of this police state, with the word Gestapo remaining as a word which even today still implies terror.

Roberts wrote that Hitler may achieve one goal by consolidating the entire nation along the lines he wanted, but he warned that 'if so the outlook for peace would still be clouded' especially 'if he persists in the policies he has enunciated, he will plunge Europe into war; if he abandons them, he can no longer maintain his position within Germany'. Many Germans thought 'he could obtain this by simply demanding rather than face war' [p.362], which was based on taking back the Rhineland and enhanced at the Munich Conference a few years later. Roberts could not be clearer in his stark warnings when he wrote that 'from whatever angle we approach the question, then, we come to the inevitability of war unless Hitler modifies his teachings and methods or unless there is a peaceful transition to some other regime'. He then added that 'the position reduces itself to this. Hitlerism cannot achieve its aims without war; its ideology is that of war', adding that 'the nation has been duped into the sense that it has been launched along a road that can only lead to disaster' (p.363) which was not a prophecy but based on sound reasoning.

Part V

Final Observations

The 1930s was a time of total confusion, divided opinions, hesitation, indecision, and deep uncertainty in Britain and in France. France and Britain had been traditional enemies for at least nine centuries, and the Napoleonic attempt to dominate Europe was ended at the Battle of Waterloo by the British and the Prussians. The twentieth century started with the *Entente Cordiale* (8 April 1904), and the French and British became firm allies during the First World War against Germany. Many of the problems on how to understand and deal with the rise of Nazism in Germany were not helped by some continuing diplomatic tensions between these two Western powers of France and Britain.

It has been noted that 'historians are very far from reaching any consensus about French policy before the war, since research had proceeded in several different directions'.[1] Amongst the speculations, it has been suggested that 'if Chamberlain had joined forces with the French and threatened war instead of opening negotiations, Hitler might have been forced to back down'.[2] The confusion over French views persists in historical accounts, with one historian noting that Daladier was more of the realist, and he knew 'that Hitler intended to destroy Czechoslovakia, and that his word could not be relied upon', seemingly much more aware of Hitler's personal driving forces than the British.[3] Another view was that the French were convinced appeasers, 'like its British counterpart, were an amalgam of many influences. Fear of Germany did not exclude a genuine desire for Franco-German reconciliation'. Secondly, 'by encouraging and exploiting British leadership France provided herself with a perfect pretext for disengagement from Central and Eastern Europe'; thirdly, French statesmen although 'cabined by circumstances' could have done more by their 'diplomatic and military advantages'.[4] The French had offered support to Czechoslovakia but Chamberlain 'refused to consider giving a British guarantee to Czechoslovakia, or to France in support of her obligations under the Czech alliance'.[5] The divisions between the Western powers were to persist into the phoney war, and postwar under de Gaulle, the relationship between France and Britain was never a case of genuine fraternity. Hitler in the 1930s recognised this feature, interpreting it as a sign of weakness, seeing Chamberlain's only weapon as his umbrella, and heeding Ribbentrop's advice that neither France nor Britain would dare declare war. The French public and political leaders were as divided as the British, with pacifism growing in popularity after the devastation of the First World War, but the failure of the politicians to work closely and in harmony led only to indecisive reactions in the various stages of crisis, as both French and British leaders may have known what was happening in Germany's build-up of military power, but they had limited knowledge and awareness of the man Adolf Hitler and his constructed regime.

In the appeasement lobby the critical figure was the British Prime Minister Neville Chamberlain, over whom, as with the French relationship just mentioned, there are diverse views and varying historical perspectives, not least with the figure of Churchill lurking in the background demanding preparation for war. Colville wrote 'One of Hitler's cleverest moves has been to make Winston Public Enemy Number One, because this fact had helped to make him Public Hero Number One at home and in the USA', which illustrated the political war zones in the House of Commons.[6] It has been argued by some historians that Chamberlain 'was a man of limited insight and imagination, repeatedly prone to wishful thinking', he also 'put too great a burden on his own abilities…he stubbornly refused to recognise reality'.[7] The problem was that Chamberlain was a driven man, driven by the ideals of peace, but the reality he and many others failed to recognise was the fundamental nature of Hitler and his created regime. As such the criticism that 'he put too great a burden on his own abilities' may well have been correct. As raised in the main text of this study there are, as always, many opinions of Chamberlain the man. Some seeing him as a highly moral person driven by the ideal for peace between nations, some seeing him as a 'blinkered horse' only seeing what he wanted to see, and others that he was dealing with *Realpolitik*. In January 1945 when Harold Macmillan was commenting on the Italians trials, he mentioned General Roatta who had gained access to all the secret British files, including one in which Chamberlain had 'offered French colonies (e.g. Tunis) to Mussolini!' Macmillan described this as a 'quite nice little problem'.[8] It raised the question of how many promises of this nature had Chamberlain made to secure peace with Italy, and evidently supported the *Realpolitik* perspective. It has been claimed that Chamberlain was 'rational to a fault, Chamberlain could not imagine that anyone in his right mind…would actually want war', but it was the failure to be aware of Hitler's mind and thinking processes.[9] Yet in one of his letters (September 1938) he wrote 'Is it not positively horrible to think that the fate of hundreds of millions depends on one man and he is half mad!'[10] It would seem from this letter that Chamberlain had reached some justifiable conclusion about Hitler, but one can describe a good friend 'as half mad', yet he missed the point that Hitler was not just half mad but psychologically warped and in charge of a major nation.

There is a tendency to see many as sympathetic to Hitler's initiative for pan-Germanism which received much support in Germany, but as Richard Evans wrote this policy was also shared by others outside Germany, such as 'the British Prime Minister Neville Chamberlain, who accepted the *Anschluss* of Austria and brokered the incorporation of the Sudetenland into Germany at the Munich Agreement in 1938'.[11] It will always be contentious as to whether Chamberlain had any sympathy for Hitler's views or was being desperately overzealous in an effort to maintain peace.

Finally, two major historical factors about Chamberlain must not be neglected. First and foremost, he was a good man, with the anti-Nazi German diplomat Ulrich von Hassell writing in his diary that 'Neville Chamberlain died on 9 November 1940, a tragic end to a man of goodwill'.[12] It was a different view held by the Nazis. Goebbels had interpreted Chamberlain's disappearance 'as scuttling off to America' when he was dying from bowel cancer.[13] He wrote that Chamberlain had 'collapsed morally and physically under the weight of our attacks, he wanted to see Hitler's downfall. We have seen his and his Empires' downfall'.[14] In his diaries Goebbels frequently called both Chamberlain and Churchill liars, but his diary reflects the gross inhumanity of the Nazi regime.

At Chamberlain's funeral in Westminster Abbey Churchill and Halifax helped as pallbearers, with Churchill later stating in the Commons that 'Neville Chamberlain acted with perfect sincerity…to save the world from the awful, devastating struggle in which we are now engaged. This alone will stand him in good stead as far as what is called the verdict of history.'

Churchill's address leads to the second factor, is that sadly, as good and humane as Chamberlain was, he was badly mistaken in his prognosis of Hitler, believing he could reason, in his terms, with a 'half mad man'. He appeared unaware of the nature of Hitler by thinking he could be reasoned with, even up to the last moment with his shuttle diplomacy of flying to Germany three times to bring Hitler to agreement.

Chamberlain and others would have needed considerable knowledge and insight into whom they were dealing with, and insights from foreign journalists in Germany, as Part Two of this study discloses, were clearly insufficient. Colville wrote (5 November 1939) that 'our Intelligence service seems very weak, despite the number of sympathisers we must have in Germany'.[15] Sometimes the news percolating out was almost unbelievable, and Colville commented on a White Paper (31 October 1939) on German concentration camps, writing it 'is a sordid document calculated to appeal to people's lowest instincts...but after all most of the evidence is produced from prejudicial sources and in any case undesirable to arouse passion before they had begun in earnest'.[16] The head of the SIS said in 1938 that 'it was peculiarly difficult to interpret intelligence from Germany'...and from other countries such as 'France, Italy, Japan, and Russia, Britain was even more poorly informed'.[17]

Politics could not be unmixed from the Foreign Office or from the Intelligence agencies. When Intelligence had suggested that Germany was going to strike at Western Europe via the Netherlands, and the Foreign Office communicated this rumour to the USA, upon which a senior Civil Servant (Sir George Mounsey) attacked MI6, not only was he dismissive of covert findings, but he 'had his own agenda: to sustain the policy of appeasement adopted by Neville Chamberlain and Lord Halifax, whom he admired prodigiously'.[18] The Foreign Office and Intelligence services were the servants of their political masters, and the truth of what was happening in Germany under the Nazi regime was best sought from German dissidents, but there were few, and those who were hoping to overthrow Hitler, were either not believed or ignored. The Intelligence services could try and supply the number of new German tanks and planes which may win a war, but above all the thought processes of the potential enemy needed the closest scrutiny first and foremost. On 1 January 1940 Colville wrote we are faced by a 'Germany armed to the teeth, loyal to its government, and ruled by an unscrupulous clique whose word was not trustworthy and whose aggressive instincts were patent to the whole world'.[19] When Colville wrote this in 1940 the war had already started, and this viewpoint had at last been realised – but a few years too late.

What was needed, which is the main argument of this study, was the need to know the mind of Hitler and therefore his regime, which reflected the nature of the dictator. There were two critical sources as this exploration has made clear. The first was *Mein Kampf* in which Hitler set forth his political agenda for Germany and his foreign policy of enlargement. The few who read it such as the British Ambassador Rumbold and the Russian Foreign Secretary Litvinov were both convinced of the extreme dangers to international peace that Hitler posed. There seems little doubt that many when they found a copy skimp-read it or regarded it as a book written by an ill-educated raving lunatic, which alone should have been a warning. What was required was to use gifted academics to analyse it in detail from several perspectives. The first reason to view it was to explore Nazi plans for the future, another perspective would be understanding the mind of the author, and possibly a moral philosopher to indicate the inherent evils of the man who dared write shall appalling views.

One academic who read it with care and then travelled to see for himself the truth of Nazi Germany, whose book is outlined in Part Four, was the Australian Stephen Roberts who wondered whether 'the mind which wrote *Mein Kampf* had changed'.[20] He did not think this was the case, as Hitler was now a popular dictator, developing an Army state which was growing in power and keeping the Führer as the figurehead. The crux of the main issue, as Roberts demonstrated, was that Hitler's ravings in *Mein Kampf* were already taking shape, and that in his book Hitler had already begun his projected plans, meaning the future was indeed bleak, but both books were mainly ignored by those in power.

This book by Roberts is not a history book, but a commentary of the day (1936) by what this gifted academic mind understood about the driving forces in Hitler's Germany. The British and French governments had their own informants, and as noted earlier in this study, there had been publications about the military buildup in Germany, and there was the ongoing clash between those who saw Germany as a potential enemy, and those who wanted peace at any cost. With the benefit of hindsight, it is all too easy to look back and identify errors of judgement, and as today, it is difficult if not impossible to predict what is around the corner, which *Mein Kampf* and Roberts had clearly indicated in the era of the Second World War.

Roberts was more than a journalist, he was not subject to having his work checked by Goebbels and his scrutiny teams, he had no senior diplomatic management urging him caution, no publisher telling him to list all the military facts and trying to influence his views. Roberts was seeing for himself how the central figure of Nazism, Hitler, was the driving force with his maniacal and criminal way of thinking, and how he was subduing an entire population to his immoral views. In his section on Jews in Germany, Roberts had made it clear that Hitler had serious psychological problems, was totally immoral, and was more criminally inclined than the Mafia. He had identified Hitler's intentions of retrieving lost territories (irredentist nationalism), of seeking *Lebensraum*, which meant expanding German borders, and his hatred of France, all of which were vast warning signals.

Estimating the danger of Hitler was not just counting up his new military weapons, but understanding who he was, what drove him, and deducing his intentions and the probability he would enact them. Roberts had met many of his henchmen and observed others, he had witnessed the enthralment of the masses, seen firsthand the criminality, and all his intelligence and human insight was telling him that war was inevitable.

Roberts' book was not a boring academic thesis, nor highly technical and filled with military data, and it did not just dwell on military concerns, making it very readable. He looked from education to youth movements, farming, economics, labour forces, religion, and every aspect of German life and how Hitler was perverting traditional Germany to a country shaped and moulded to his warped thinking processes. He also boldly described Hitler as a liar and a person who could not be trusted in what he claimed, including the keeping of treaties and pacts. At times he did his absolute best to try and see the Nazi perspective, and he was only hoodwinked once by the cunning Himmler.

His concluding chapter was a last-gasp warning of the inevitability of a major war, and this was written in 1936–7. Given his academic background and his training in analysis, he was a person whose views should have been read with keen interest by national leaders, as it would have been seen as a red alert of what was down the road, thus giving more time for suitable preparation, but he was 'the man who was ignored' in the very places and by the very people who should have known better.

Had this book been read and scrutinised by academics who had read *Mein Kampf*, it would have been only a matter of connecting the dots. When Roberts had travelled across 1935 Germany, meeting some of the Nazi leaders and public, it had dawned on him that what Hitler had demanded in *Mein Kampf* was already starting in a remorseless fashion. Roberts' predictions of future years were uncomfortably correct with the benefit of hindsight. Had he not been ignored it would have offered critical foresight and influenced the future for the better.

Notes

Introduction
1. Shirer, William, *20th Century Journey* (Little, Brown and Company: Boston, 1984), p.137
2. Ibid., p.181

Part One: Appeasement and Divided Opinions
1. Cato (Michael Foot, Frank Owen, Peter Howard), *Guilty Men* (London: Faber & Faber, 2011)
2. Finney, Patrick, *Remembering the Road to World War Two* (London: Routledge, 2011), p.216
3. Bouverie, Tim, *Appeasing Hitler* (London: Vintage, 2019), p.11
4. Elborough, Travis, *Our History of the Twentieth Century: As Told in Diaries, Journals and Letters* (London: Michael O'Mara Books, 2017), p.195
5. See Colville, John, *The Fringes of Power: Downing Street Diaries 1939–1955* (London: Hodder and Stoughton, 1985), p.66
6. Taylor, Fred (Ed. and translator), *The Goebbels Diaries* (London: Hamish Hamilton, 1982), p.97
7. See Burleigh, Michael, *The Third Reich* (London: Pan Books, 2001), p.472
8. Ibid., p.590
9. Ferguson, Niall, *The War of the World: History's Age of Hatred* (London: Allen Lane, 2006), p.325
10. See Schmidt, Paul, *Hitler's Interpreter* (Cheltenham: History Press, 2016), pp.77–8
11. Ibid., p.28
12. Ibid., p.31
13. Ibid., p.32
14. Ibid., p.34
15. Eden, Anthony, *The Eden Memoirs: Facing the Dictators* (London: Cassell, 1962), p.7
16. Schmidt, Paul, *Hitler's Interpreter*, pp.45ff
17. Eden, Anthony, *The Eden Memoirs: Facing the Dictators*, p.43
18. Schmidt, Paul, *Hitler's Interpreter*, p.49
19. Finney, Patrick, *The Origins of the Second World War* (London: Arnold, 1997), p.200
20. Schmidt, Paul, *Hitler's Interpreter*, p.53
21. Ibid., p.57
22. See Bouverie, Tim, *Appeasing Hitler*, p.128
23. Elborough, Travis, *Our History of the Twentieth Century: As Told in Diaries, Journals and Letters*, p.173
24. Bouverie, Tim, *Appeasing Hitler*, p.141
25. Feiling, Keith, *The Life of Neville Chamberlain* (London: Macmillan, 1946), p.332
26. Eden, Anthony, *The Eden Memoirs: Facing the Dictators*, p.567
27. Burleigh, Michael, *The Third Reich*, p.739

28. Eden, Anthony, *The Eden Memoirs: Facing the Dictators*, p.573
29. Ibid., p.549
30. See Sangster, Andrew, *The Futile Pursuit of Power* (Dunbeath: Whittles Publishing, 2023)
31. Eden, Anthony, *The Eden Memoirs: Facing the Dictators*, p.582
32. Ciano Papers, (Ed.) Muggeridge, *Ciano's Diplomatic Papers* (London: Odhams Press, 1948), p.171
33. Ibid., p.183.
34. Bouverie, Tim, *Appeasing Hitler*, p.190
35. Elborough, Travis, *Our History of the Twentieth Century: As Told in Diaries, Journals and Letters*, p.177
36. Ferguson, Niall, *The War of the World: History's Age of Hatred*, p.349
37. Boyne, Walter, *The Influence of Air Power upon History* (New York: Pelican Publishing Company, 2003), p.15
38. See Bouverie, Tim, *Appeasing Hitler*, pp.42ff
39. Churchill Winston, *The Second World War Volume 1* (London: Cassell, 1948), p.7.
40. Bryant Mark, *World War II in Cartoons* (London: Grub Street, 2009), p.11
41. Hastings, Max, *Catastrophe* (London: William Collins, 2013), p.563.
42. Kissinger Henry, *A World Restored: Metternich, Castlereagh, and the Problems of Peace 1812–1822* (Boston: Houghton Mifflin, 1973), p.138.
43. Schmidt, Paul, *Hitler's Interpreter*, p.64
44. Ibid., p.67
45. Schmidt, Paul, *Hitler's Interpreter*, p.79
46. Elborough, Travis, *Our History of the Twentieth Century: As Told in Diaries, Journals and Letters*, p.160
47. Schmidt, Paul, *Hitler's Interpreter*, p.85
48. Ibid., p.63
49. Eden, Anthony, *The Eden Memoirs: Facing the Dictators*, p.504
50. Neville, Peter, *Appeasing Hitler: The Diplomacy of Sir Nevile Henderson 1937–39* (London: Macmillan, 1999), p.267
51. Goldstein, Eric, Neville Chamberlain, the British Official Mind and the Munich Crisis contained in: Lukes, Igor and Goldstein, Eric (Eds) *The Munich Crisis, 1938: Prelude to World War II* (London: Frank Cass, 1999), p.282
52. See Henderson, Nevile, *Failure of a Mission: Berlin 1937–1939* (London: Readers Union, 1940)
53. Burleigh, Michael, *Sacred Causes* (London: Harper Press, 2006), p.226
54. Quoted in Ferguson, Niall, *The War of the World: History's Age of Hatred*, p.354
55. Eden, Anthony, *The Eden Memoirs: Facing the Dictators*, p.598
56. Ciano, Galeazzo, *Diary 1937–1943* (London: Phoenix, 2002), p.126
57. Schmidt, Paul, *Hitler's Interpreter*, p.99
58. Ibid., p.100
59. Ibid., p.101
60. See Bouverie, Tim, *Appeasing Hitler*, p.259
61. Schmidt, Paul, *Hitler's Interpreter*, p.104
62. Ibid., p.112
63. Bullock, Alan, *Hitler: A Study in Tyranny* (London: Penguin Books, 1990), p.470
64. Ciano, Galeazzo, *Diary 1937–1943*, p.135
65. Schmidt, Paul, *Hitler's Interpreter*, p.115
66. Ibid., p.116

67. Quoted in Bouverie, Tim, *Appeasing Hitler*, p.289
68. Schmidt, Paul, *Hitler's Interpreter*, p.118
69. Ibid., p.119
70. Ibid., p.120
71. Ciano, Galeazzo, *Diary 1937–1943*, p.136
72. Bullock, Alan, *Hitler: A Study in Tyranny*, p.471
73. Hassell, Ulrich von, *The Ulrich von Hasell Diaries, 1938–1944* (London: Frontline Books, 2011), pp.1–2
74. Hart-Davis (Ed.), *King's Counsellor – Abdication and War: The Diaries of Sir Alan Lascelles* (London: Weidenfeld & Nicolson, 2006), p.271
75. Evans, Richard J., *The Third Reich in History and Memory* (London: Abacus, 2016), p.254
76. See Bouverie, Tim, *Appeasing Hitler*, p.306
77. Ciano, Galeazzo, *Diary 1937–1943*, p.171
78. Ibid., p.176
79. Ibid., p.176
80. Ibid., p.201
81. See Schmidt, Paul, *Hitler's Interpreter*, p.129
82. Eberle, Henrik and Uhl, Matthias (Eds), *The Hitler Book: The Secret Dossier Prepared for Stalin* (London: John Murray, 2006), p.42
83. Bullock, Alan, *Hitler: A Study in Tyranny*, p.482
84. Colville John, *The Fringes of Power: Downing Street Diaries 1939–1955*, p.34
85. Ibid., p.25
86. Evans, Richard J., *The Third Reich in History and Memory*, p.259
87. See Ferguson, Niall, *The War of the World: History's Age of Hatred*, p.376
88. Schmidt, Paul, *Hitler's Interpreter*, p.135
89. Ferguson, Niall, *The War of the World: History's Age of Hatred*, p.377
90. Finney, Patrick, *The Origins of the Second World War*, p.47
91. Ferguson, Niall, *The War of the World: History's Age of Hatred*, p.335
92. See Colville, John, *The Fringes of Power: Downing Street Diaries 1939–1955*, p.72
93. Schmidt, Paul, *Hitler's Interpreter*, p.146
94. Ciano, Galeazzo, *Diary 1937–1943*, p.265
95. See Ibid., p.266
96. See Colville, John, *The Fringes of Power: Downing Street Diaries 1939–1955*, p.110
97. Ciano, Galeazzo, *Diary 1937–1943*, p.269
98. Schmidt, Paul, *Hitler's Interpreter*, p.154
99. Ibid., p.159
100. Colville, John, *The Fringes of Power: Downing Street Diaries 1939–1955*, p.53
101. Ibid., p.44
102. Ibid., p.45
103. Ibid., p.58
104. Ibid., p.29
105. Alanbrooke, Field Marshal Lord, *War Diaries 1939–1945* (London: Weidenfeld & Nicolson, (2001), p.25

Part Two: Literary Efforts to Reveal the Truth

1. Schmidt, Paul, *Hitler's Interpreter*, p.86
2. Ferguson, Niall, *The War of the World: History's Age of Hatred*, p.339
3. Ibid., p.336

4. See Bouverie, Tim, *Appeasing Hitler*, p.327
5. Shirer, William, *20th Century Journey*, p.29.
6. Ibid., p.118
7. Ibid., p.138
8. Ibid., p.139
9. Ibid., p.156
10. Ibid., p.161
11. Ibid., p.192
12. Ibid., p.206, footnote
13. Ibid., p.217 & p.219
14. Ibid., p.222
15. Ibid., p.255
16. Ibid., p.299
17. Ibid., p.320
18. Ibid., p.323
19. Ibid., p.434
20. See Bartlett, Vernon, *Nazi Germany Explained* (London: Victor Gollancz, 1933)
21. Woodman, Dorothy, *Hitler Rearms* (London: John Lane the Bodley Head Ltd, 1934), p.9
22. Ibid., p.47
23. Ibid., p.85
24. Ibid., p.101
25. Ibid., p.114
26. Bouverie, Tim, *Appeasing Hitler*, p.21
27. Woodman, Dorothy, *Hitler Rearms*, p.153
28. Ibid., p.162
29. Ibid., p.166
30. Ibid., p.201
31. See Infield, Glen, *Disaster at Bari* (New York: Bantam, 1988)
32. Atkinson, R., *The Day of the Battle: The War in Sicily and Italy 1943–44* (London: Abacus, 2013), p.367
33. Woodman, Dorothy, *Hitler Rearms*, p.293
34. Ibid., p.326
35. Ibid., p.327

Part Three: *Mein Kampf*
1. Bouverie, Tim, *Appeasing Hitler*, p.199
2. Shirer, William, *20th Century Journey*, p.215
3. Ibid., p.215
4. Ibid., p.217
5. Bouverie, Tim, *Appeasing Hitler*, p.18

Chapter One: Hitler, the Man and His Views
1. Heiber Helmut, *Göbbels* (New York: Hawthorn Books, 1972), p.96
2. Ebermayer, Erich and Meissner, Hans-Otto, *Evil Genius: The Story of Joseph Göbbels* (London: Allan Wingate, 1953), p.97.
3. Shirer, William, *20th Century Journey*, p.120

Part Four: Introduction
1. Wood, David, *Stephen Henry Roberts* (Sydney, Australia: University of Sydney, 1986), p.29
2. Ibid., p.30
3. Ibid., p.30
4. Bouverie, Tim, *Appeasing Hitler*, pp.173–4
5. Eden, Anthony, *The Eden Memoirs: Facing the Dictators*, p.571
6. Ibid., p.570
7. Wood, David, *Stephen Henry Roberts*, p.35

Chapter One: The Early Days
1. Litchfield, David, *Hitler's Valkyrie* (Stroud: The History Press, 2013), p.50
2. Shirer, William, *20th Century Journey*, p.181

Chapter Two: Four Years of Power
1. Ibid., p.181 and p.194

Chapter Five: Hitlerism and the World
1. Ibid., p.314

Part Five: Final Observations
1. Finney, Patrick, *The Origins of the Second World War*, p.19
2. See Evans, Richard J., *The Third Reich in History and Memory*, p.254
3. Ibid., p.255
4. Finney, Patrick, *The Origins of the Second World War* (London: Arnold, 1997)
5. Bullock, Alan, *Hitler: A Study in Tyranny*, p.437
6. Colville, John, *The Fringes of Power: Downing Street Diaries 1939–1955*, p.112
7. Quoted in Evans, Richard J., *The Third Reich in History and Memory*, p.253
8. Macmillan, Harold, *War Diaries* (London: Macmillan, 1984), p.645
9. Quoted in Evans, Richard J., *The Third Reich in History and Memory*, p.260
10. Finney, Patrick, *The Origins of the Second World War*, p.43
11. Evans, Richard J., *The Third Reich in History and Memory*, p.217
12. Hassell, Ulrich von, *The Ulrich von Hasell Diaries, 1938–1944*, p.104
13. Taylor, Fred (Ed. and translator), *The Goebbels Diaries*, p.160
14. Ibid., p.169
15. Colville, John, *The Fringes of Power: Downing Street Diaries 1939–1955*, p.48
16. Ibid., p.46
17. Finney, Patrick, *The Origins of the Second World War*, p.43
18. Hastings, Max, *The Secret War* (London: William Collins, 2015), pp.14–15
19. Colville, John, *The Fringes of Power: Downing Street Diaries 1939–1955* (London: Hodder and Stoughton, 1985), p.64
20. Roberts, Stephen H., *The House that Hitler Built* (London: Methuen Publishers, 1937), p.359

Bibliography of Cited Texts

Alanbrooke Field Marshal Lord, *War Diaries 1939–45* (London: Weidenfeld & Nicolson, 2001)
Atkinson, Rick, *The Day of the Battle, The War in Sicily and Italy 1943–44* (London: Abacus, 2013)
Bartlett, Vernon, *Nazi Germany Explained* (London: Victor Gollancz, 1933)
Bouverie, Tim, *Appeasing Hitler* (London: Vintage, 2019)
Boyne, Walter, *The Influence of Air Power upon History* (New York: Pelican Publishing Company, 2003)
Bryant, Mark, *World War II in Cartoons* (London: Grub Street, 2009)
Bullock, Alan, *Hitler: A Study in Tyranny* (London: Penguin Books, 1990)
Burleigh, Michael, *The Third Reich* (London: Pan Books, 2001)
Burleigh, Michael, *Sacred Causes* (London: Harper Press, 2006)
Cato (Michael Foot, Frank Owen, Peter Howard), *Guilty Men* (London: Faber & Faber, 2011)
Churchill, Winston, *The Second World War Volume 1* (London: Cassell, 1948)
Ciano Papers, (Ed.) Muggeridge, *Ciano's Diplomatic Papers* (London: Odhams Press, 1948)
Ciano, Galeazzo, *Diary 1937–1943* (London: Phoenix, 2002)
Colville, John, *The Fringes of Power: Downing Street Diaries 1939–1955* (London: Hodder and Stoughton, 1985)
Eberle, Henrik and Uhl, Matthias (Eds), *The Hitler Book: The Secret Dossier Prepared for Stalin* (London: John Murray, 2006)
Ebermayer, Erich and Meissner, Hans-Otto, *Evil Genius: The Story of Joseph Göbbels* (London: Allan Wingate, 1953)
Eden, Anthony, *The Eden Memoirs: Facing the Dictators* (London: Cassell, 1962)
Elborough, Travis, *Our History of the Twentieth Century: As Told in Diaries, Journals and Letters* (London: Michael O'Mara Books, 2017)
Evans, Richard J., *The Third Reich in History and Memory* (London: Abacus, 2016)
Feiling, Keith, *The Life of Neville Chamberlain* (London: Macmillan, 1946)
Ferguson, Niall, *The War of the World: History's Age of Hatred* (London: Allen Lane, 2006)
Finney, Patrick, *The Origins of the Second World War* (London: Arnold, 1997)
Finney, Patrick, *Remembering the Road to World War Two* (London: Routledge, 2011)
Goldstein, Eric, Neville Chamberlain, the British Official Mind and the Munich Crisis contained in: Lukes, Igor and Goldstein, Eric (Eds.) *The Munich Crisis, 1938: Prelude to World War II* (London; Frank Cass, 1999)
Hart-Davis (Ed), *King's Counsellor – Abdication and War: The Diaries of Sir Alan Lascelles* (London: Weidenfeld & Nicolson, 2006) p.271
Hassell, Ulrich von, *The Ulrich von Hasell Diaries, 1938–1944* (London: Frontline Books, 2011)
Hastings, Max, *The Secret War* (London: William Collins, 2015)
Hastings, Max, *Catastrophe* (London: William Collins, 2013)
Heiber, Helmut, *Göbbels* (New York: Hawthorn Books, 1972)
Henderson, Nevile, *Failure of a Mission: Berlin 1937–1939* (London: Readers Union, 1940)

Hitler, Adolf, *Mein Kampf* (London: Pimlico, 1992)
Infield, Glen, *Disaster at Bari* (New York: Bantam, 1988)
Kissinger Henry, *A World Restored: Metternich, Castlereagh, and the Problems of Peace 1812–1822* (Boston: Houghton Mifflin, 1973)
Litchfield, David, *Hitler's Valkyrie* (Stroud: The History Press, 2013)
Lukes, Igor and Goldstein, Eric (Eds.) *The Munich Crisis, 1938: Prelude to World War II* (London: Frank Cass, 1999)
Macmillan, Harold, *War Diaries* (London: Macmillan, 1984)
Neville, Peter, *Appeasing Hitler: The Diplomacy of Sir Nevile Henderson 1937–39* (London: Macmillan, 1999)
Roberts, Stephen H., *The House that Hitler Built* (London: Methuen Publishers, 1937)
Sangster, Andrew, *The Unknown Field Marshal* (Oxford & Philadelphia: Casemate, 2020)
Sangster, Andrew, *The Futile Pursuit of Power* (Dunbeath: Whittles Publishing, 2023)
Schmidt, Paul, *Hitler's Interpreter* (Cheltenham: History Press, 2016)
Shirer, William, *20th Century Journey* (Little, Brown and Company: Boston, 1984)
Taylor, Fred (Ed. and translator), *The Goebbels Diaries* (London: Hamish Hamilton, 1982)
Wood, David, *Stephen Henry Roberts* (Sydney, Australia: University of Sydney, 1986)
Woodman, Dorothy, *Hitler Rearms* (London: John Lane the Bodley Head Ltd, 1934)

Index

Amann, Max, 154
Anglo-French relationships, 9, 12, 22, 34, 36, 38, 51, 56, 59, 162, 175
Anschluss, 15, 20, 22, 63, 66, 98, 166, 177
Anti-Semitism, 3, 5–6, 44, 58, 67, 89–91, 95, 107–108, 116, 122, 150, 156–7, 167, 180
Aryan myth, 73, 88, 90–1, 93, 95–7, 99, 108, 122, 154, 158, 160
Astor, Nancy, 44
Attlee, Clement, 37, 42
Attolico, Italian Ambassador, 53

Baldwin, Stanley, 5, 7, 11, 14
Barth, Karl, 158
Beaverbrook, newspaper magnate, 3
Beck, General Ludwig, 25, 32, 137
Beneš, Edvard, 32–3, 36, 38–40, 46, 66, 167
Blomberg, General, 20, 136
Blood and Soil belief 85, 126, 145, 146, 156
Blum, Léon, 6
Bonnet, French Foreign Minister, 6
Bracken, Brendan, 23
Brest-Litovsk Treaty, 164
Brooke, General Alan, 20, 58
Brownshirts, Observations on, 133–4
Brüning, Heinrich, 145, 148
Buch, Walter, 129, 130, 131

Canaris, Admiral, 32, 42, 46
Central Directorate of the Party, 129
Chamberlain, Austen, 8, 13–14, 17
Chamberlain, Neville,
 attitudes towards him, 2, 17, 19, 33, 36, 43, 45, 49, 57, 176–7
 character, 7, 9, 14, 18, 23–4, 35, 48, 52
 his attitudes, 5, 7, 15, 17, 21, 31–3, 47, 56, 114

Channon, Henry 'Chips', 16, 30
Churchill, Winston, 3–5, 7–8, 11, 13–15, 17, 19–23, 26–30, 33–4, 37, 42–3, 48, 50, 52–4, 56–7, 59, 62, 70, 76, 115, 176–8
Ciano, Galeazzo, 18–19, 35, 39, 41, 45–6, 53, 170
Colville, John, 47–8, 55, 57, 176, 178–9
Colvin, Ian, journalist, 62
Communism, Western fear of, 3, 30, 49, 163
Concordat with Rome, 88
Cooper, Duff, 33
Czechoslovakia Problem, 21–5, 32–5, 38–40, 43, 46–7, 154, 165, 168, 175

Dachau, 3, 132, 154
Dahlerus, Birger, 53–4
Daladier, Édouard, 6, 38–40, 42, 47, 175
Danzig issue, 32, 51, 53–4, 165, 168
Darlan, Admiral, 71
Darré, Walter, 126, 145, 171
Dawson, Editor of *The Times*, 62, 64
de Gaulle, Charles, 176
Dibelius, Martin, 158
Disarmament Conference, 5, 26–7, 161
Dodd, American Ambassador, 64
Dollfuss, Engelbert, 30, 162, 166
Drexler, Anton, 117, 124
Duke of Windsor, *see* Edward VIII

Ebbutt, Norman, journalist, 64, 66
Economic Observations, 141–2, 144, 146
Eden, Anthony, 8–12, 17–19, 21, 23, 27–8, 31, 34–5, 40, 114
Edward VIII, King, 30
Epp, Ritter von, 171
Ernst, Karl, 134
Euthanasia Decree, 82

First World War, ramifications, xii, 17, 58, 76, 85
Fisher, Robert, 26
Flandin, Pierre-Étienne, 12
Franco, Francisco, 14, 106, 139, 170
François-Poncet, French Ambassador, 26
Frick, Wilhelm, 123

George V, King, 11
George VI, King, 20, 41–2
Gleiwitz incident, 54
Goebbels, Joseph, 6, 16, 25, 30–1, 35, 44, 46, 62–3, 65–7, 73, 79, 111, 119, 122, 127, 129, 131, 136, 145, 153–5, 164, 171, 177, 180
Göring, Hermann, 15–16, 25, 29, 31, 39, 45, 47, 50, 53, 56, 64, 70, 107, 119, 121, 127–32, 134, 136–9, 144, 160, 171
Grandi, Dino, 17–19
Grüber, Kurt, 147
Guilty Men, 1940 published book, 1

Hácha, Emil, 46, 47
Halder, General, 42
Halifax, Viscount, 15–17, 20–1, 25, 32, 34, 36–7, 45–6, 49, 52–3, 57, 62, 107, 177–8
Hanfstaengl, Dr Ernst, 63
Hankey, Maurice, 22, 26, 29
Hassell, Ulrich von, 41, 177
Hauer, Wilhelm, 158
Henderson, Nevile, 21, 25, 31–4, 46, 50–2, 54
Henlein, Konrad, 22, 33, 35, 167
Hess, Rudolf, 76, 113, 122–3, 131, 151
Himmler, Heinrich, 25, 72, 113, 122, 130–1, 157, 180
Historical Revisionism, 2
Hitler,
  as a young man, 117–18, 120
  attitudes, 10, 37, 42
  character, 9, 20, 22, 27, 29, 35, 38–40, 44, 50, 71, 77, 79, 81, 84, 91, 93, 102, 107, 120
  his views, 13, 34, 36, 85–90, 94–6, 98–9, 101, 103, 105
Hitler Youth, 29, 32, 70, 87, 107, 111, 143, 147–8, 158
Hoare-Laval Agreement, 11

Hoare, Samuel, 8, 11–12, 20, 22, 47
Hore-Belisha, Leslie, 5–6, 34, 46
House that Hitler Built, The, 111–13, 115

Inskip, Thomas, 13
Intelligence services, 27, 46, 178
Ironside, General, 51
Irredentist Nationalism, 11, 22, 47, 58, 95, 103, 165, 180

Journalists, xi, 21, 29, 43, 61–5, 68, 77, 111, 154, 178

Keitel, General, 23
Kellogg-Briand Pact, 4
Kennedy, Joseph, 23
Keynes, John Maynard, 28
Kristallnacht, 44

Labour Party, 5, 7, 14, 34, 37, 43, 57, 68
Labour Service, 70, 111, 148
Labour service camps, 143, 149
Landsberg prison, 93
Lascelles, Alan, 41
Laval, Pierre, 5, 10–11
League of Nations, 4, 9–11, 13, 26, 51, 128, 161, 163, 167–8
Lebensraum, 22, 26, 56, 73, 78, 95, 99–100, 105, 108, 116, 123, 135, 144, 146, 180
Ley, Robert, 103, 130, 149–50, 154
Litvinov, Maxim, 49, 77, 179
Lloyd George, David, 4, 28–9, 48, 100
Locarno Treaty, 4, 59
Londonderry, Lord, 29, 44
Lothian, Marquess of, 28
Low, David, cartoonist, 61

MacDonald, James Ramsay, 5, 11
Macdonald Peace Plan, 162
Macmillan, Harold, 23, 176
Mannerheim, Baron, 169
Marx, Karl, 92, 140, 164
Masaryk, Tomáš, 66, 167
Mein Kampf, xii, 20, 22, 26–7, 34, 39, 44, 73, 75–8, 80, 83, 85, 91, 94–5, 98, 100, 102, 106–109, 111, 113–15, 117–18, 120, 122, 128, 135–6, 149–50, 153–4, 169, 171–2, 179–81
Memel issue, 165, 168–9

Molotov, Vyacheslav, 49, 51
Morton, Desmond, 27
Mosley, Oswald, 4
Müller, Bishop Ludwig, 88, 157–8
Munich crisis,
　Part One at Berchtesgaden, 32
　Part Two at Godesberg, 36
　Part Three at Munich, 38
Munich Putsch, 76, 106, 119
Murrow, Ed, broadcaster, 63, 66
Mussolini, Benito, 3, 9–11, 13–14, 17–21, 24, 35, 39–41, 45–6, 48, 50, 53–4, 72, 106, 162, 170, 176

Nazi Regime and the Law, 159–60
Nazi Regime and Women, 151–2
Nazis Movement, early days, 123
Neo-Darwinism, 83
Niemöller, Pastor, 64, 158
Night of the Long Knives, 30, 36, 124, 134, 139
NSDAP, 85, 92–3, 102, 124, 127
Nuremberg Race Laws, 64, 156
Nuremberg Rally, 1936, 139

Pacifism, 5, 26
Pan-Germanism, 22, 51, 73, 95, 108, 165, 171–2, 177
Phipps, Eric, 8, 26, 29–31
Phoney War, 54
Pope Pius XII, 32
Prague, Germans occupy, 46
Propaganda, 55, 84
Public reaction, xii, 1, 4, 11, 19, 21, 23, 34, 38, 49–50, 59

Racism, 85, 90–1, 96–8, 108, 120, 123
Realpolitik, and Appeasement, vii–ix, 2, 176
Rhineland Occupation, 11–13, 65, 91, 104, 162–3, 173
Ribbentrop, Joachim von, 6, 10, 21, 23, 30, 35, 45, 50, 54, 113, 161, 176
Roatta, General, 176
Roberts, Stephen, 113, 115, 179–80

Röhm, Ernst, 30, 124, 132, 134–5
Roosevelt, President, 6, 17, 19, 23, 38, 44, 67
Rosenberg, Alfred, 29, 73, 123, 125, 153, 158, 161, 164
Rothermere, Lord, 28
Rumbold, Horace, 26–7, 31, 75, 179
Runciman, Lord, 25, 33, 36

Schacht, Hjalmar, 12, 65, 113, 141, 144, 171
Schirach, Baldur von, 147, 153, 157
Schleicher, General Kurt von, 134–5
Schuschnigg, Kurt, 166
Seeckt, General von, 7, 69–70, 136–7
Seeds, William, British Ambassador, 49
Shirer, William, xi, 31, 63–5, 67, 78, 80, 121, 131
Simon, John, 8–9, 11
Spanish Civil War, 14
Speer, Albert, 83
Stab-in-the-back myth, 90, 136
Strasser brothers, 129, 135
Strength through Joy, 103, 150
Stresa Agreement, 9–11, 162
Sudetenland, 22, 25, 34–5, 37, 42, 177

Ten Year Rule Policy, 7
Thompson, Dorothy, journalist, 63
Todt, Fritz, 152
Trade Unions, 102, 149

Vansittart, Robert, 26, 28, 32
Versailles Treaty, 4, 10–11, 15, 28, 31, 58, 69, 85, 94–5, 108, 124, 135–6, 161–3, 165, 169
Völkischer Beobachter, 154
Völkisch movement, 85

Weltanschauung, 125
Wiedemann, Captain Fritz, 25
Wigram, Ralph, 27
Wilson, Horace, 27, 37
Woodman, Dorothy, 68–70, 72–4

Dear Reader,

We hope you have enjoyed this book, but why not share your views on social media? You can also follow our pages to see more about our other products: facebook.com/penandswordbooks or follow us on X @penswordbooks

You can also view our products at www.pen-and-sword.co.uk (UK and ROW) or www.penandswordbooks.com (North America).

To keep up to date with our latest releases and online catalogues, please sign up to our newsletter at: www.pen-and-sword.co.uk/newsletter

If you would like a printed catalogue with our latest books, then please email: enquiries@pen-and-sword.co.uk or telephone: 01226 734555 (UK and ROW) or email: uspen-and-sword@casematepublishers.com or telephone: (610) 853-9131 (North America).

We respect your privacy and we will only use personal information to send you information about our products.

Thank you!